APERTURE

AF252022

Beyond Wilderness

Entering the final decade of the millennium, the terror of nuclear war has been joined by a new set of terrors—global warming, acid rain, dead oceans, mutations and cancers caused by radiation and toxic waste. A series of environmental disasters, from Bhopal to Chernobyl, Three Mile Island to the *Exxon Valdez,* have brought forth an unprecedented array of political forces, from the Green party in Western Europe to Greenpeace and Earth First! activists in the United States. The endangered environment has become a universal concern.

As Barry Lopez argues in his essay "Unbounded Wilderness," the crisis is not simply one of laws and economics, but of culture. In the past, landscape photography borrowed the model of romantic European landscape painting, seeing nature as a place out there, where people have no right to be. This remains the operative style of much landscape photography, and is promulgated with continuing effectiveness in many books, calendars, and exhibitions. But such a prettified view of the land ignores the real threats—from chemical pollution, deforestation, nuclear contamination, and the ravages of extractive mining and drilling—that now face not only lands designated as "wild," but everywhere.

What seems to be needed is a new attitude toward the land and our place in it. The wilderness—defined as a place where humans have never been—is largely a fiction; Native Americans roamed Yellowstone and Yosemite for thousands of years before whites first "discovered" those areas. We need to move beyond the idea of wilderness, and to recognize our inevitable implication in every aspect of the land. As Wes Jackson argues in his essay "Wilderness as Saint," we must learn to grant as much significance to inner-city slums and working farms as to the national parks.

In recent years a series of photographers have extended the terms of landscape photography to encompass these new ecological imperatives. This issue features the work of many of these picturemakers, along with essays that address these and related questions. Robert Dawson, for example, documents the central importance water holds in the deserts of the American West, while John Pfahl deploys a sharp wit in his lusciously picturesque images of factory smoke and nuclear power plants tucked into scenic settings. Richard Misrach records antinuclear protests in the Nevada desert, while other photographers provide graphic images of the terrible effects of environmental depredation.

Through the work of these and other photographers and writers, "Beyond Wilderness" attempts to direct public debate away from questions of preserving an artificial wilderness and toward a new and enlightened stewardship of the earth—our only earth, where we and our children live. For in considering the future of our endangered land we are considering our own future as well.

THE EDITORS

2 UNBOUNDED WILDERNESS
By Barry Lopez
Photographs by William Clift, Barbara Bosworth, A. J. Meek, Robert Dawson, Alan Tibbetts, and Mark Klett

16 LAND AND LANDSCAPE
By Charles Hagen
Photographs by Philip Hyde and Robert Glenn Ketchum

24 POWER AND SMOKE: TWO STATEMENTS
Photographs by John Pfahl

30 RECLAIMING HISTORY: RICHARD MISRACH AND THE POLITICS OF LANDSCAPE PHOTOGRAPHY
By Rebecca Solnit
Photographs by Richard Misrach

36 A GROWING AWARENESS: ENVIRONMENTAL GROUPS AND THE MEDIA
By Joel Connelly
Photographs by Gary Braasch, Ken Graham, Michael Baytoff, and Sam Kittner

44 OUT OF THE GARDEN
Photographs by Len Jenshel

50 WILDERNESS AS SAINT
By Wes Jackson
Photographs by Terry Evans

56 WATER IN THE WEST
By Gerald Haslam
Photographs by Robert Dawson

64 OF HOUSES AND HIGHWAYS
By J. B. Jackson
Photographs by Peter deLory, John Ganis, Masumi Hayashi, and Stuart Klipper

72 PEOPLE & IDEAS
The Legacy of Ansel Adams: Debts and Burdens
By Mark Klett
Topographic Translations
By Nan Richardson
Evans in the Night of Photography
By Edmundo Desnoes

Unbounded Wilderness

By Barry Lopez

The fate of the American landscape, its ponds and hollows, its creeks and forests, its prairies, wet glades, and canyons, cannot be addressed solely in terms of "wilderness" or be solved by "wilderness preservation." What we face now in North America—and, of course, elsewhere—is a crisis in land use, in how we regard land.

With the impending failure of vast but finite underground aquifers, the loss of animals and topsoil, and the intractability of certain forms of pollution, it has become clear that we need to rethink our relationship to the entire landscape. How we farm, where we place roads, how we design cities, limit real estate development, and how we mine, fish, and log are all now crucial questions. To have this fundamental problem of land ethics defined, or understood, as mainly "a fight for wilderness" hurts us in two ways. It preserves a misleading and artificial distinction between "holy" and "profane" lands, and it continues to serve the industries that most seriously threaten wilderness. By focusing public attention on "a fair division" of the relatively few parcels of land that are still candidates for wilderness designation, and on the roughly two percent of federal land that has already been locked up (in their phrase), these industries hope to continue to mine, log, dam, graze, and drain the remaining ninety-six percent of federal land with minimal interference. Many of them cynically assume, in addition, that what has been locked up can, and will, be opened up.

The kind of management plan the extractive industries do not want to hear—and so far they haven't had to—is one based on responsible use, not this false dichotomy. As long as the argument remains "wilderness" versus "non-wilderness," the timber industry (the only extractive industry excluded from wilderness areas) will be happy to appear gracious in trading two high-altitude, rockbound parcels of land suitable for wilderness designation for one parcel of low-altitude forest land. The real issue—the responsible management of *all* land—remains obscured. And the apparent graciousness of the timber industry's gesture founders when, with stunning hypocrisy and insensitivity, it expresses "concern" because wilderness areas may exclude the handicapped.

What we face is a crisis of character. Our relationships with the land are essentially still colonial—exploitive, indifferent, romantic, and cruel. They are largely untouched by a sense of wonder or by the sense of a universe shaped by other than human perception and orderings. We are, it is possible to argue, blind to creation; we do not scruple or hesitate to improve upon it or to disturb it.

In wilderness, the threads of evolution and all the synapses of the food web, theoretically, are free of the social and economic schemes of human beings. Ozone depletion, acid rain, and the labyrinthine cycling of manmade chemicals through the food chain make this intended ideal something of a romance, but we persist in securing wilderness—taking land out of the cycle of manufacturing—for excellent reasons, both moral and practical. Haunted by a sense that we do not have the right to appropriate everything, we seek, on moral grounds, to leave some land untouched (and even to repair or make restitution through the relocation and reintroduction of species). And hearing, for example, of the utility of some exotic plant in treating cancer, we see a practical advantage in leaving these "blueprint" landscapes undisturbed.

Our desire to preserve wild places is, unarguably, wise; and the fight to preserve them is waged furiously now all over the world. (A striking difference in these separate battles is the extent to which low-tech, small-scale human life is incorporated into the meaning of wilderness in various cultures.) But the fight for wilderness is a holding action. The social and economic forces that would dismantle wilderness are, again, pleased to focus a public relations campaign or their considerable political and legal power on this narrow front. It is on a broader, overriding front, the responsible management of public and private lands for future generations, that they do not wish to be challenged. Such management would include candor

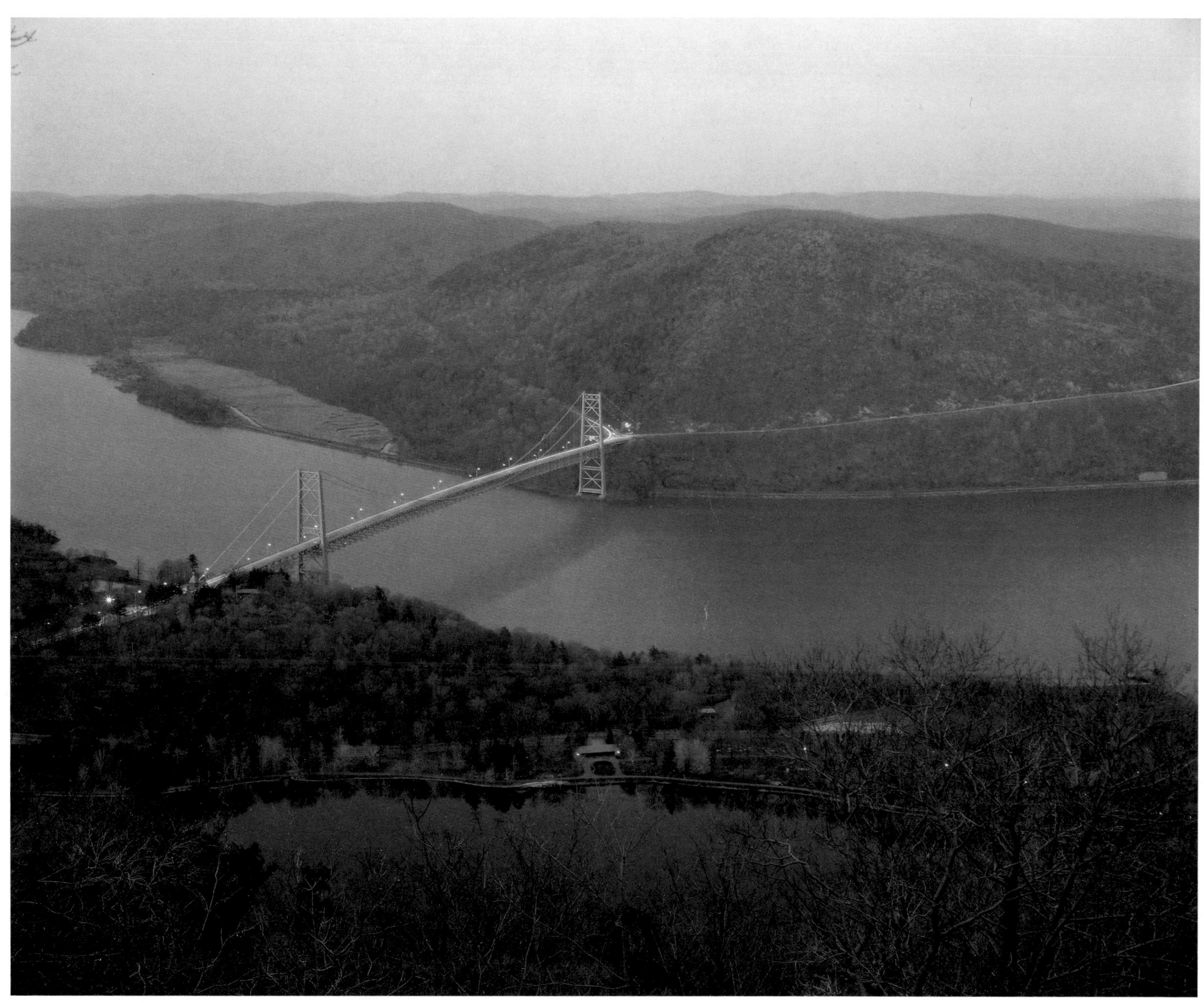

William Clift, *Evening, Bear Mountain Bridge, Hudson River, New York*, 1986

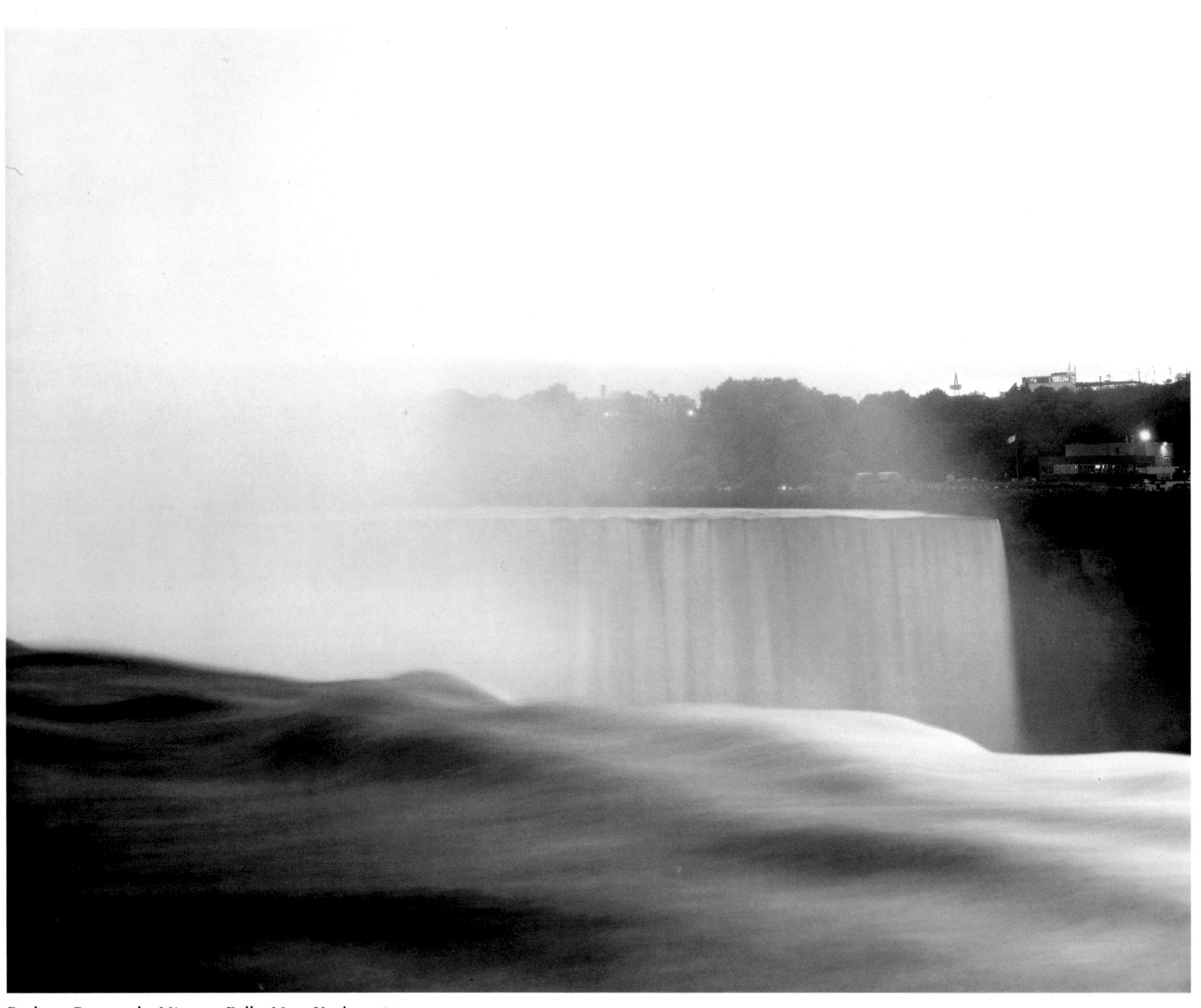

Barbara Bosworth, *Niagara Falls, New York,* 1986

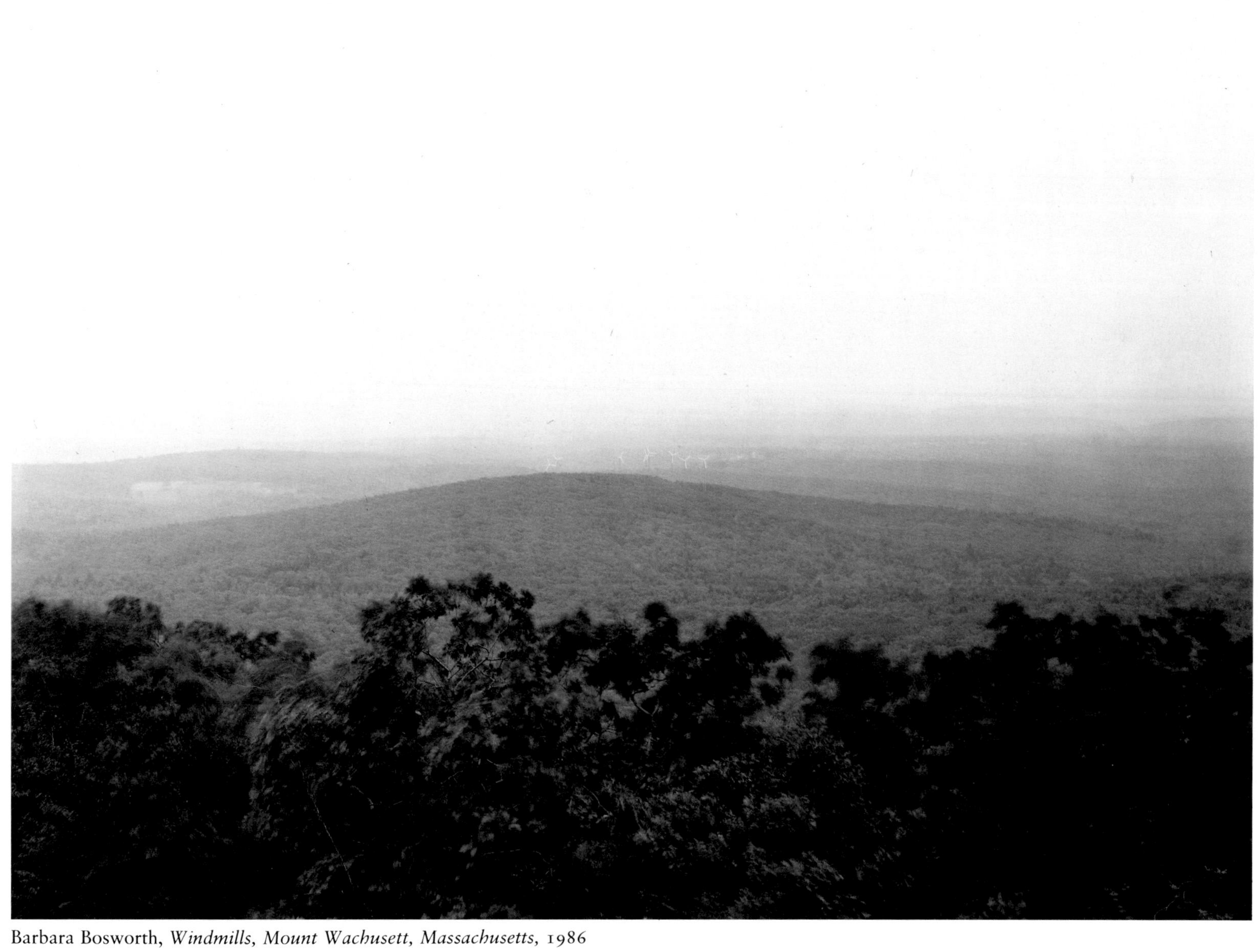

Barbara Bosworth, *Windmills, Mount Wachusett, Massachusetts,* 1986

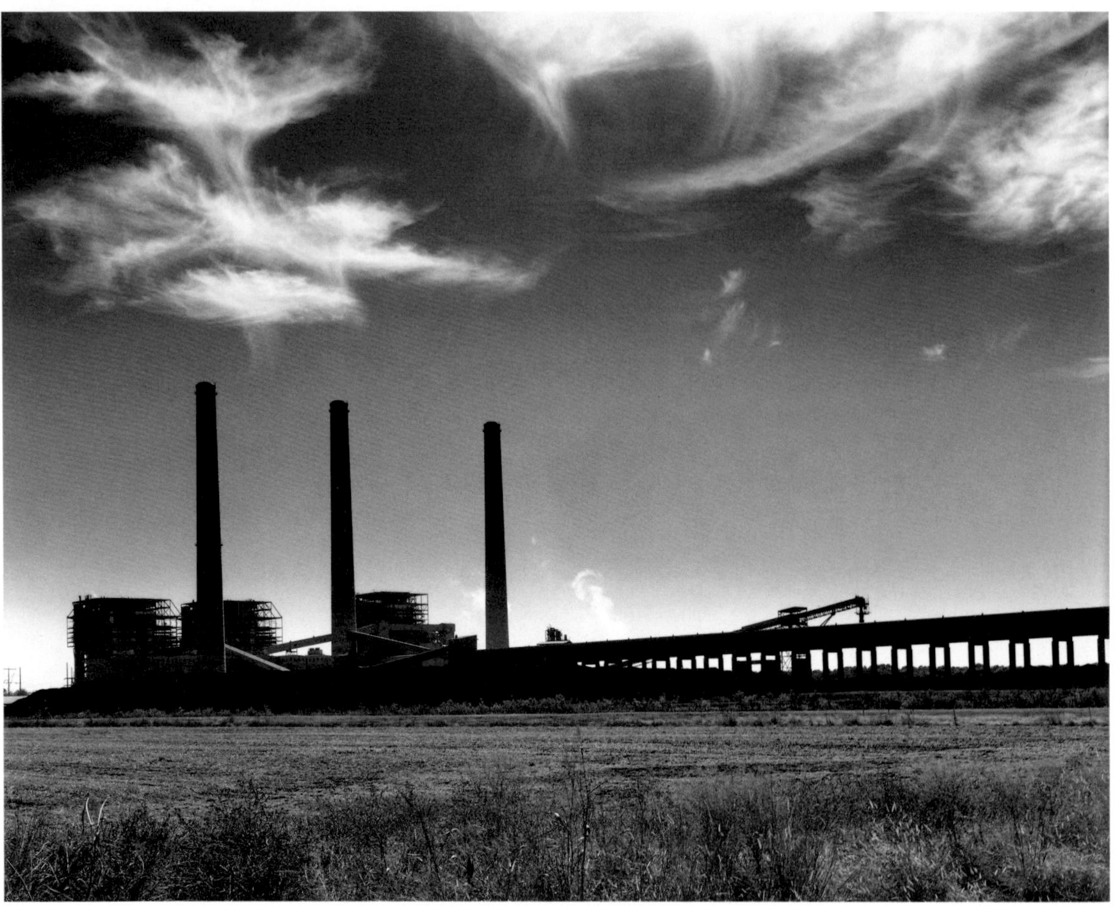

A. J. Meek, *Golf Course and Chemical Plant near Donaldsonville, Louisiana*, 1988

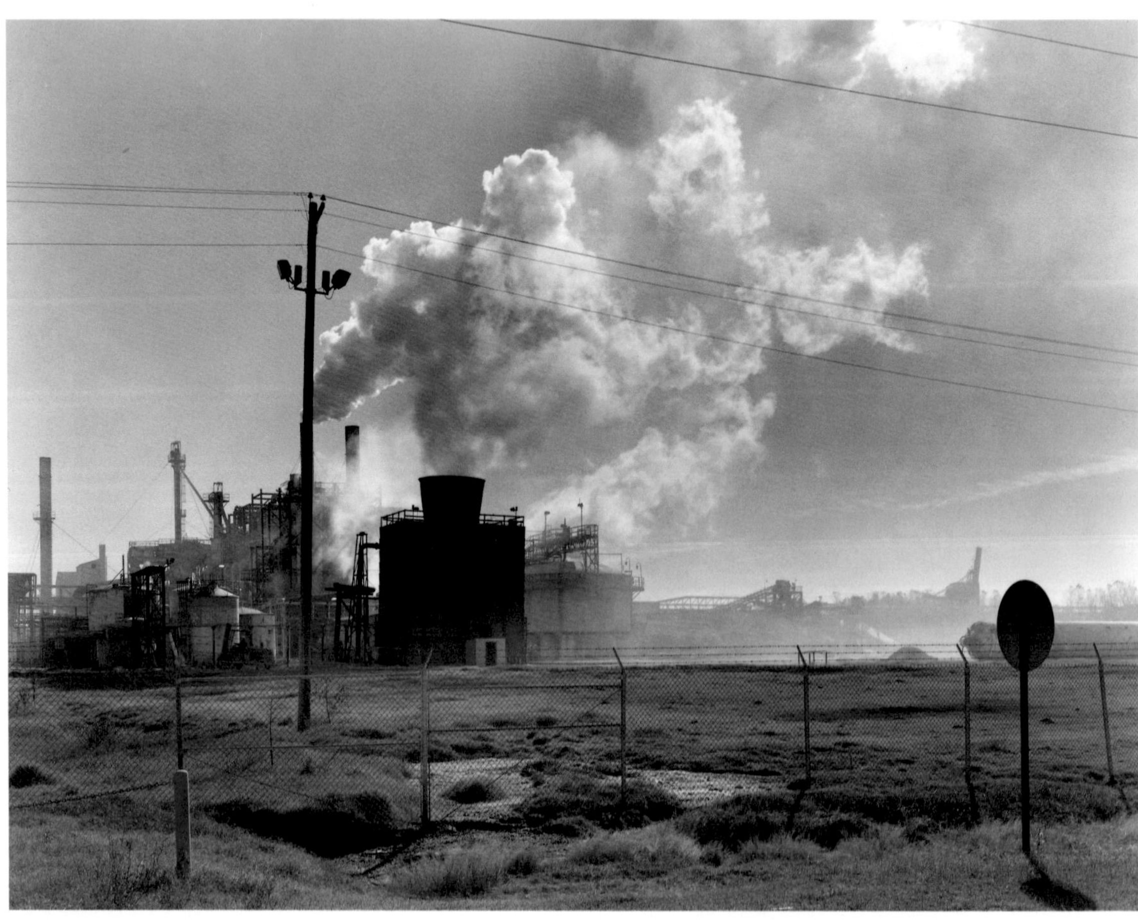

A. J. Meek, *View looking through a fence, Big Cajun Power Plant, New Roads, Louisiana*, 1987

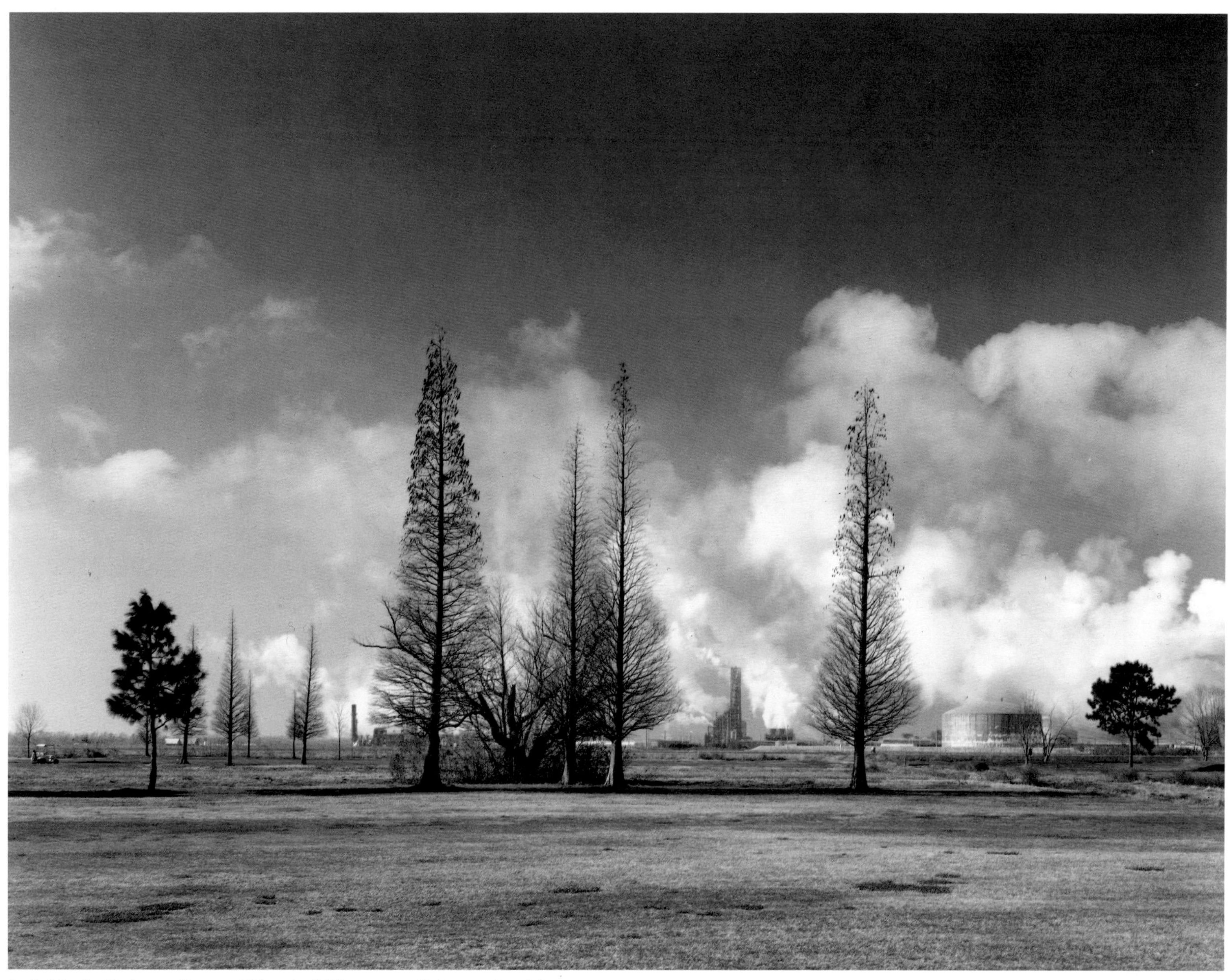

A. J. Meek, *Geismar Dragon/Chemical Plant near Geismar, Louisiana,* 1988

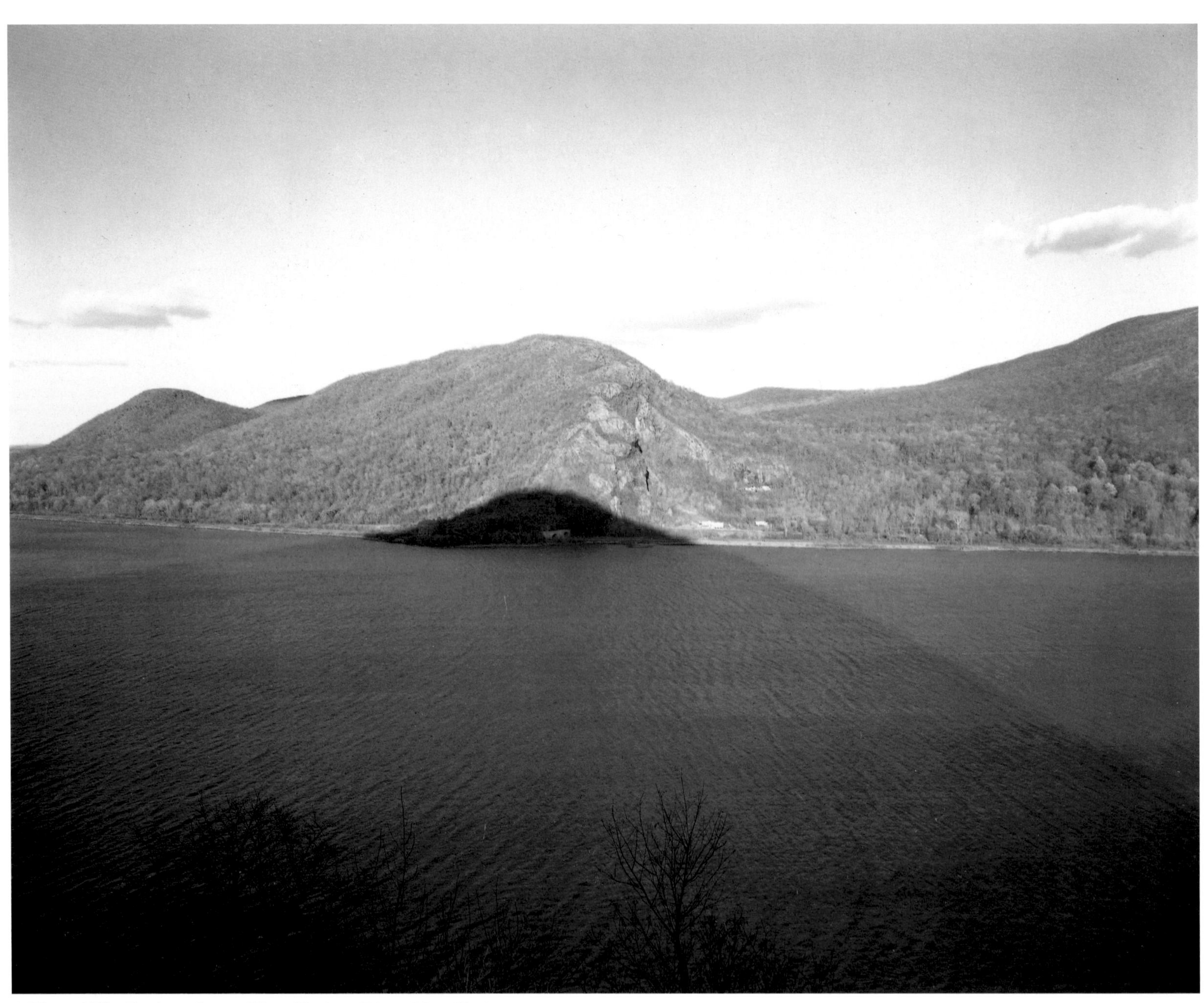

William Clift, *Shadow, Storm King, Hudson River, New York*, 1988

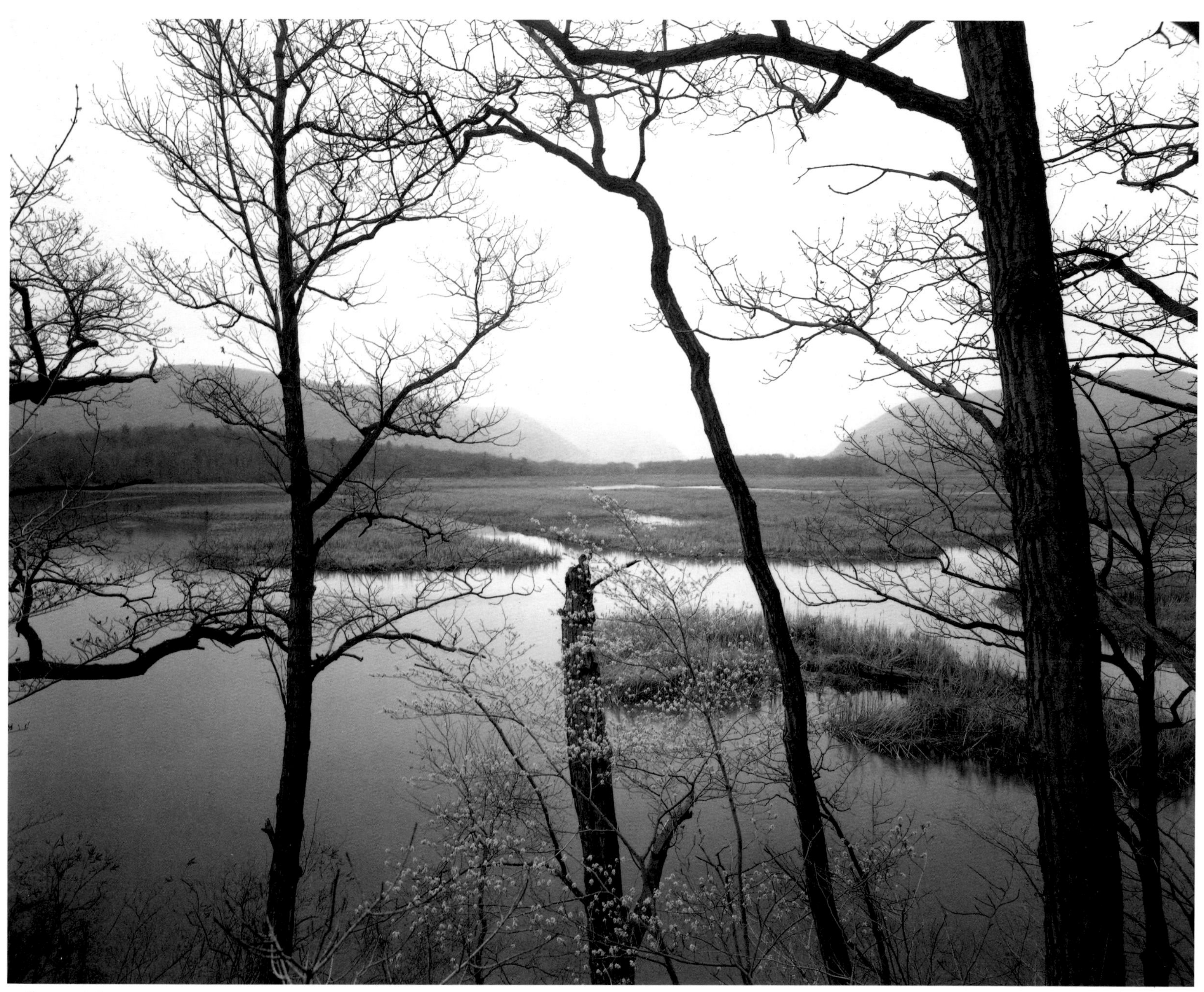

William Clift, *Constitution Marsh, Hudson River, New York,* 1987

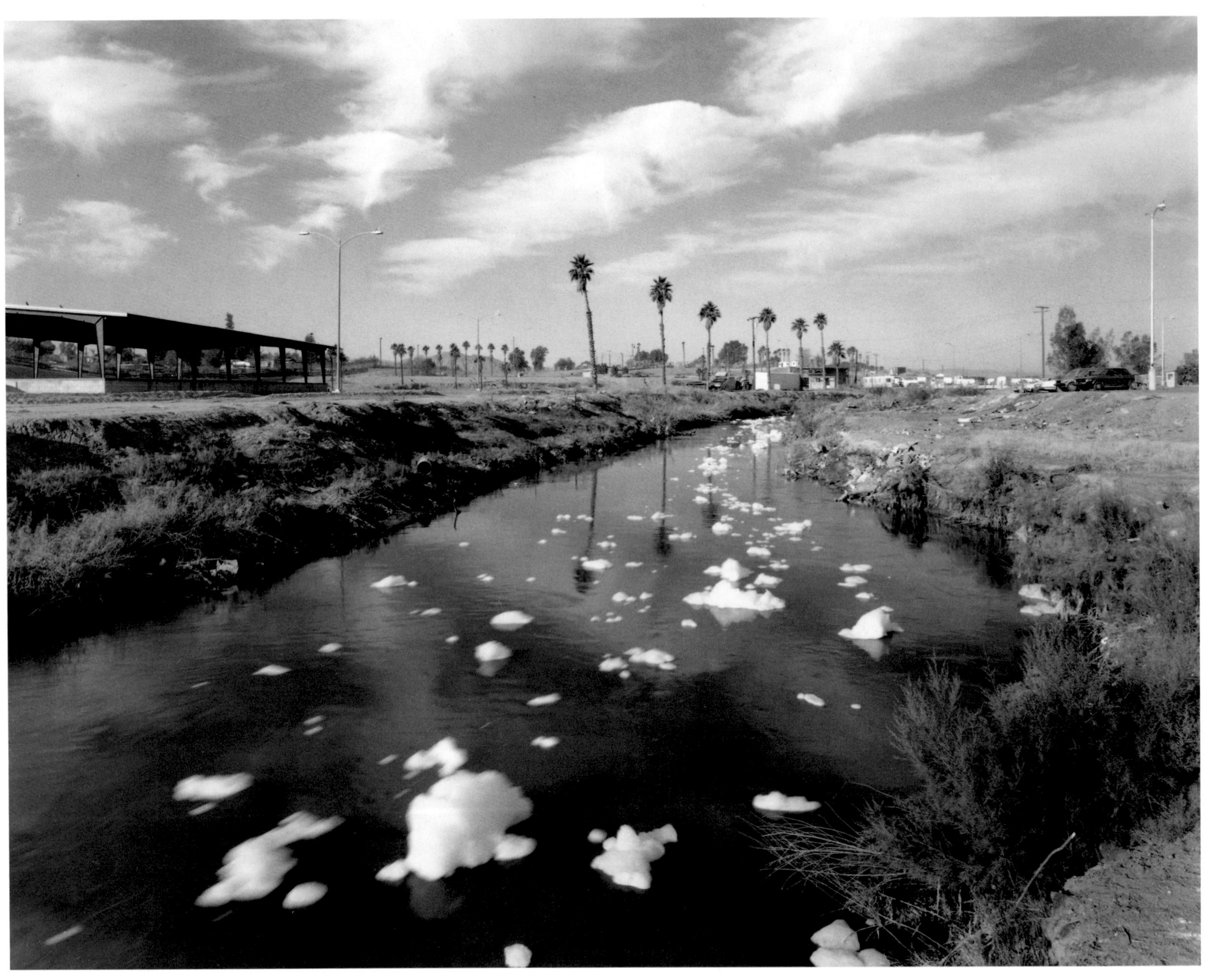

Robert Dawson, *Polluted New River, Calexico, California,*
from the "California Toxics Project," 1989

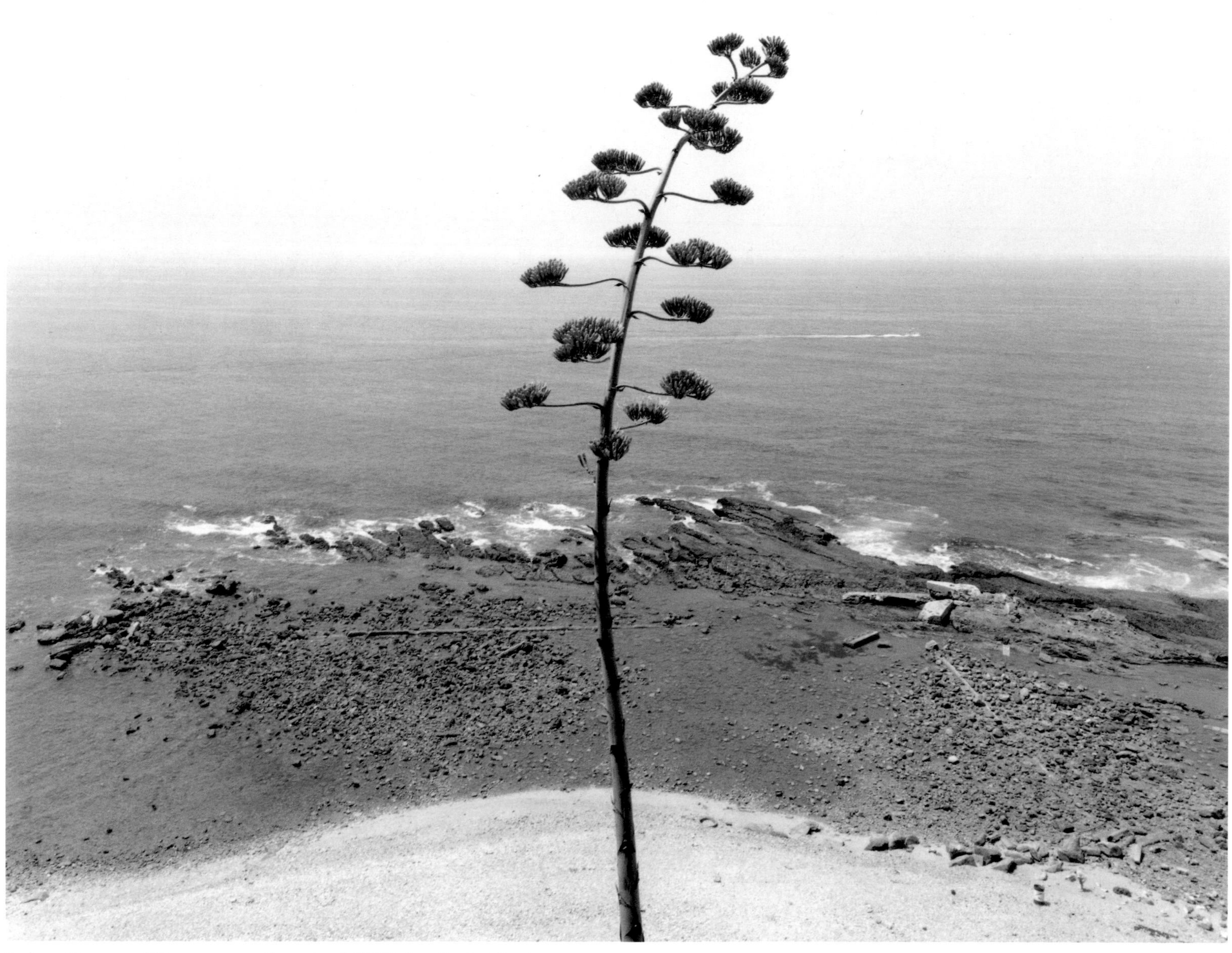

Robert Dawson, *Where 55,000 Pounds of DDT Are Buried Underwater,*
Santa Monica Bay, California, from the "California Toxics Project," 1989

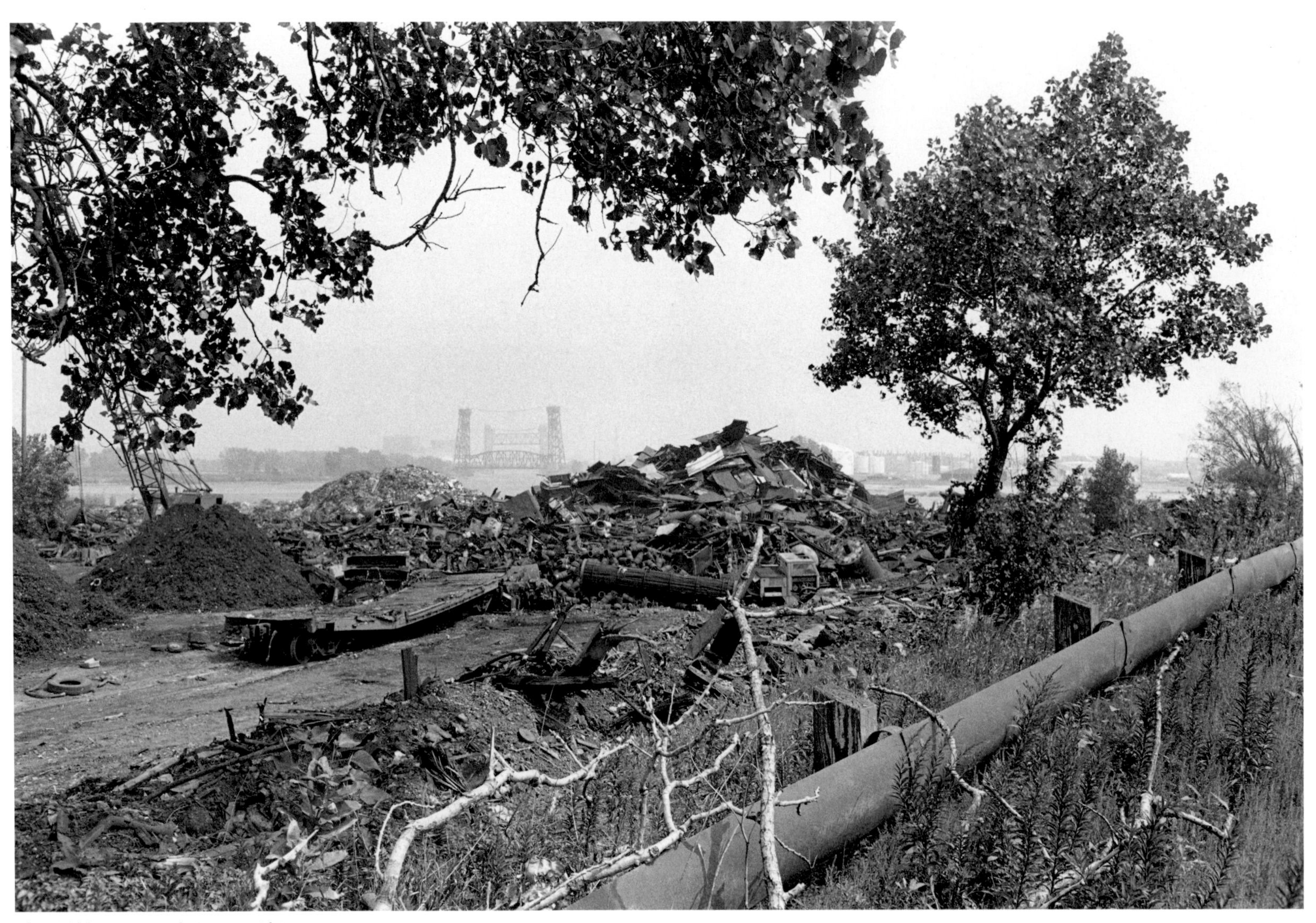

Alan Tibbetts, *130th Street, Chicago, 1988*

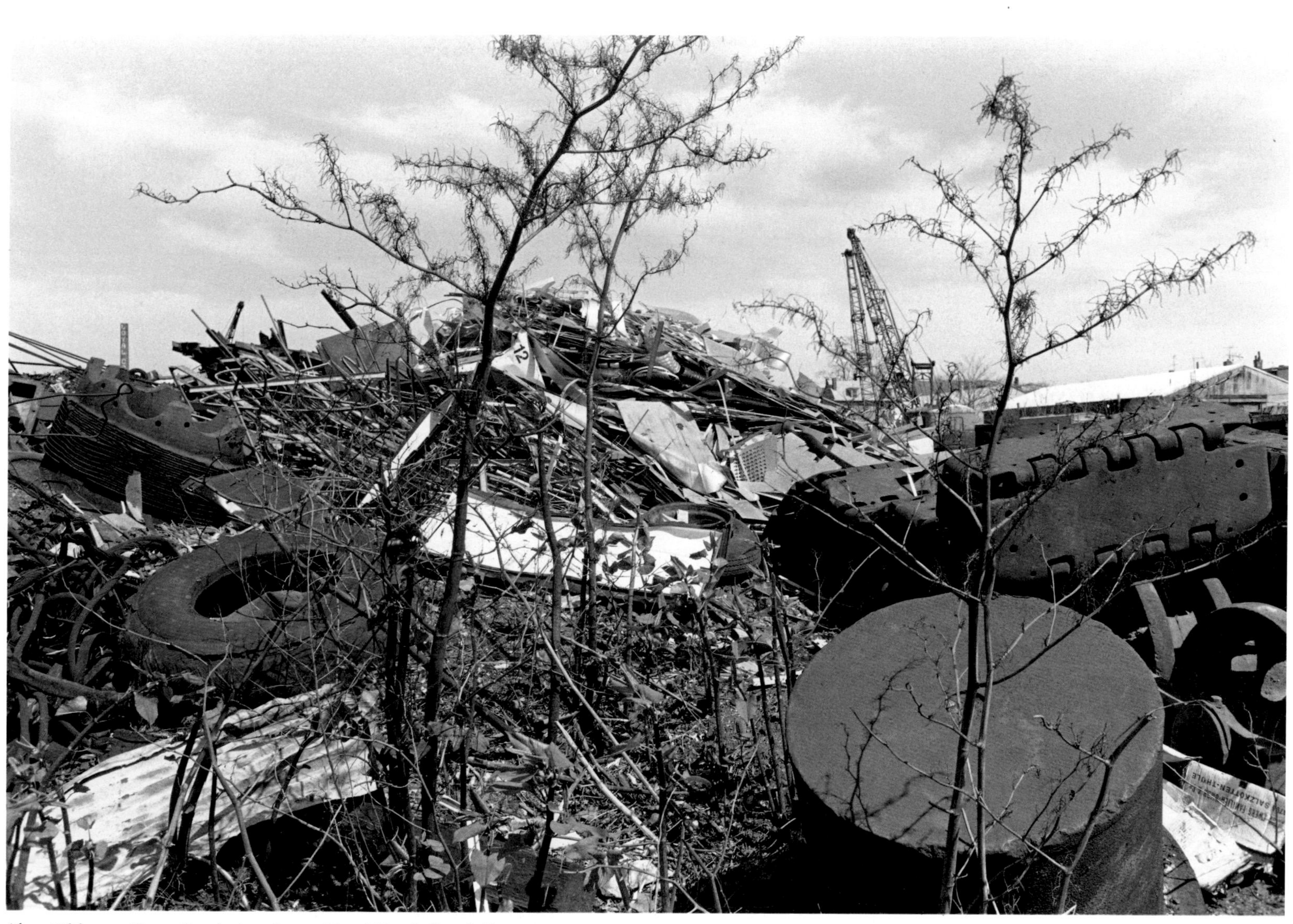

Alan Tibbetts, *Trees Bordering Scrap Metal Yard, South Boston,* 1989

about the social cost of dams, the second, poisonous life of mine tailings, and the methodical killing of black bears to protect stands of commercial timber.

We need another kind of relationship with the earth, a wiser, humbler, more deferential association, a more informed reciprocity. We share a biology. If we have a decision to ponder now, it is how to (re)incorporate the lands we occupy, after millennia of neglect, into our moral universe. We must incorporate not only our farmsteads and the retreats of the wolverine but the land upon which our houses, our stores, and our buildings stand. Our behavior, from planting a garden to mining iron ore, must begin to reflect the same principles.

In an essay called "Photographing Evil," the photographer Robert Adams addresses issues of artistic responsibility and social reform and considers photography's limits in dealing with the "certainty of evil." A curious reverberation in this essay is how, in his own photographs, Adams captures our corrosive relations with the land. He does so, in part, by avoiding the summary effect, the exclusionary aspect, of "pinup" nature photography. It is easier, certainly, to photograph what is beautiful in nature than what is dark, but the desire to *see* the other side of nature is a longing for wholeness we need to attend to. We need to see the wildness in wilderness if we are ever to grasp our differences and concordances with nature. Similarly, in considering how we will care for the earth (i.e., how we will care for ourselves), we must broaden our definition of landscape writing and landscape photography to include more than visions of wilderness and sojourns in wild lands. Such writing and photography must now convey the sense of an unbroken pattern of land and our responsibility for maintaining a commensal relationship with it.

The value of de facto and de jure wilderness is indisputable, and the need to protect it is essential. But the deeper, more pervasive issue—how we farm, how we log, how we fish— includes this intelligence. Our crisis is not a crisis of technology or law, of administration or professional skill, but a crisis of culture. The predicament has been elucidated straightforwardly in the work of Aldo Leopold, Rachel Carson, the late Lewis Mumford, the late Edward Abbey, and perhaps most forcefully in the work of Wendell Berry. The thinking is not esoteric or radical. A cursory reading of ethnographic reports from around the earth makes it clear that the *aberration* in human history is recent, short, and ours—a geography stripped of dignity and ethical responsibility.

Wild landscapes are necessary to our being. We require them as we require air and water. But we need, at the same time, to create a landscape in which wilderness makes deep and eminent sense as part of the whole, a landscape in which wilderness is not an orphan. □

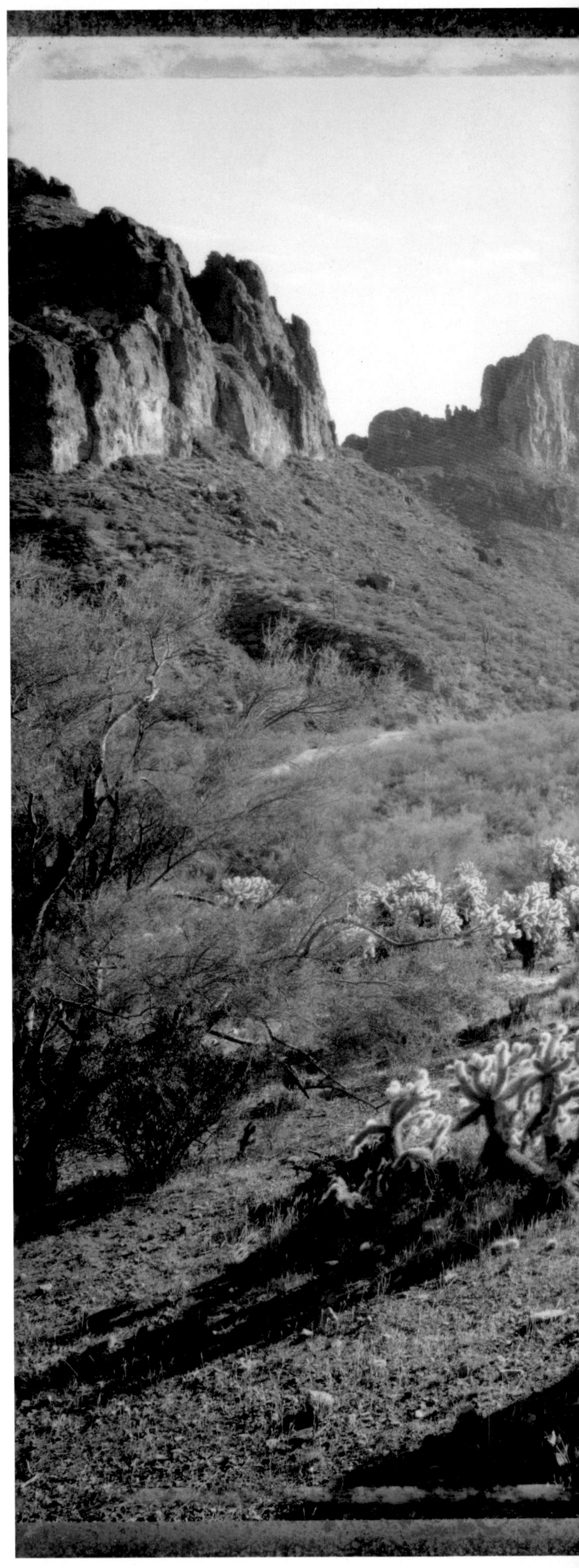

  Mark Klett, *Daytrip into the Superstitions, Arizona,* 1989

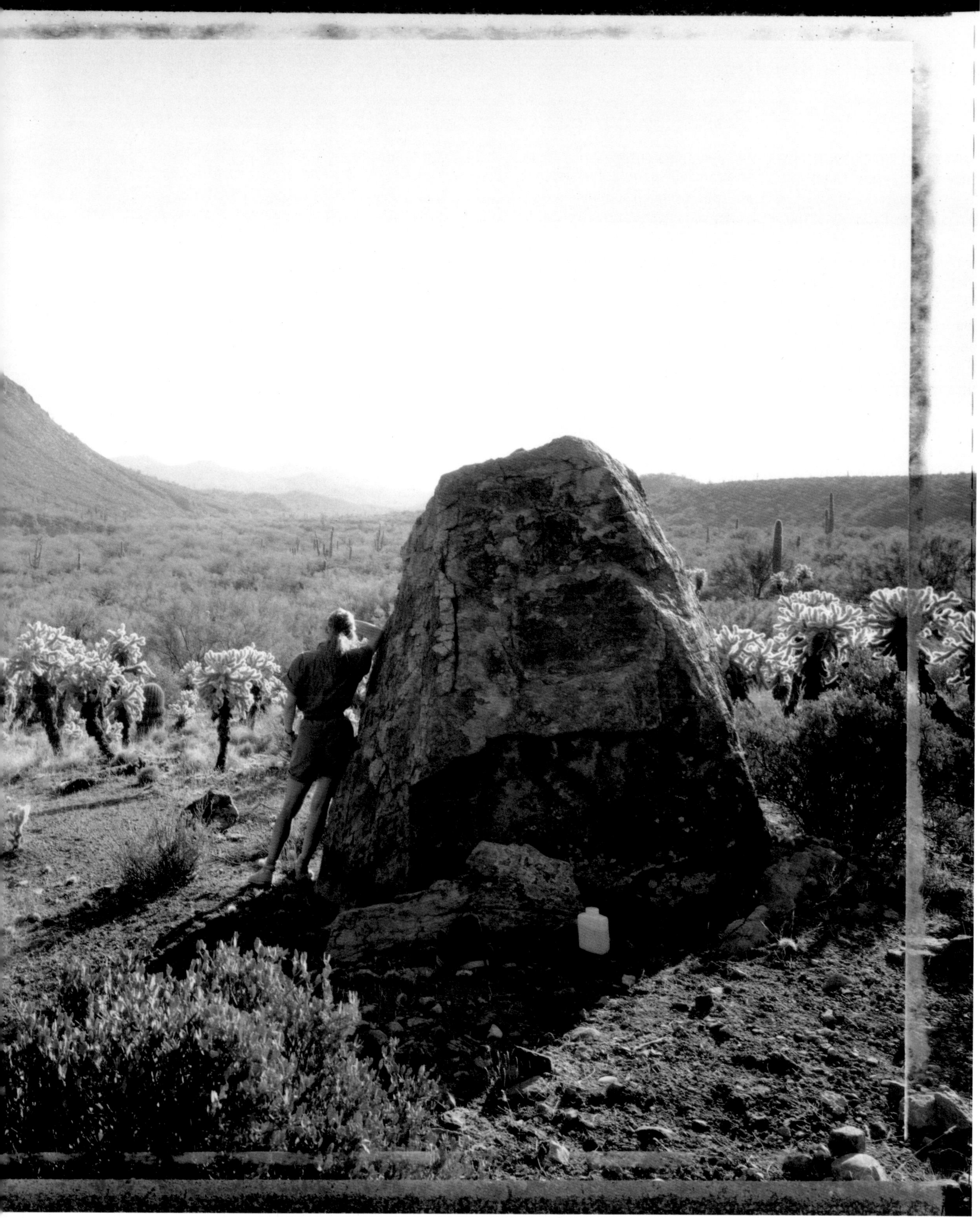

Land and Landscape

By Charles Hagen

From the first, photography of the American landscape has been tied up with the politics of the land. The photographs of T. H. O'Sullivan, William Bell, and others who accompanied the geological surveys of the West after the Civil War not only provided pictorial evidence of the regions the survey teams traveled through, but also were used to secure funding for further exploration. In a similar way, William Henry Jackson's photographs of Yosemite, along with Thomas Moran's paintings, are credited with helping persuade Congress to set aside land there for the first national park, while in the 1930s Ansel Adams's photographs were used to lobby Congress to pass further conservation legislation.

Beginning in the 1960s this process was continued by the Sierra Club, under the direction of David Brower, now head of Earth Island Institute. The first of the Club's famous "exhibit format" books, *This Is the American Earth,* was published in 1960, with photographs by Ansel Adams and others, and texts by Nancy Newhall. Oversized and beautifully printed, with luscious wilderness photographs accompanied by poetic texts, these "exhibit format" books proved enormously popular. Twenty-three have been published in the series to date, according to Jon Beckmann, the publisher of Sierra Club Books; however, the most recent title in the series was published in 1984, and by far the greatest number were published between 1960 and 1970, during Brower's tenure as director.

Some of the books were explicitly celebrations of the beauty of the American landscape. *"In Wildness Is the Preservation of the World",* published in 1962, paired Eliot Porter's photographs with excerpts from the writings of Henry David Thoreau. Other Sierra Club books from the time were what Philip Hyde, who photographed for the Club for many years, terms "battle books"—volumes that addressed a specific environmental or wilderness conservation issue. Perhaps the most celebrated of these was *The Place No One Knew: Glen Canyon on the Colorado* (1963), with photographs by Porter and others, which recorded the canyon drowned by Lake Powell at the height of the government dam-building mania that swept the West in the 1950s and early '60s. "That was a turning point in the conservation movement," Hyde recalls. "There weren't enough people who'd seen Glen Canyon and who'd raised their voice against the dam." But as a result of the book, Hyde argues, "a lot of people woke up to what had been lost." And the following year, when the Bureau of Reclamation proposed building two dams in the Grand Canyon, Brower published *Time and the River Flowing: The Grand Canyon,* which featured Hyde's photographs. "That was a battle book," Hyde says. "Its chief purpose was to fight the Grand Canyon dams." And the fight was successful: "the Bureau of Reclamation lost that fight, and they went into decline after that."

"We feel a great sense of reverence about them," Beckmann says today of the exhibit-format books. Moreover, he adds, "they built up the membership of the Club phenomenally. Basically, the Sierra Club grew from a somewhat parochial West Coast organization to national prominence because of those books." The Sierra Club now publishes a wide range of environmental and outdoors books, including travel guides and activist-oriented titles. Nevertheless, picture books remain among the group's most popular titles.

While Sierra Club Books may have moved away from the exhibit-format books, the series has had an enormous impact both on the environmental movement and landscape photography. "I think there are few people who weren't profoundly affected by Brower's exhibit format books in the '60s," says T. H. Watkins, editor of *Wilderness,* the monthly magazine of the Washington-based Wilderness Society. "I think they had an impact comparable to that of Thomas Moran's paintings of the Yellowstone in the 1880s."

Today, the idea behind the exhibit-format books lives on in the Club's calendars. Begun in the mid 1960s and now published in five different models, the calendars sell over a million copies a year all told. While they have spawned a host of imitators, the calendars have become a focus of criticism from photographers and naturalists alike. The "most basic message" of the calendars, Beckmann says, is of "the beauty of nature— they're wonderful photographs produced well. It annoys me that the photo world looks down their noses at the calendar," he continues. "But we think the success of what we've done, and the fact there are some really wonderful photographers in them, justifies them."

Photographs play a major role in the work of many other environmental organizations as well. Watkins reports that *Wilderness* is "using more photographs than at any time in the history of the magazine. People can't save what they don't know, and photography is still the best medium for getting this across." *Wilderness*'s extensive use of photography, Watkins argues, adds to the effectiveness of the organization's efforts to lobby Congress and increase public awareness of environmental issues. "Photography gives the magazine tremendous weight on the Hill and among TV and newspaper people," he reports.

Another approach to the use of photographs and other media in environmental battles has been taken by Greenpeace, the activist group whose many demonstrations and other staged events have drawn enormous media attention. "There's a Greenpeace action somewhere in the world every day," reports Jay Townsend, director of photography for Greenpeace U.S.A. And media coverage of these events is "absolutely essential," he adds. "The events themselves last only a short period, but the photos are printed over and over, and so short-term events

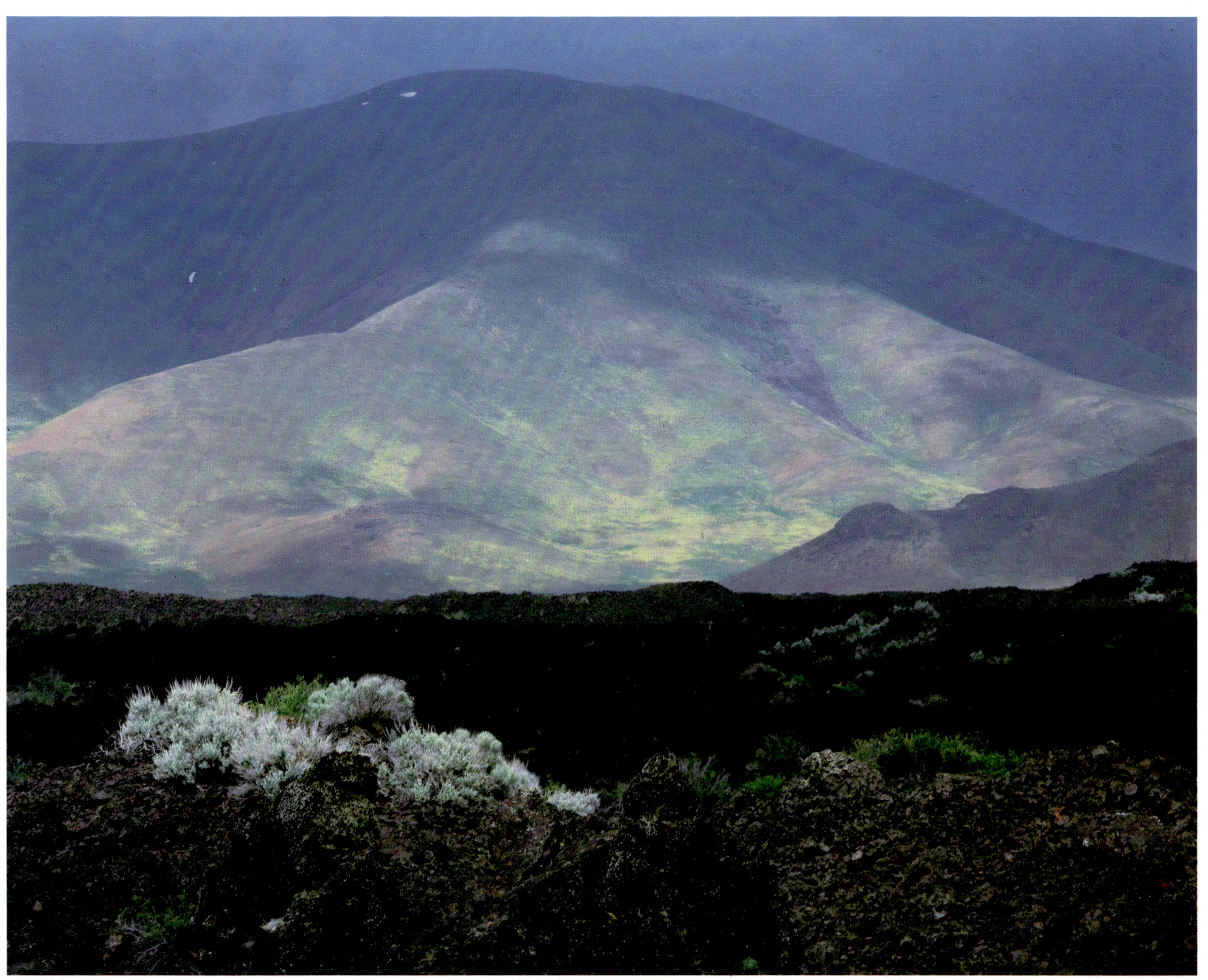

Philip Hyde, *Sunset on Las Tres Virgenes, Baja California, Mexico,* 1981

*I look for things that express nature as it is—not how I might mold it into
something else. I guess I'm somewhat of a realist—whatever that means.
I'm interested in communicating what I see. I want nature to speak
directly, and not get too much in the way of that.*

PHILIP HYDE

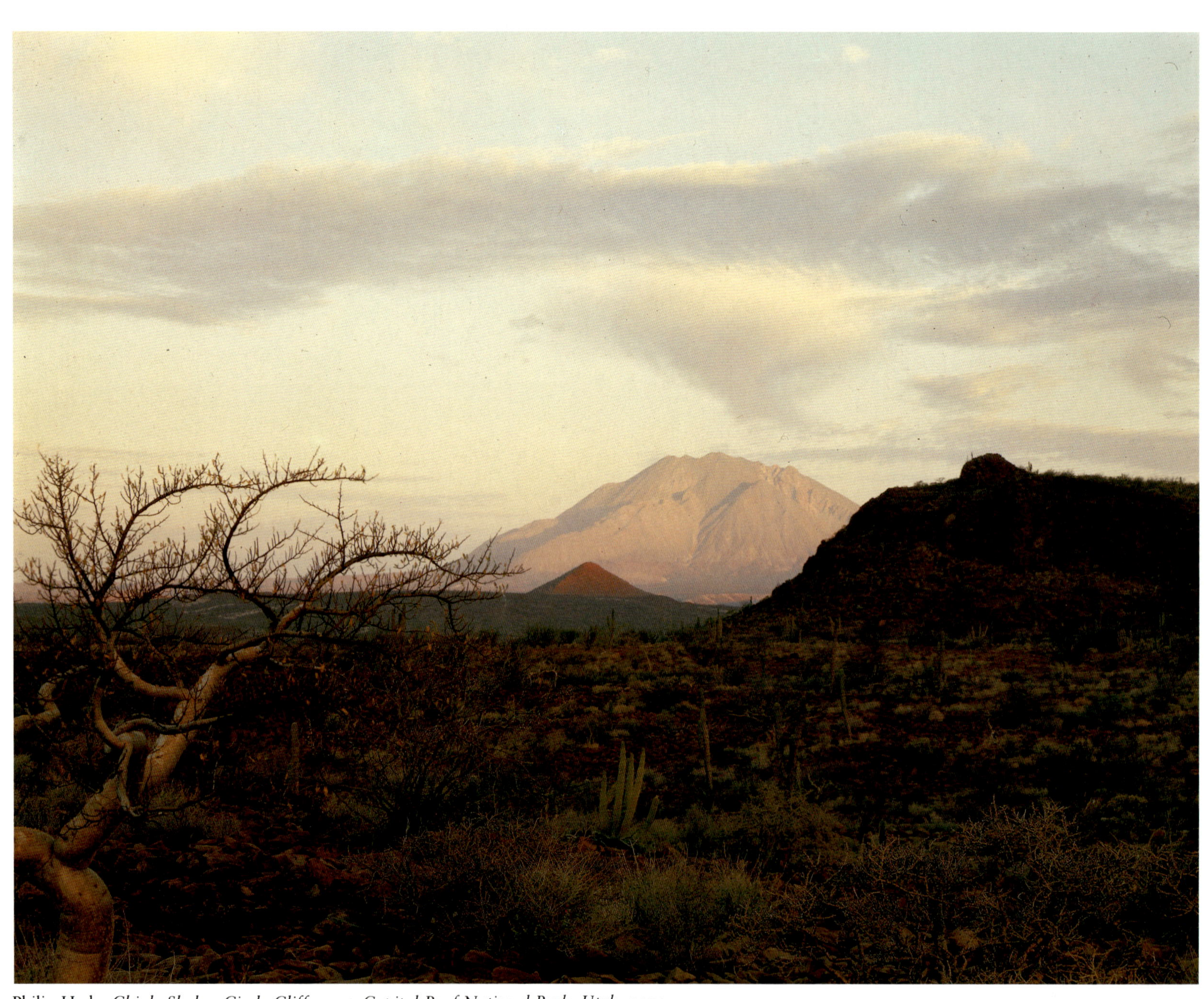

Philip Hyde, *Chinle Shales, Circle Cliffs, near Capitol Reef National Park, Utah,* 1970

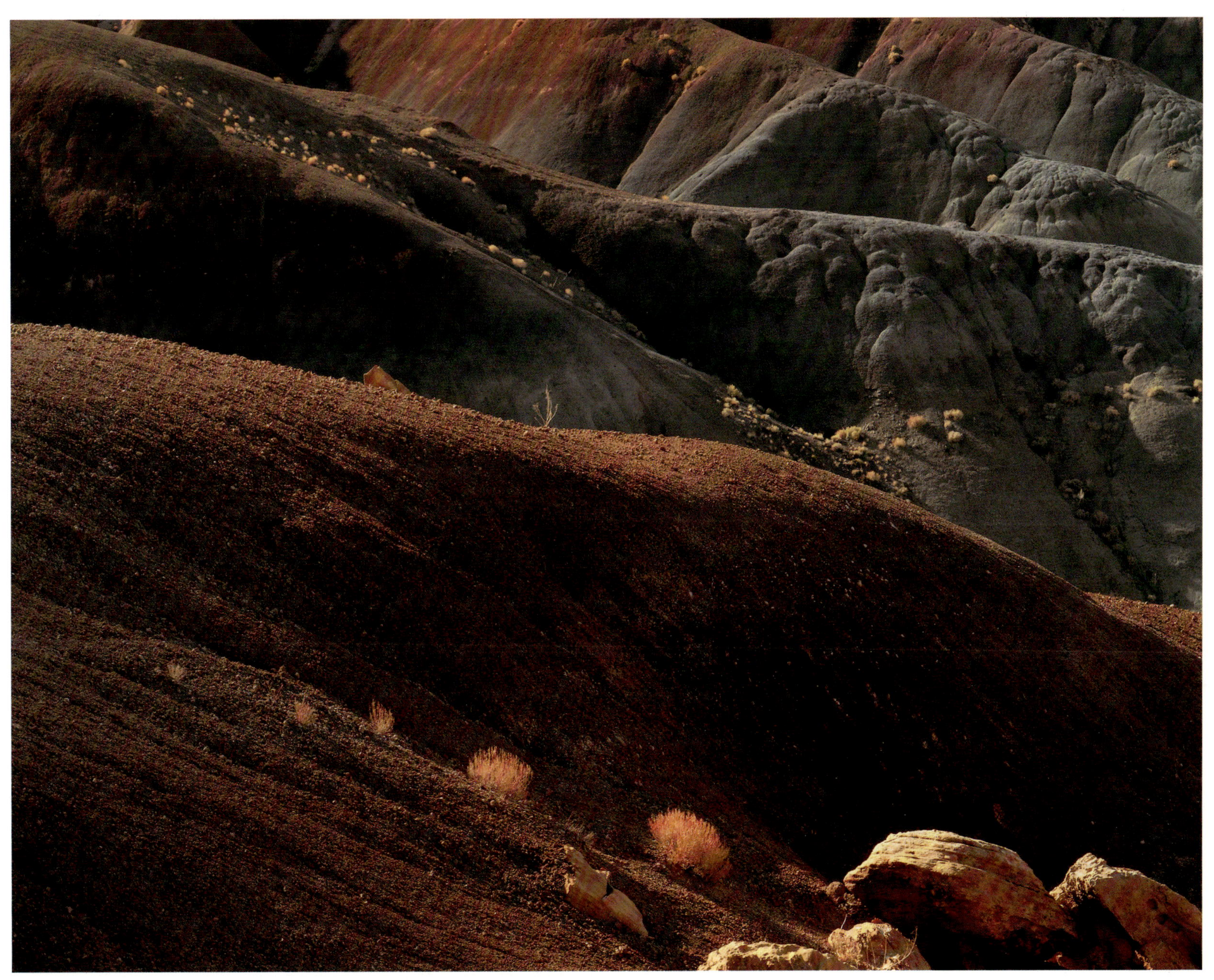

Philip Hyde, *Lava Flow, Flowers on Hills, Craters of the Moon National Monument, Idaho,* 1987

can have long-term effects. All of our actions are done with the impact of the media in mind," Townsend explains. "If a tree falls in the woods and nobody sees it, how do you know it fell? But if you have a dozen photographers there to document it, everyone knows. We do a lot of stuff that isn't necessarily set up for the media," Townsend notes. "But we see photo ops as an effective tool—one of many tools we use."

Despite this innovative use of photographs to address environmental problems directly, the dominant style of depicting the land remains the beautiful, fully detailed large-format style of Ansel Adams, Eliot Porter, and their artistic descendants. Recently, though, a number of photographers have begun to question traditional landscape photography for not adequately reflecting the embattled nature of the American Western landscape and for producing what writer Barry Lopez has termed, in another context, "pinups" of a pristine wilderness. As Colorado photographer Robert Adams puts it, "It just seems to me that that style is not particularly accurate. I see pictures of untrammelled nature as so freakish."

Watkins, though, rejects such charges. "I've been in the wilderness," he says. "It looks like that. Nobody who's ever spent any amount of time in the wilderness is going to say those photographs are lying—they ain't!" Robert Glenn Ketchum also believes that such pictures are not in themselves false. "I don't agree with people who say the wilderness doesn't exist anymore," he argues. "I spend too much time out in those wild lands. I know it's still out there. I think the wilderness is still legitimate as subject matter—but it's not all that's out there."

Hyde, too, has thought about what the most appropriate way to photograph the land might be. "I've always tried to seek out places that had some controversy about them," he says. But "I've never been an enthusiast of what we used to call 'dirty pictures,' " photographs that emphasized environmental problems directly. "My objective was to show the place as beautiful as it was, and I always felt that would be all that was needed."

The Western landscape has changed radically since Hyde began to photograph it. In recent years, he has photographed extensively in the desert—and, he says, "there's been a real change there—military air pollution, you could call it. There are millions of acres that the military controls and has totally ruined, by bombing them. That's an issue I'd like to see a lot more attention paid to."

"I come out of the Ansel Adams school," says Ketchum, whose books include *The Hudson River & the Highlands* (1985) and *The Tongass: Alaska's Vanishing Rain Forest* (1987). But in addition to pictures that are "definitely a celebration, jubilant photographs," Ketchum says he tries to depict "the hard facts of the new American landscape"—clear-cuts, nuclear power plants, polluted rivers. "I make elegant, beautiful photographs of these horrible scenes," Ketchum explains; as a result, "people have a strong approach-avoidance conflict in dealing with the pictures." What he tries to do, Ketchum says, is to make "a beguiling photograph out of a difficult subject, so people will not just walk by." To reach an audience, Ketchum argues, it's important to make the pictures beautiful: "If you only had tough pictures, no one would look at them. The trick is to keep people engaged."

"Art brings me a podium from which to discuss the politics of the scenes I photograph," says Ketchum. "That's the same thing Ansel was doing. I'm just turning up the heat, and bringing in the books as a vehicle for the politics—which Ansel never did. He made political speeches, but his active aesthetic work did not engage landscape in a directly political way."

The question of how to photograph the land is not simply one of aesthetics, but has economic and political ramifications as well. Robert Adams argues that beautiful pictures of untarnished wilderness can lull people into ignoring what's actually happening to the land. "Few people in the East realize what's happened out here," he says. "Much of this stuff—one thinks primarily of the military and its nuclear weapons and waste—has been dumped on the West by people in the East." Adams regards many of the landscape books published today as essentially nostalgic, celebrating a landscape that has been irreversibly altered. "Those places have been so damaged," he notes. "Books of that sort are like keepsakes, to remind us of what the places were like." Today, Adams says, "the publishing market is awash in sentimental, rather formulaic landscape books. It makes it hard to find a publisher for pictures that are less immediately ingratiating. It's the old 'give 'em what they want' syndrome. And you can see it throughout the culture. It's a very serious problem."

What is the appropriate way today to depict the landscape? "I come back to the idea that on the whole it's better to try to tell as broadly accurate a truth as possible," Adams says. "I have sympathy for people wanting that other kind of picture," Adams continues. "But I'm afraid it's an escapist instinct, and a dangerous one—though we all share it."

In the end the debate over landscape photography is about the competing demands of art and politics—and it's a debate in which there are no easy answers. On the one hand, photographers try to use their medium to its fullest capabilities, to provide a convincing and moving image of the world. On the other hand, to be politically effective these photographers must reach a broad audience—and the temptation is to make pictures that will be easily acceptable to that audience. For Adams, though, nature as it is now includes the presence of people. "The more you can include bits of the chaos of our everyday world" in landscape photographs, he argues, "the more convincing it will seem."

Just how much evidence of mankind's involvement with the land to include is a tricky question. Even Greenpeace has been forced to make some concessions in this regard, in a calendar they produce. "People don't want pictures of dying dolphins on their walls all month long," says Townsend. "So we do use beautiful nature shots as the main pictures. The tougher pictures are there, just smaller—in the calendar grid."

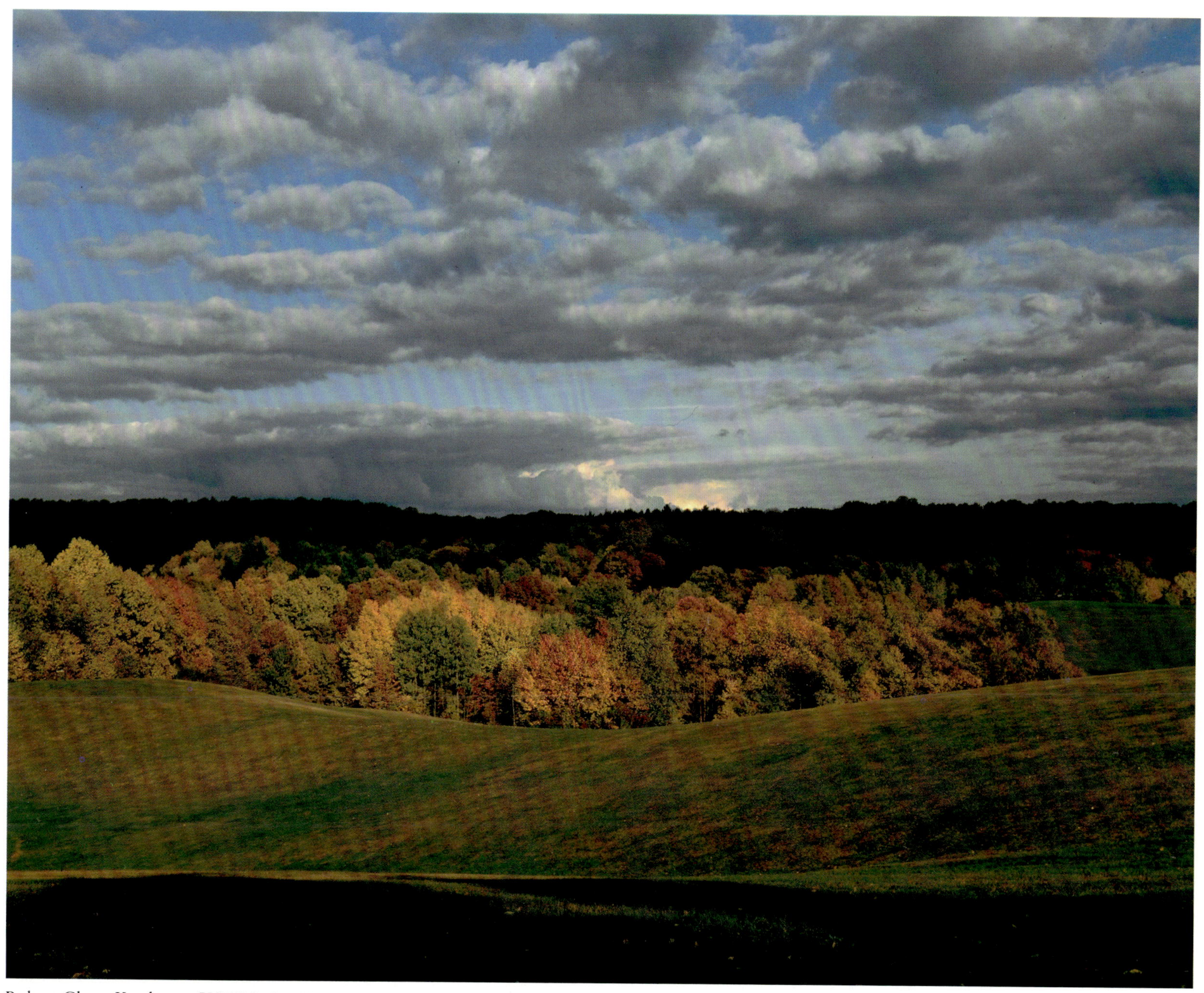

Robert Glenn Ketchum, *CVNRA # 462,* 1987

I try to make a beguiling photograph out of a difficult subject, so people will not just walk by. If you only had tough pictures, no one would look at them. The trick is to keep people engaged.

ROBERT GLENN KETCHUM

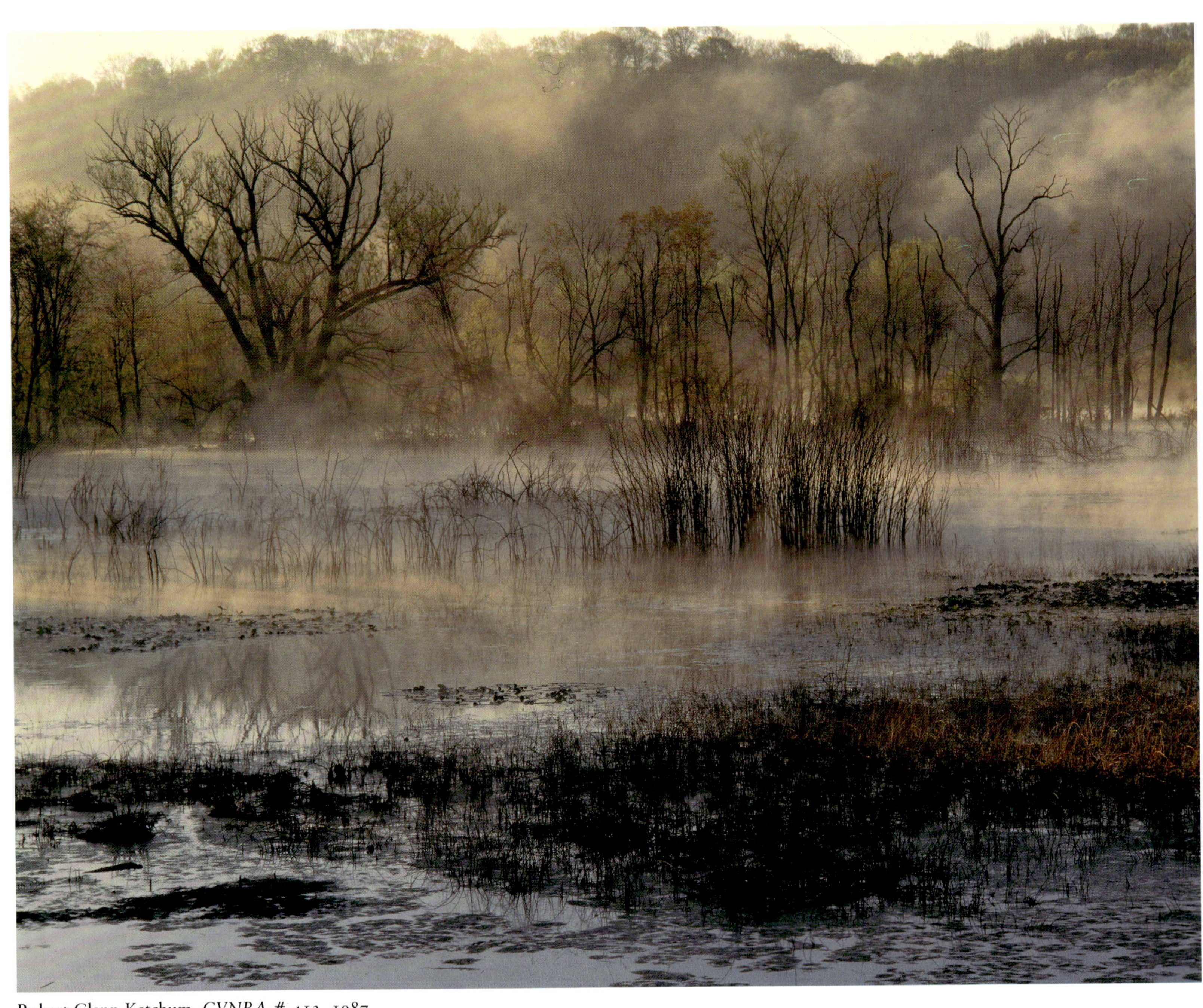

Robert Glenn Ketchum, *CVNRA # 412, 1987*

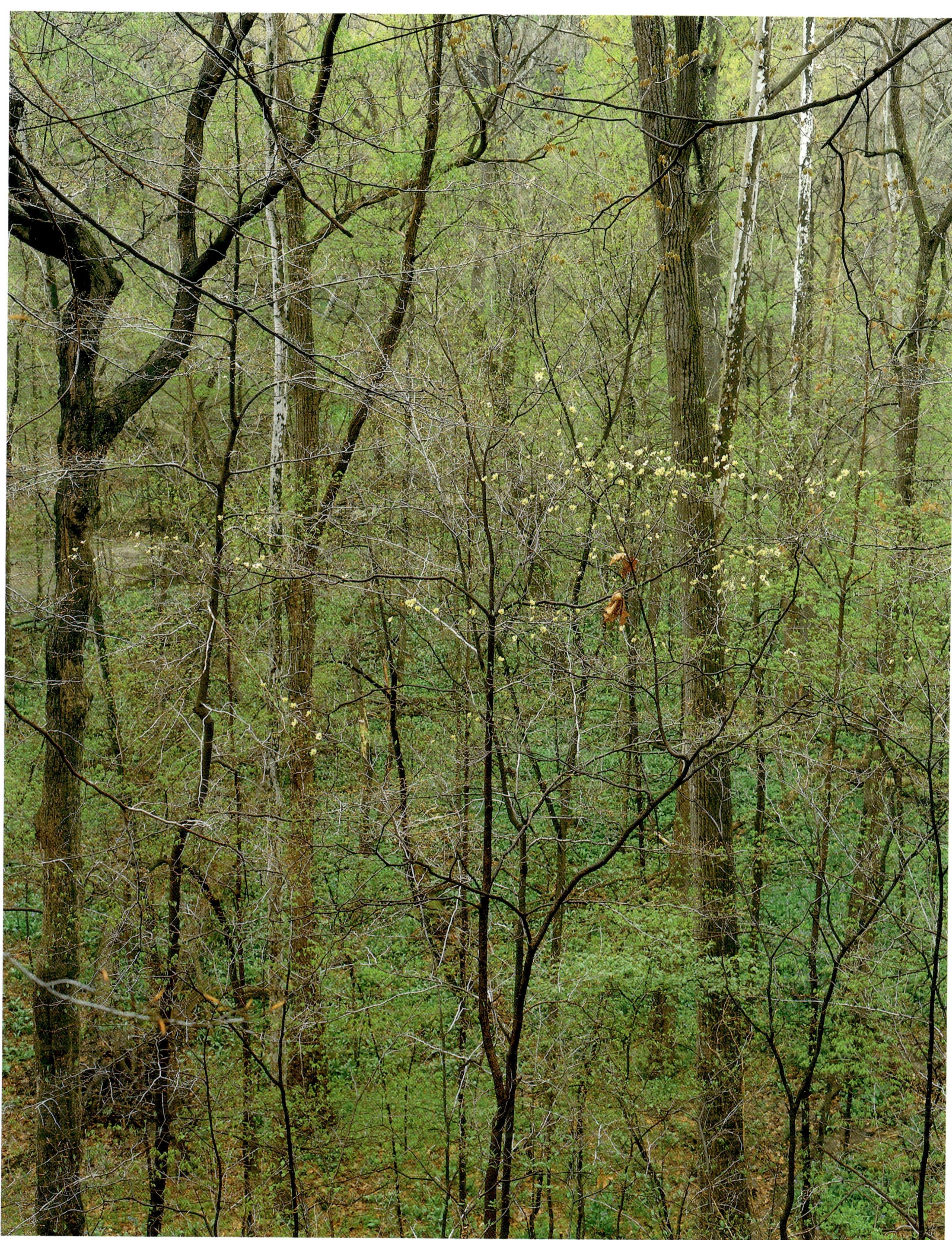

Robert Glenn Ketchum, *CVNRA # 945, 1988*

Power and Smoke: Two Statements

By John Pfahl

I have frequently noticed that the electric-power companies have chosen the most picturesque locations in America in which to situate their enormous plants. This is likely due to a need for rivers and waterfalls to propel their turbines, or for lakes and oceans to cool their reactors. It may also attest to the importance placed upon being isolated from large population centers for safety considerations. Whatever the reason, it sometimes seems that there is an almost transcendental connection between power and the natural landscape. Even the names given to the plants conjure up an Arcadian vision of the land: Seabrook, Crystal River, Indian Point, Palo Verde.

For me, power plants in the natural landscape represent only the most extreme example of man's willful domination over the wilderness. It is the arena where the needs and ambitions of an ever-expanding population collide most forcefully with the finite resources of nature.

It is not without trepidation that I have appropriated the codes of "the Sublime" and "the Picturesque" in my work. After all, serious photographers have spent most of this century trying to expunge such extravagances from their art. The tradition lives on, mostly in calendars and picture postcards. I was challenged to rework and revitalize that which had been so roundly denigrated. However, by making the landscape appear so romantic, would it promote the naive impression that these power plants were living in blissful harmony with nature? Would my work be co-opted by industry? I needn't have worried. For the most part, the work has been received in the same spirit as it was intended.

In order to make my observations rise to the metaphoric plane, I deliberately searched out a variety of power sources in addition to nuclear, including fossil fuel, hydro, wind, solar, and geothermal. I felt that concentrating on nuclear power alone would detract from my larger ambitions and reduce the project to a specific political agenda. I gradually learned that the other, supposedly more benign, sources of energy all had their dark sides, that the *actual* harm done to the environment was at least as disturbing as the potential harm from nuclear mishaps. Familiar dangers seem to get preempted by unfamiliar ones.

There seems to be no easy, black-and-white solution to the environmental dilemma. I have become uncomfortable with reducing the tangle to a generic, ideologically correct version of reality. As Estelle Jussim wrote, it is almost impossible for a single photograph to state both the problem *and* the solution. I want to make photographs whose very ambiguity provokes thought, rather than cuts it off prematurely. I want to make pictures that work on a more mysterious level, that approach the truth by a more circuitous route.

(Artist's statement)

The prodigious display of smoke bursting forth from the stacks of the Bethlehem Steel coke operation in Lackawanna, New York, can best be seen from a low slag bluff overlooking the plant from the north. A narrow boat channel of dark water separates me from the silhouetted factory buildings bathed in the radiance of Lake Erie. By the simplest act of looking through the enormous telephoto lens of my Hasselblad, I thrust myself into a phantasmagoria of light and color. Simultaneously attracted and repelled, I feel myself engulfed in a truly awesome spectacle of nature. It is like suddenly being hurled into a roaring cataract, an erupting volcano, or a violent storm at sea. Alarm whistles blow and smoke discharges into the sky, expanding and changing form far more rapidly than I can imagine possible, and, at its absolute zenith, dissipating into thin air before I can take another breath.

The presentation has its own geyserlike rhythms and rationale, and fifteen to twenty minutes pass before another discharge takes place. Doubtless the efficiencies of the internal workings of the mill dictate a logic for the timings, but from my removed vantage point I can only see them as part of an irrational process, terrifying in its capriciousness. I wait again for what seems an interminable time, and just when I impatiently fear that the workmen have closed down the line ending the show for the day, the whole process suddenly starts over again. New colors, shapes, and textures arise from other stacks in different, hallucinatory combinations.

By good fortune, the prevailing winds blow the smoke away from where I like to stand, and I can see the dark bundles make their way inland. Occasionally, however, the clouds come right at me and I become immersed in a lung-searing atmosphere of toxicity. I grab at my equipment and stumble back to the car, trying all the while not to inhale too deeply. I recall the recent newspaper stories reporting that this particular plant is first in statewide rankings of highly toxic emissions, discharging 1.4 million tons of benzene alone into the air each year.

Later, at home, it strikes me that the smell of the smoke, overpowering at full strength, is unnervingly familiar to me. In much more dilute form, it wafts by on certain balmy days when I am working in the garden. I am hardly conscious of it. It is one of the many familiar aromas, along with the newly turned earth and the freshly cut grass, that I have come to identify with the notion of home.

(Adapted from *A Distanced Land: The Photographs of John Pfahl*, forthcoming from University of New Mexico Press.)

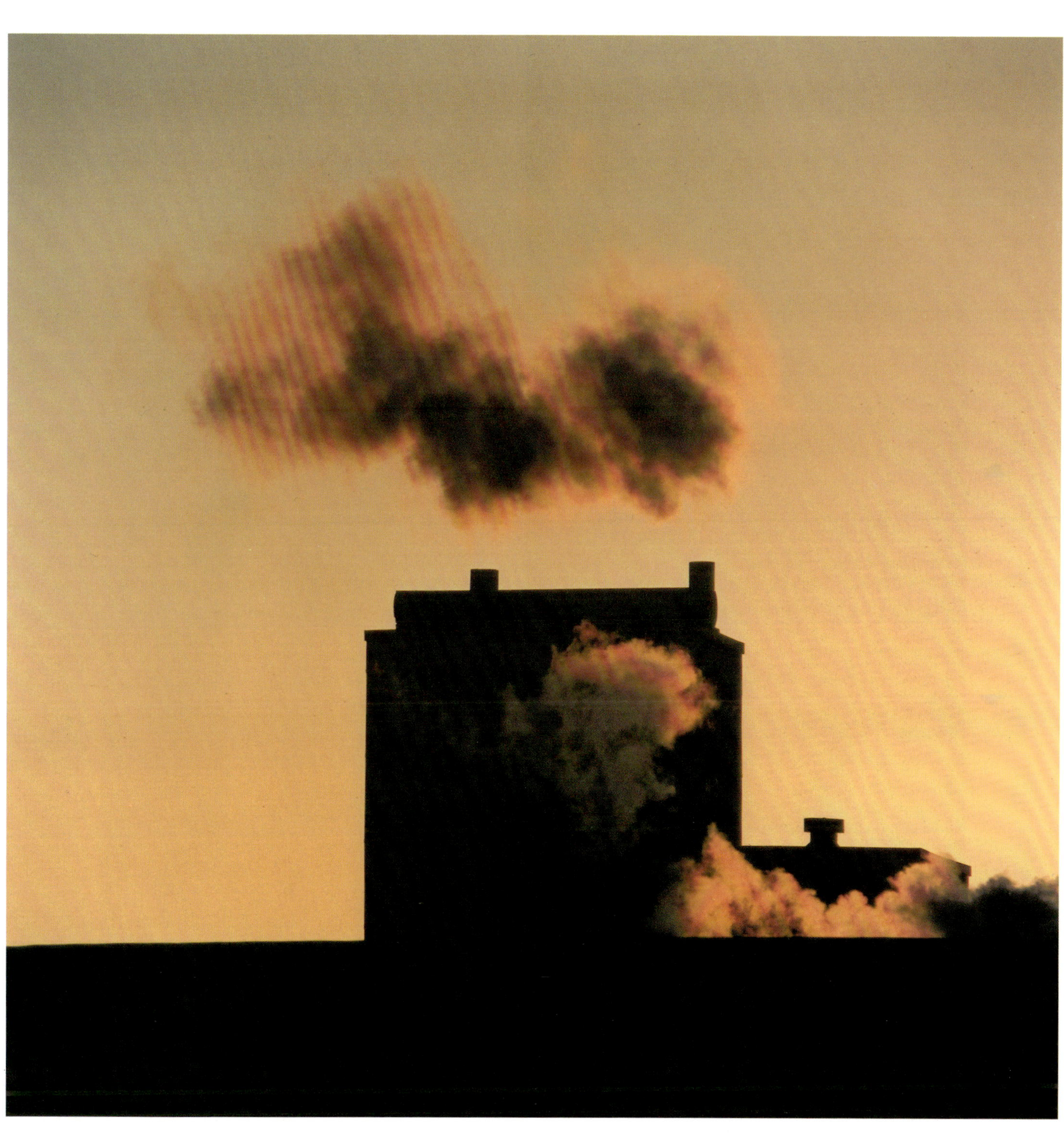

John Pfahl, *Goodyear Smoke*, 1989

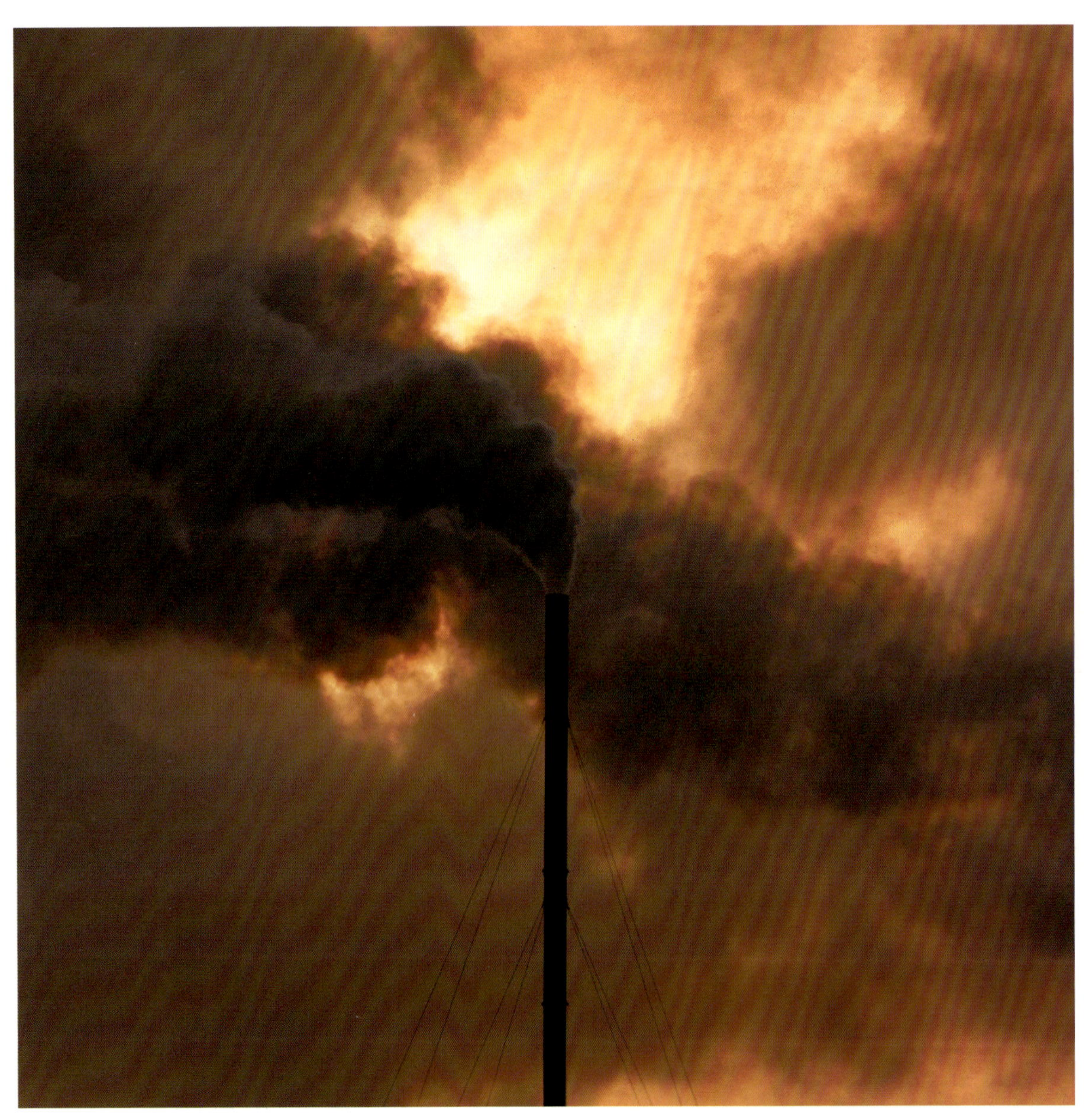

John Pfahl, *O-Cel-O Smoke*, 1989

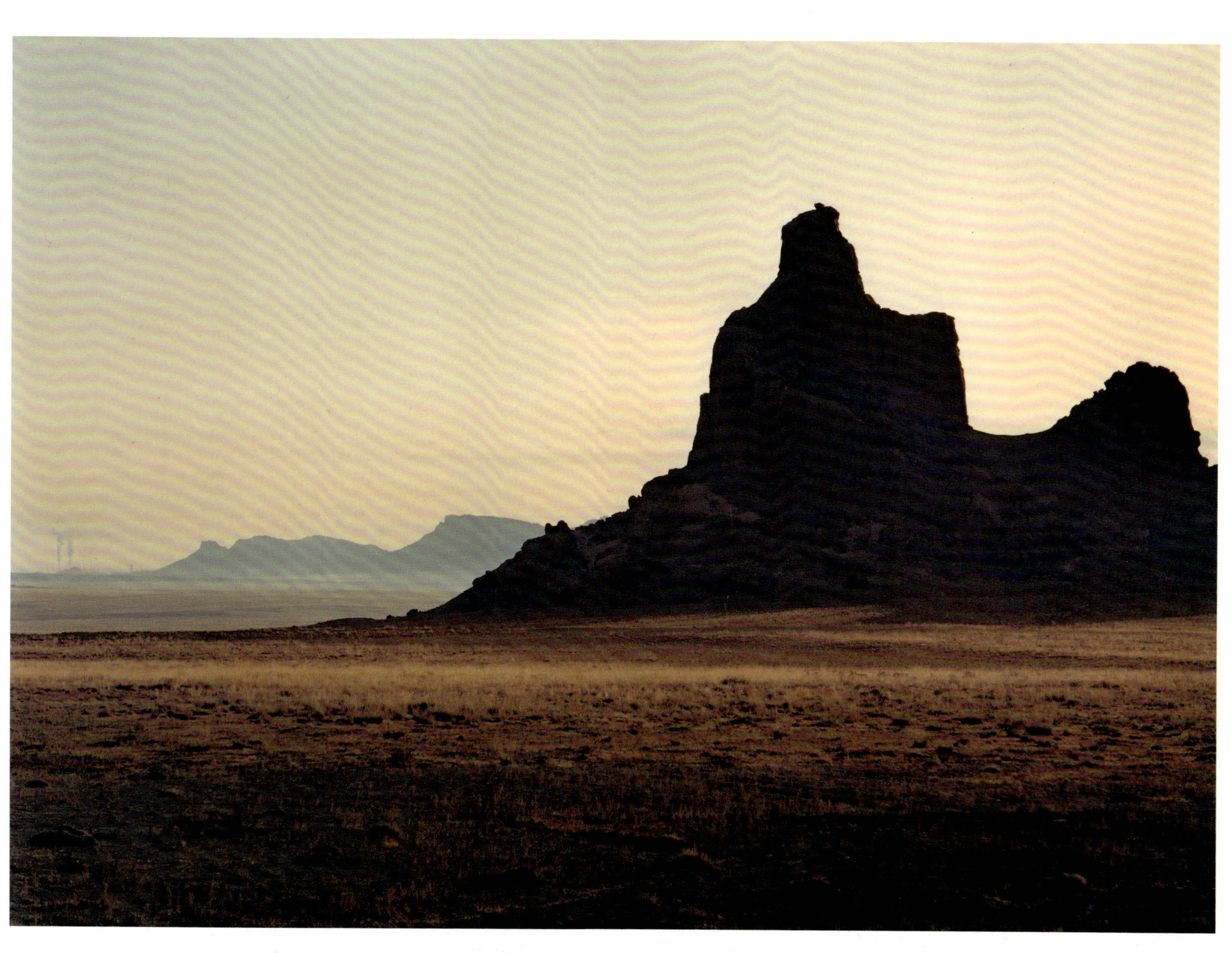

John Pfahl, *Four Corners Power Plant (morning), Farmington, New Mexico,* 1982

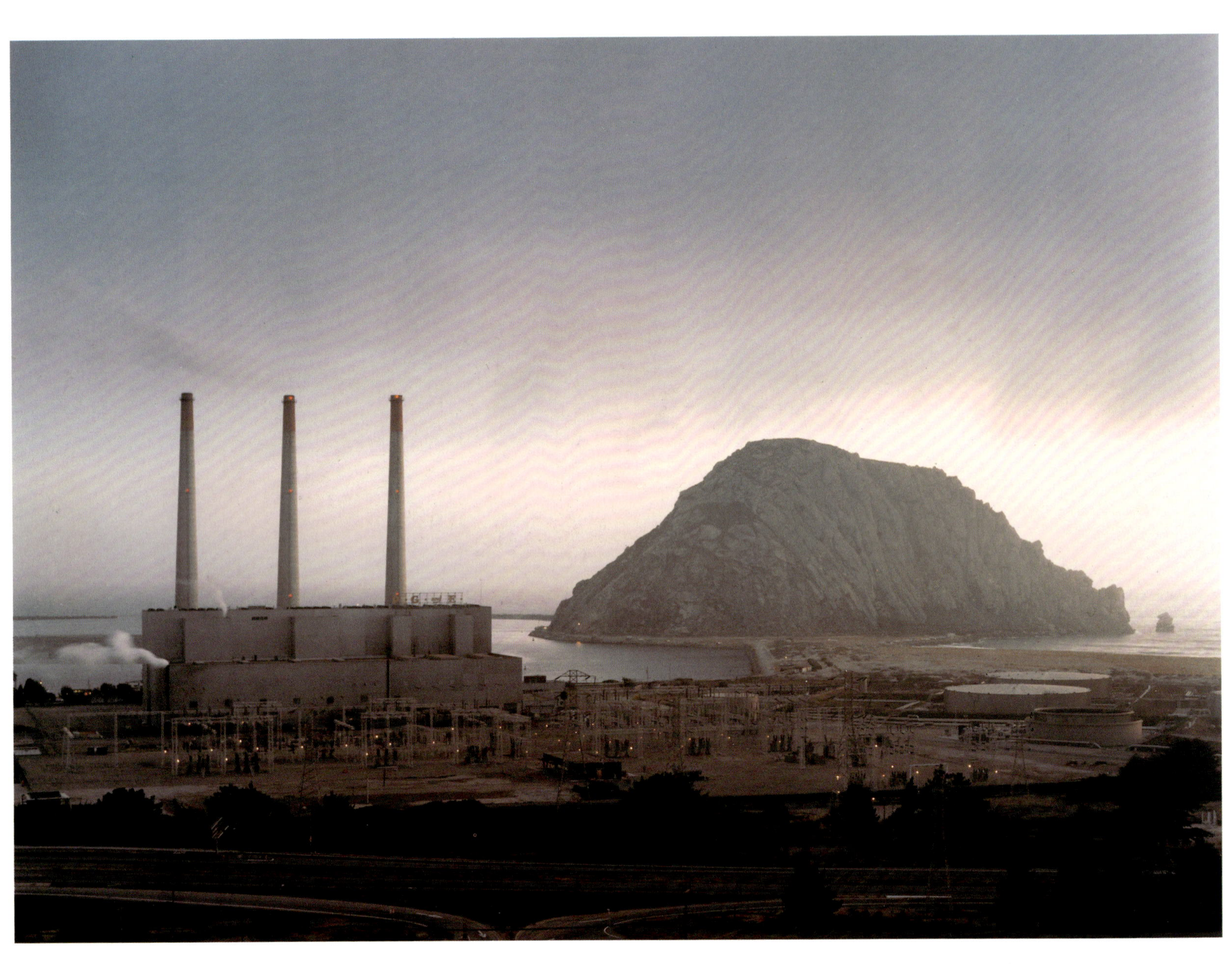

John Pfahl, *Pacific Gas and Electric Plant, Morro Bay, California,* 1983

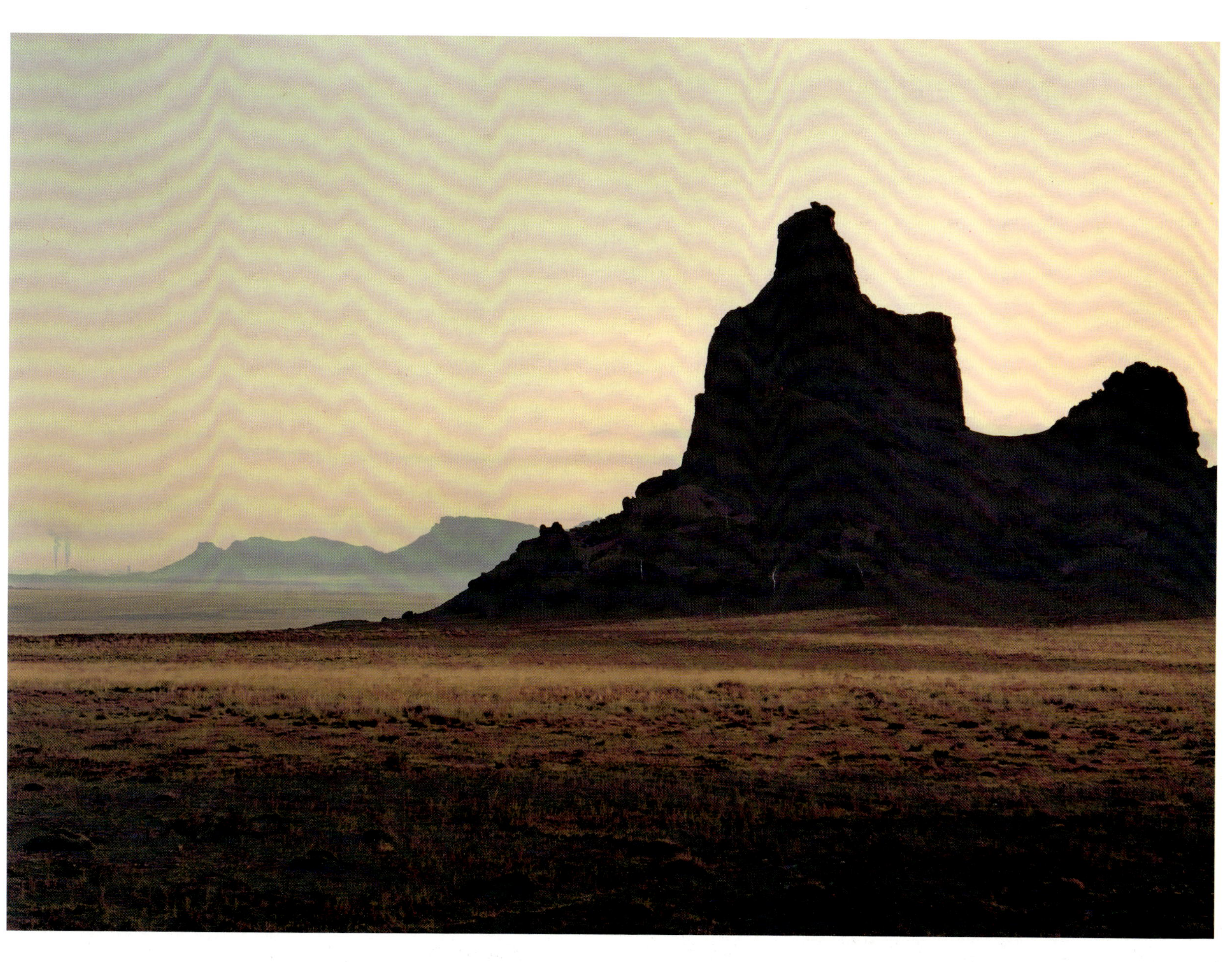

John Pfahl, *Four Corners Power Plant (morning), Farmington, New Mexico,* 1982

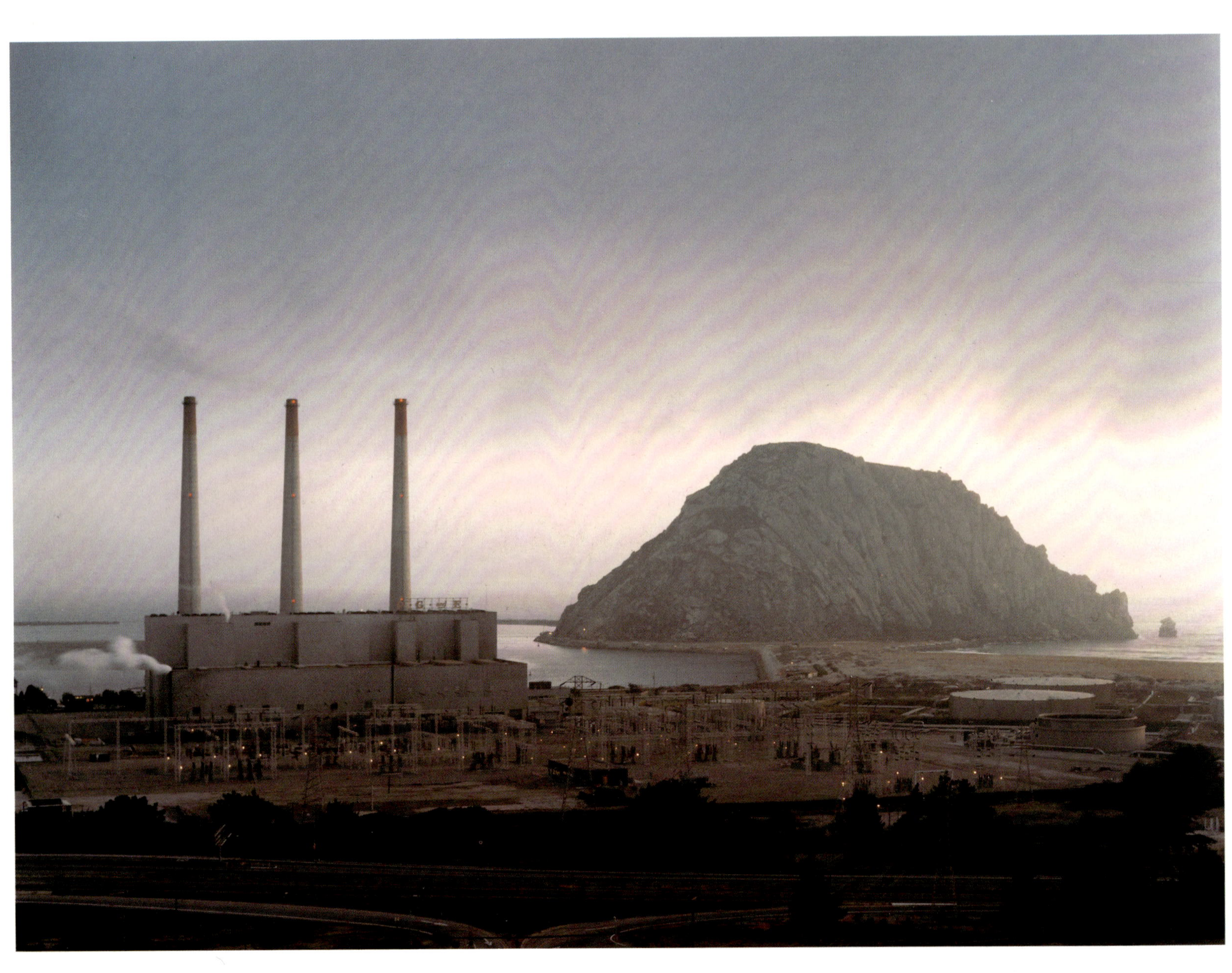

John Pfahl, *Pacific Gas and Electric Plant, Morro Bay, California*, 1983

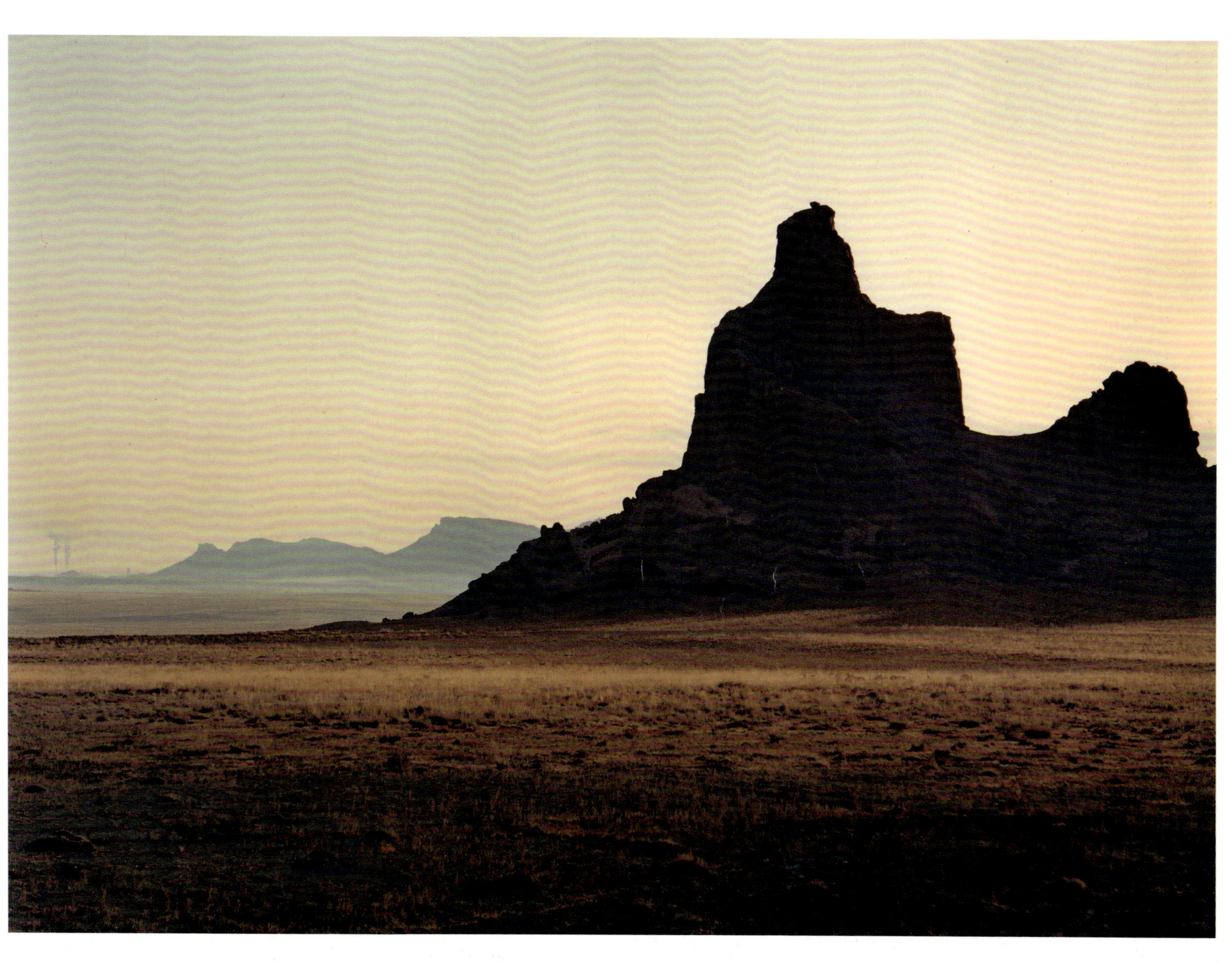

John Pfahl, *Four Corners Power Plant (morning), Farmington, New Mexico*, 1982

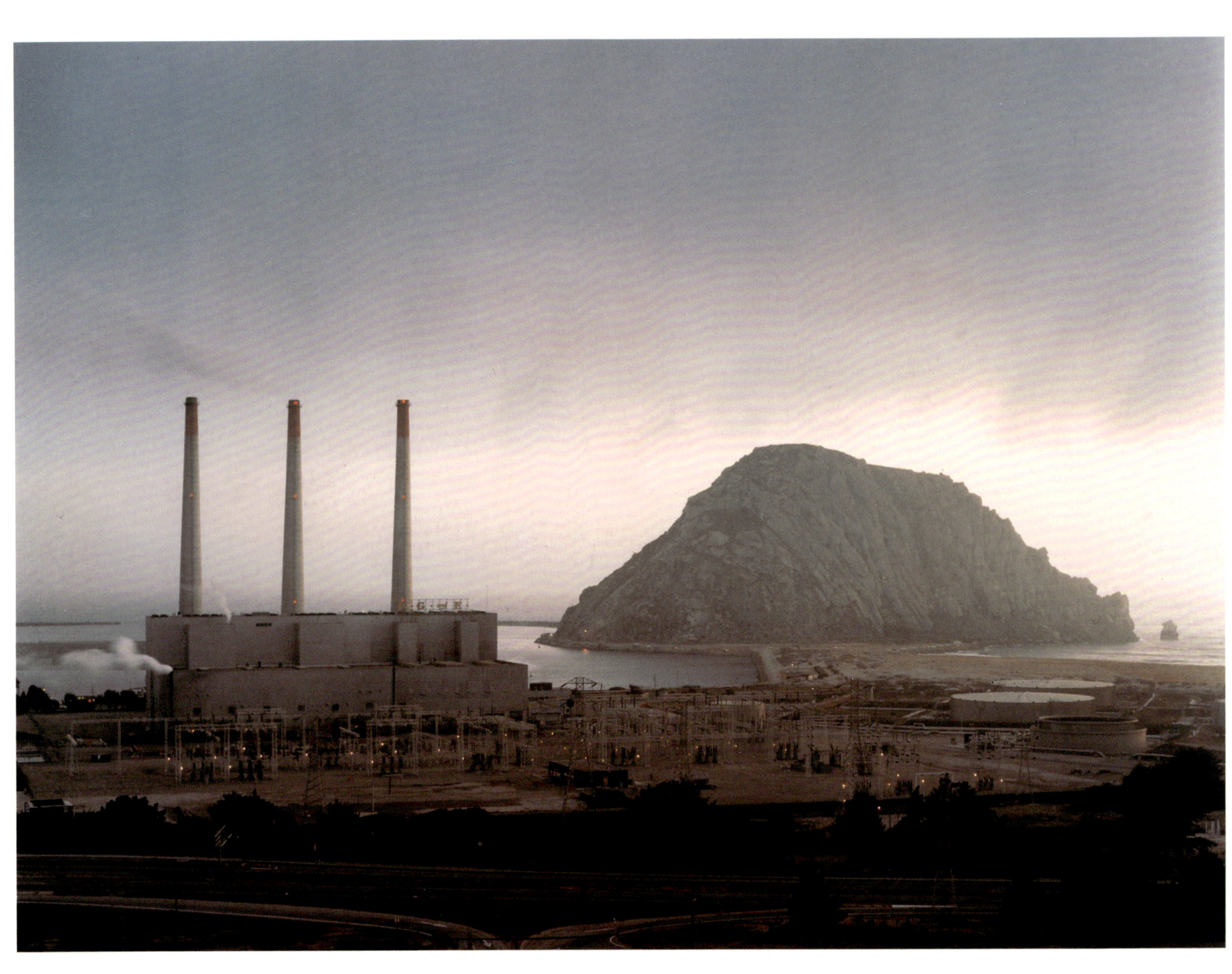

John Pfahl, *Pacific Gas and Electric Plant, Morro Bay, California,* 1983

John Pfahl, *Occidental Smoke,* 1989

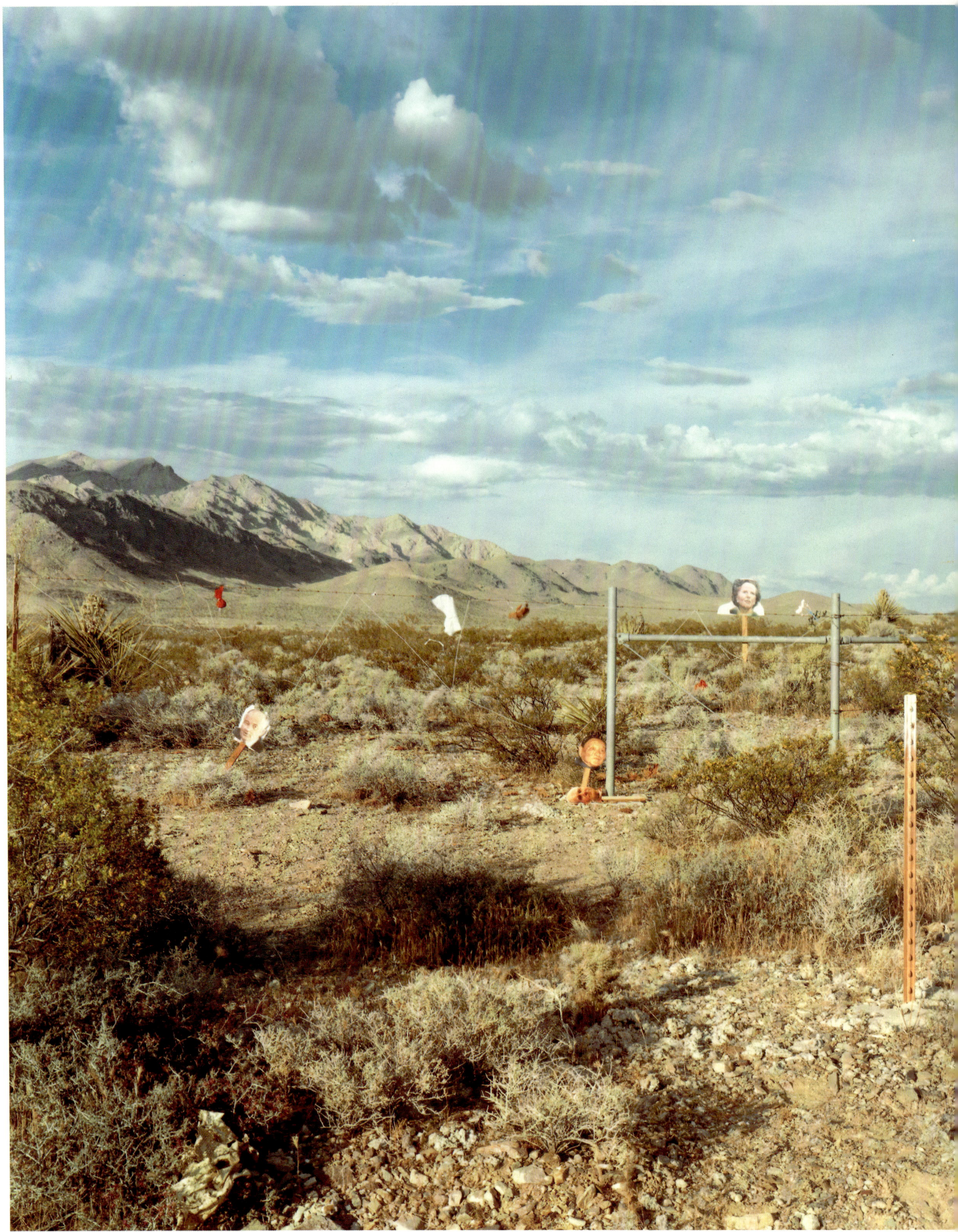

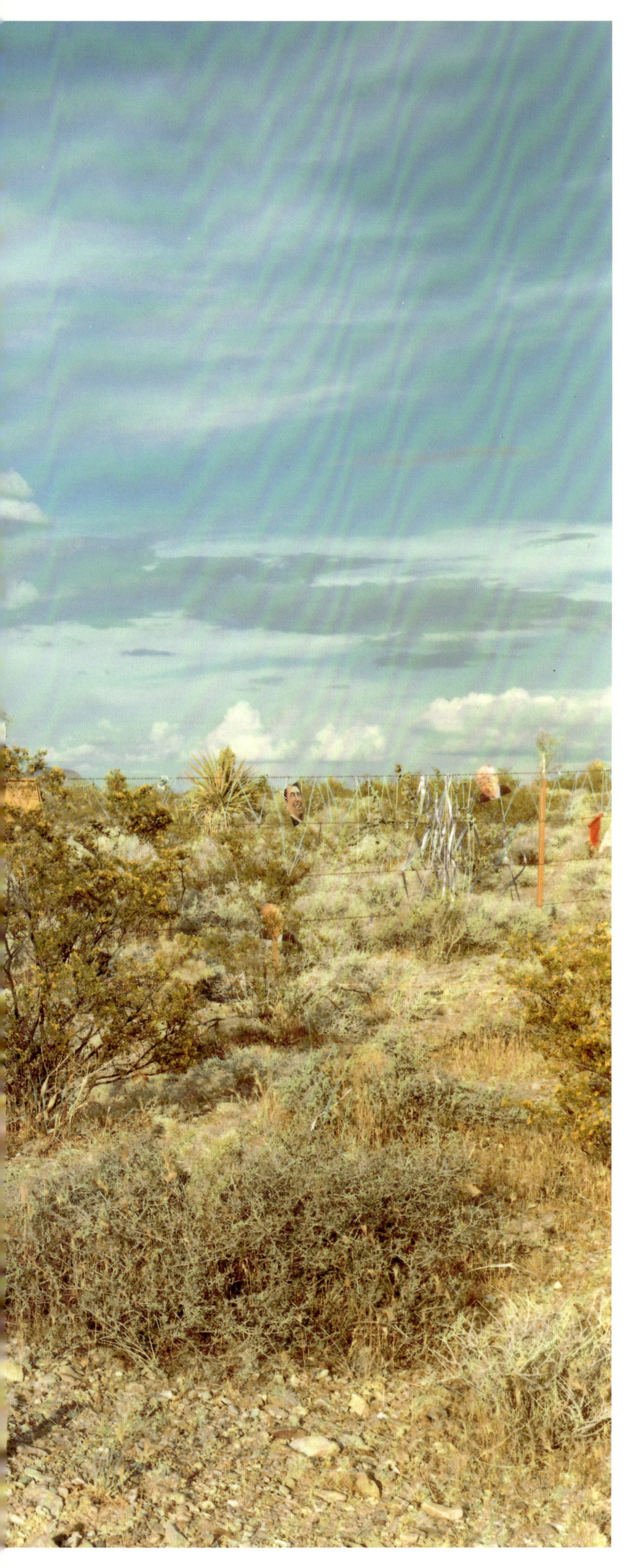

Reclaiming History:
Richard Misrach and the Politics
of Landscape Photography

By Rebecca Solnit

Interstate 95 from the main gate of the Nevada Test Site, where all the nation's nuclear weapons are tested, to the town of Beatty runs through nearly seventy miles of long vistas and sparse settlement. The day after the big 1990 demonstration against nuclear testing Las Vegas activist Chris Brown drove me along that route, telling me stories that the landscape prompted: about the geologic past evident in the volcanoes and the tilted strata of mountains and mesas, about the brief downpours of January and long 110-degree days of summer, and about the human strata of mining, ranching, and military operations that have been overlaid on this landscape in the past century. A few miles into the trip we passed Yucca Mountain, a dark ridge to the east where the Department of Energy wants to dump high-level radioactive waste that would boil underground for a thousand years. Later we passed the largest cyanide pond in the world, a pretty gleam on the other side of the road, the residue of modern gold-mining techniques. Most of the land that makes up the 3.1 million acres of Nellis Air Force Base, which includes the test site, had been stolen in 1951 from the Shoshone, the region's indigenous inhabitants, and several of them had led the demonstrations the day before. I heard about activists' feats of daring and endurance in occupying the military land, about cattle driven mad and ranchers forced out by low-level military flights, about huge tracts of public land being appropriated to add to the 25 million acres the U.S. military already controls in Nevada.

People used to go to the West to see wilderness. "The West of which I speak is but another name for the Wild," said Henry David Thoreau in the line used as the epigraph for Eliot Porter's *In Wildness Is the Preservation of the World* (1962). Wilderness is the quixotic American myth of an ideal landscape, a white myth of a place unknown, unnamed, and unpossessed. It has also been largely a male myth, in which words like "pure" and "unsullied" recur, of a place to be encountered in heroic journeys. The wilderness myth arose when the U.S. was searching for a cultural identity in the first half of the nineteenth century and found the vast Western expanse of unsettled land the most impressive feature distinguishing it from Europe. As virgin wilderness it signified the moral purity of the new

Richard Misrach, *Political Effigies, Nuclear Test Site*, 1987

nation, as boundless resource it signified the magnificent future that would characterize the country without a past. We have finally inhabited the American West long enough to discover the myth's implicit pessimism, its lack of a middle ground for coexistence. Wilderness was the creation of a profoundly dualistic imagination, an absolute nature incompatible with a culture without restraint.

This pessimism was fundamental to the early history of the U.S. conservation movement: Yosemite was set aside as a state preserve and then, like Yellowstone, a national park in order to protect it from commercial exploitation. Actually, the first white visit to the valley had been a military excursion in 1851 for the purpose of rounding up, relocating, and, if necessary, wiping out the native inhabitants of Yosemite. Thus the pristine solitude idealized as its natural state is itself an aggressive cultural imposition. Yosemite was set aside as sublime scenery, and the Sierra Club was founded twenty years later to "preserve the nation's scenic resources." The recurrence of *scenery*, a word borrowed from theater, is another key to the contradictory love of landscape. After all, the compositional strategy that landscape photography inherited proposed the landscape as a stage with humanity as its drama. The dearth of people in the American landscape painting and photographic traditions signifies that the drama has not yet begun; the lone foreground figure is an observer, a stand-in for the viewer. Defining landscape as visual spectacle suggests that detached spectatorship—tourism—is the normal and proper way to be in the landscape.

The conservation movement arose to set aside scenic wilderness where human presence would be purely touristic, and the lyrical vision of the nation's two greatest conservation photographers, Ansel Adams and Eliot Porter, celebrated this vision of purity and spectatorship. Their work excluded politics along with every other human trace, though politics became the context in which their pictures were presented. Untouched beauty was the incentive for conservation, from Adams's 1930s photographs of Kings Canyon that were used to lobby Congress for its preservation as a national park to Porter's '60s elegy for Glen Canyon, whose destruction by damming galvanized concern about the vanishing of natural places. Conservation was the strategy of an era that has largely passed, of a time when you could go West to see wilderness, and save wilderness by setting it aside. Rachel Carson's *Silent Spring* (1962) revealed that our invasion of the landscape is less geographical than chemical—and invisible. No longer only a spectacle to be valued for its psychological effect, nature became the terms of our survival, and environmentalism has grown from a modest lobby to a broad movement questioning nearly all the social structures underlying a fragmented and alienated human condition viewed as the true source of our ecological crises. Politics

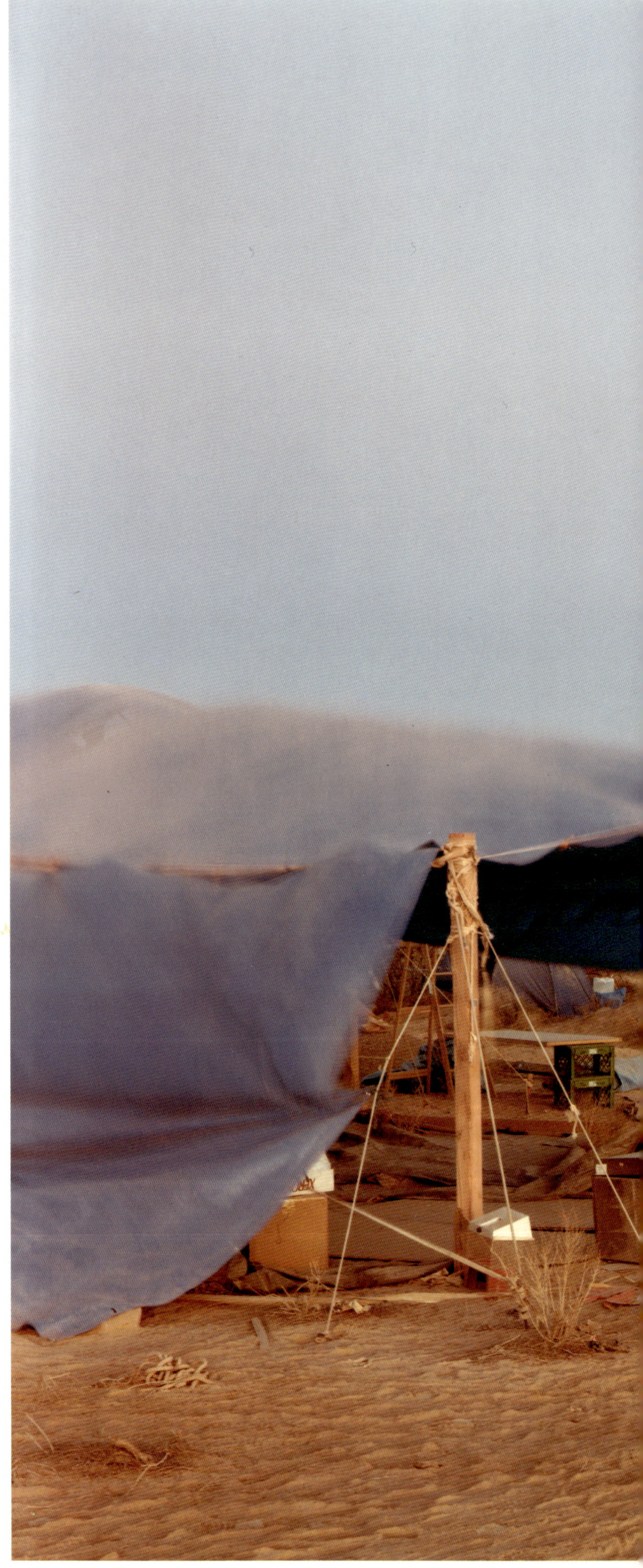

Richard Misrach, *Dr. Doom's Doomsday Machine and Reagan, Nuclear Test Site*, 1988

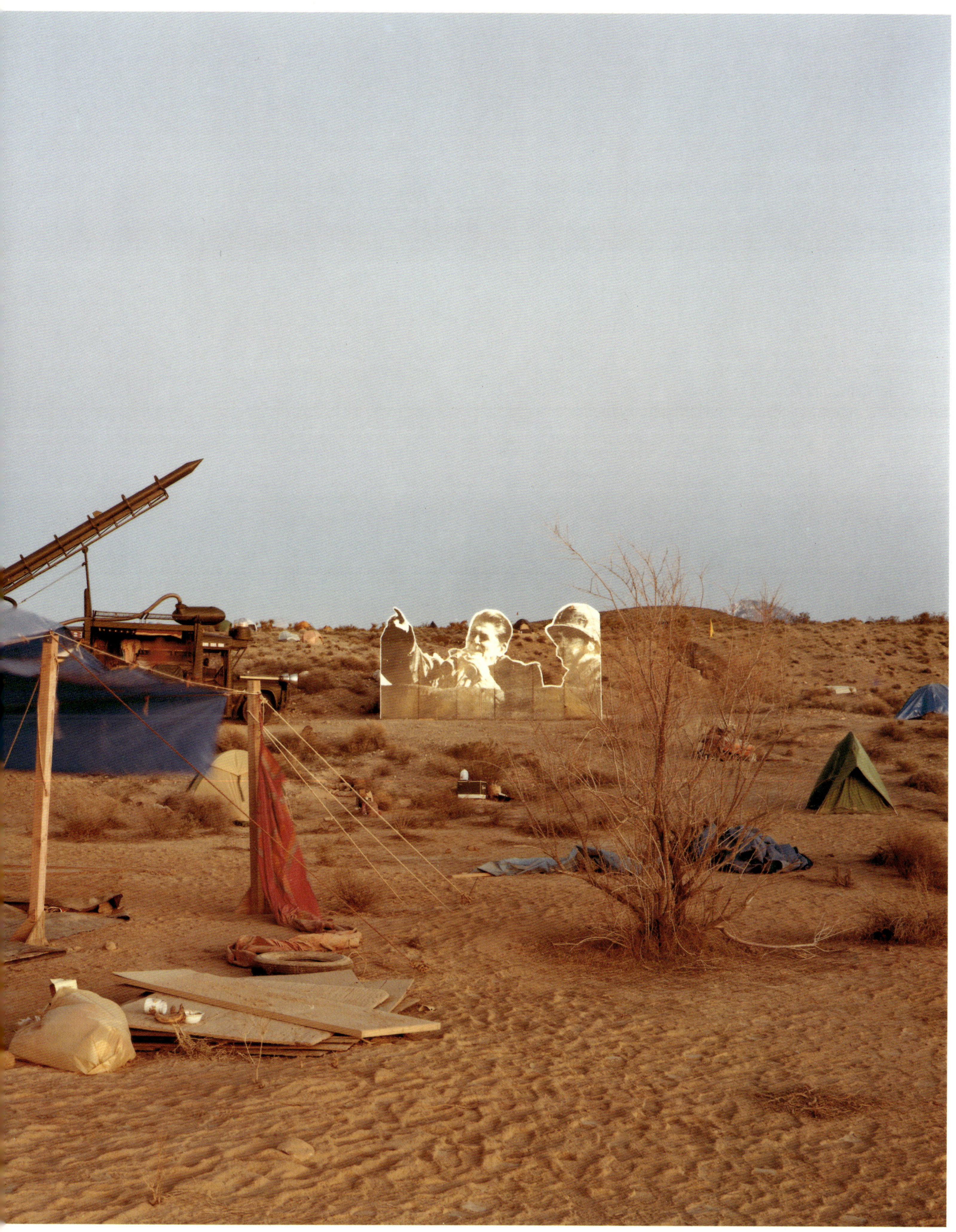

is no longer outside the frame of the landscape photograph, and the landscape itself is no longer an aesthetic refuge, but a battleground.

After giving up on politically engaged photography, Richard Misrach set out in the late 1970s for the wilderness—but in the most remote fastnesses of the Southwest he found the U.S. military. By the mid '80s, human folly had become central to his images of the space shuttle landing, or of manmade fires and flood. For the past several years Misrach has been photographing military territory in the West, from the *Enola Gay* hangar in Utah to the Bravo 20 Bombing Range in Nevada, making huge color prints that subvert the aesthetics of wilderness and nature photography. "The Pit," a series of images of a dump for dead livestock in Nevada, gives a subject that would normally be handled only by photojournalism the treatment of the lushest nature photography: big, sharp, closeup images without the relief of a horizon, pictures that allow appreciation of the rich texture and subtle color of dust, hide, decaying flesh, and bone.

The tremendous traditional beauty of Misrach's photographs and their complex political implications aren't congruous. He presents us with images that don't correspond to a theoretical interpretation of the West, but confront us with the failure of our myths in the face of our recent history. The surrounding facts undermine the aesthetic appreciation these images elicit, making such pure response almost an act of complicity. In many of Misrach's landscape images only the titles or accompanying texts reveal the military history or radiation contamination that disorients their beauty. Others, such as the photographs for the forthcoming book *Bravo 20: The Bombing of the American West* (Johns Hopkins), depict a landscape whose beauty is clearly ravaged by shrapnel, craters, and the unexploded bombs of the U.S. Navy bombing range that is the subject of the photographs. This is no longer the landscape of spectatorship. Its occupants are corpses, war machines, and activists, and the photographer himself discards the role of disengaged observer to polemicize, contextualize, propose.

In introducing politics to landscape photography Misrach seems to be moving toward something akin to history painting, a vehicle for epic, for narrative, for exhortation to morality and examination of the national conscience. His photographs don't, however, address themselves to art history, but to our history: to secret military appropriations and the devastation of tens of millions of acres of the American West, to an invisible arms race located in a magnificent landscape, to eighty-two documented accidents and atmospheric leaks from underground nuclear tests, and to the activists who interpose their bodies between the landscape and the military.　□

Richard Misrach, *Princesses of Plutonium, Nuclear Test Site,* 1988

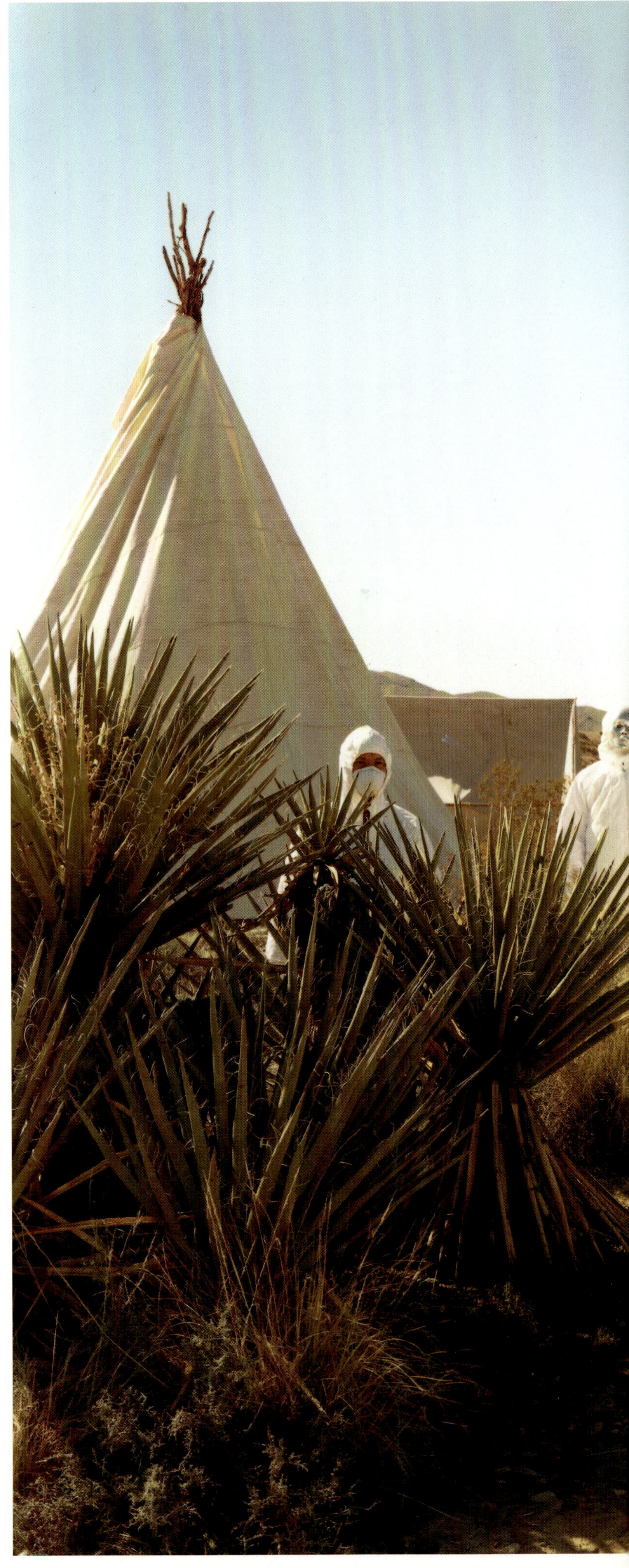

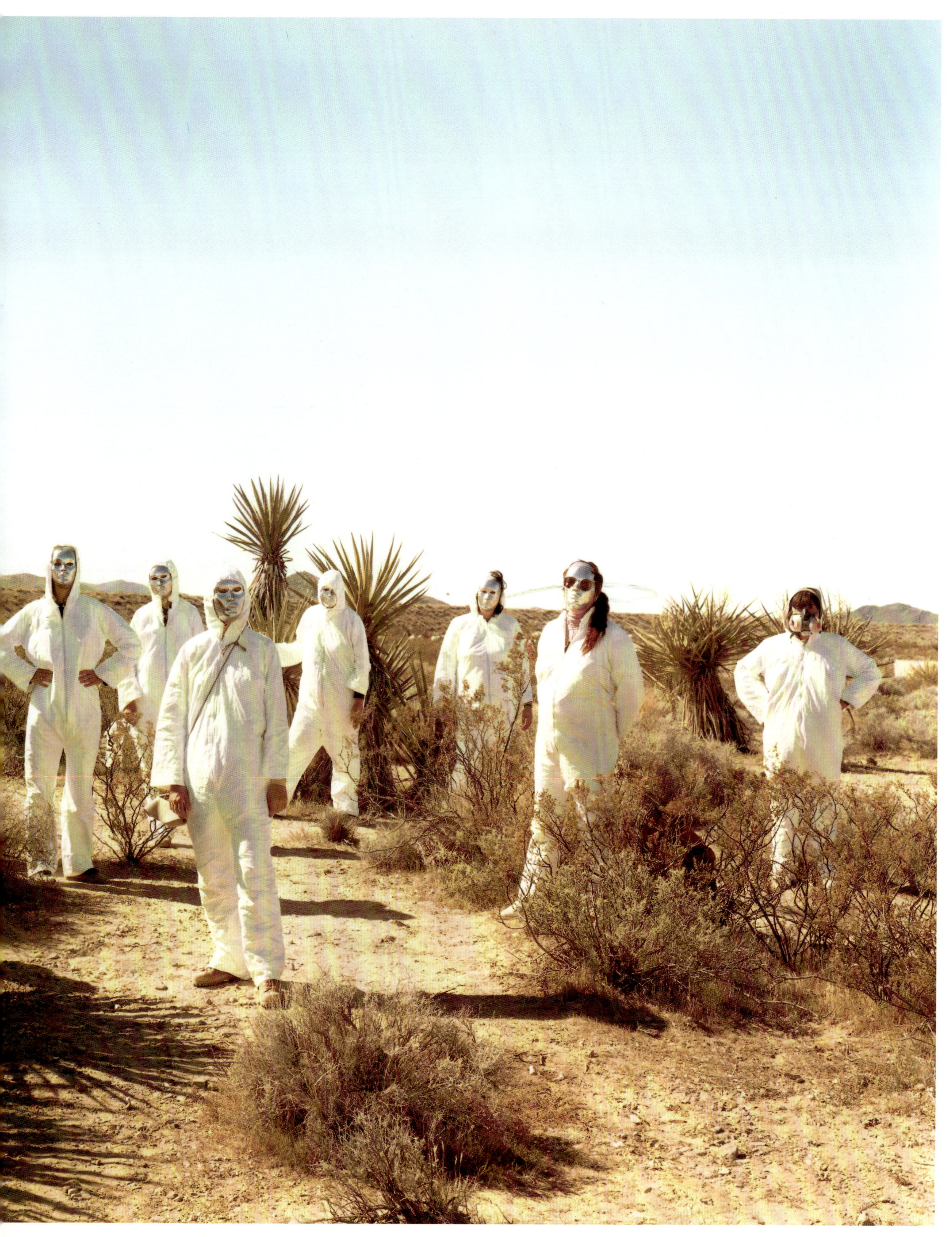

A Growing Awareness:
Environmental Groups
and the Media

By Joel Connelly

A half century ago, Mao Zedong taught his followers that political power grows out of the barrel of a gun. In the world of the 1990s, however, political and societal change flow through the lens of a camera. Environmentalists learned this lesson long ago. These days the "green lobby" packs political clout in many countries. In its infancy, however, the movement found that the only way to save species and preserve wild places was to arouse the public with visual images. Some of these images, both the brutal and the beautiful, will remain in our memories for a long time.

A pioneer in the use of visual images to alert the public to environmental threats was Dr. Fred Darvill, a Mt. Vernon, Washington, family doctor. Darvill was among the first to deploy images of sublime places followed by the horrors that awaited them. Over twenty years ago, Darvill flew to New York armed only with a painting of Image Lake, a 10,000-foot-high tarn in Washington's Glacier Peak Wilderness Area, some slides, and three shares in the Kennecott Copper Company. He was bound for the annual meeting of the multinational mining company, which proposed to build a half-mile-wide open-pit copper mine in the wilderness area. Kennecott had the legal right to do so, in the form of a mining claim that predated the Wilderness Act. Darvill set out to test the company's will. "The Sierra Club had alerted the wire services," he recalls. "I showed the painting of Image Lake, and explained what a mine would do in the area. I mentioned that it would be so big it could be seen through a telescope from the moon."

The presentation received nationwide publicity. It also attracted the eye of David Brower, then executive director of the Sierra Club and a man who pioneered the use of visual images in conservation battles. A full-page ad appeared in the *New York Times* under the heading: "AN OPEN PIT LARGE ENOUGH THAT IT CAN BE SEEN FROM THE MOON." Readers were presented with a picture of alpine glory beside one of a gouged-out open-pit mine in Utah.

In the end Kennecott never touched the wilderness. Brower would later deploy the same sorts of imagery—in a style described by John McPhee as "Early Paul Revere"—to stop two planned dams in the Grand Canyon. Above a canyon sunset picture was the classic headline: "WOULD YOU FLOOD THE SISTINE CHAPEL SO TOURISTS COULD GET CLOSER TO THE CEILING?" The Sierra Club lost its tax-exempt status, but the Grand Canyon was saved. Congressman Morris Udall of Arizona later paid grudging tribute to Brower's genius for capturing public attention, and for stopping an unwise project that Udall at the time had supported.

A prime goal of conservationists, according to Brock Evans

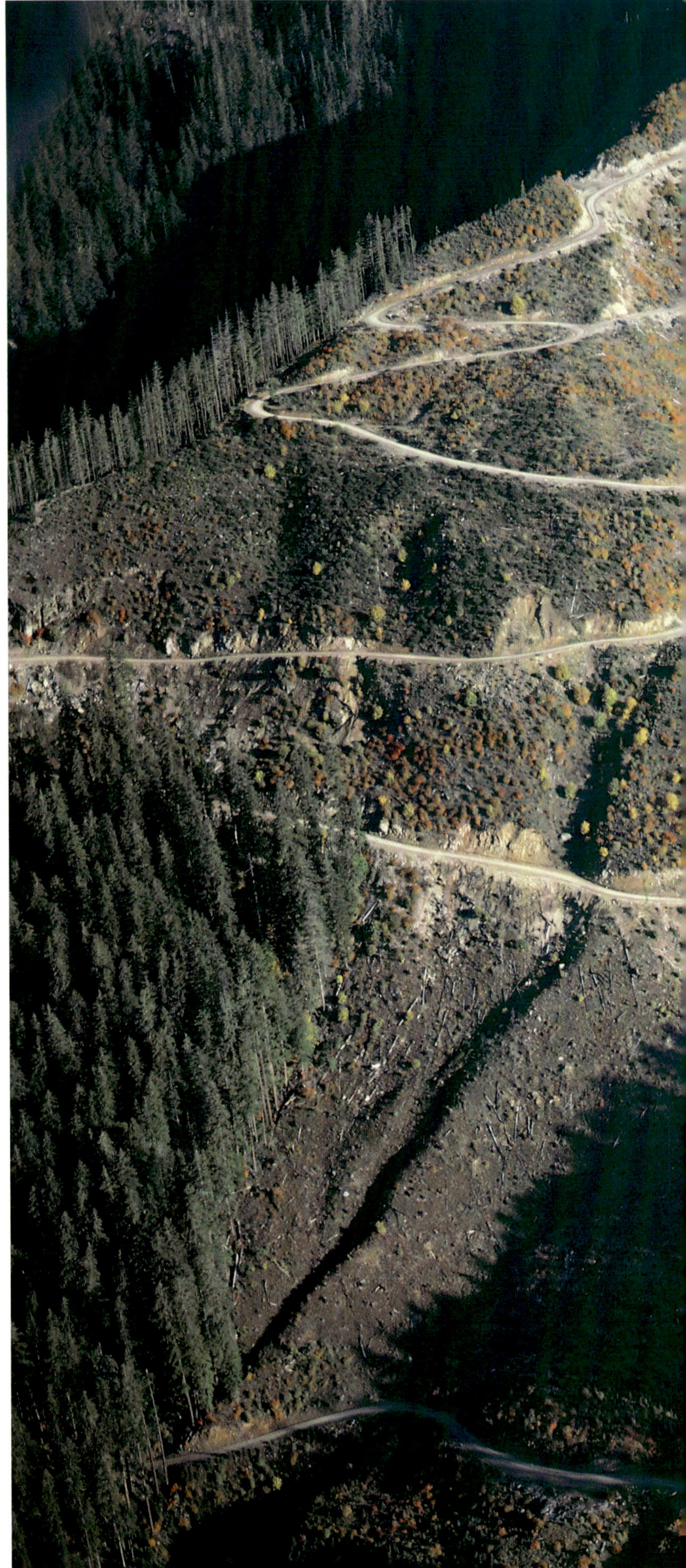

Gary Braasch, *Boundary between Weyerhauser on left, Willamette National Forest on right, North Santiam River, Oregon, 1983*

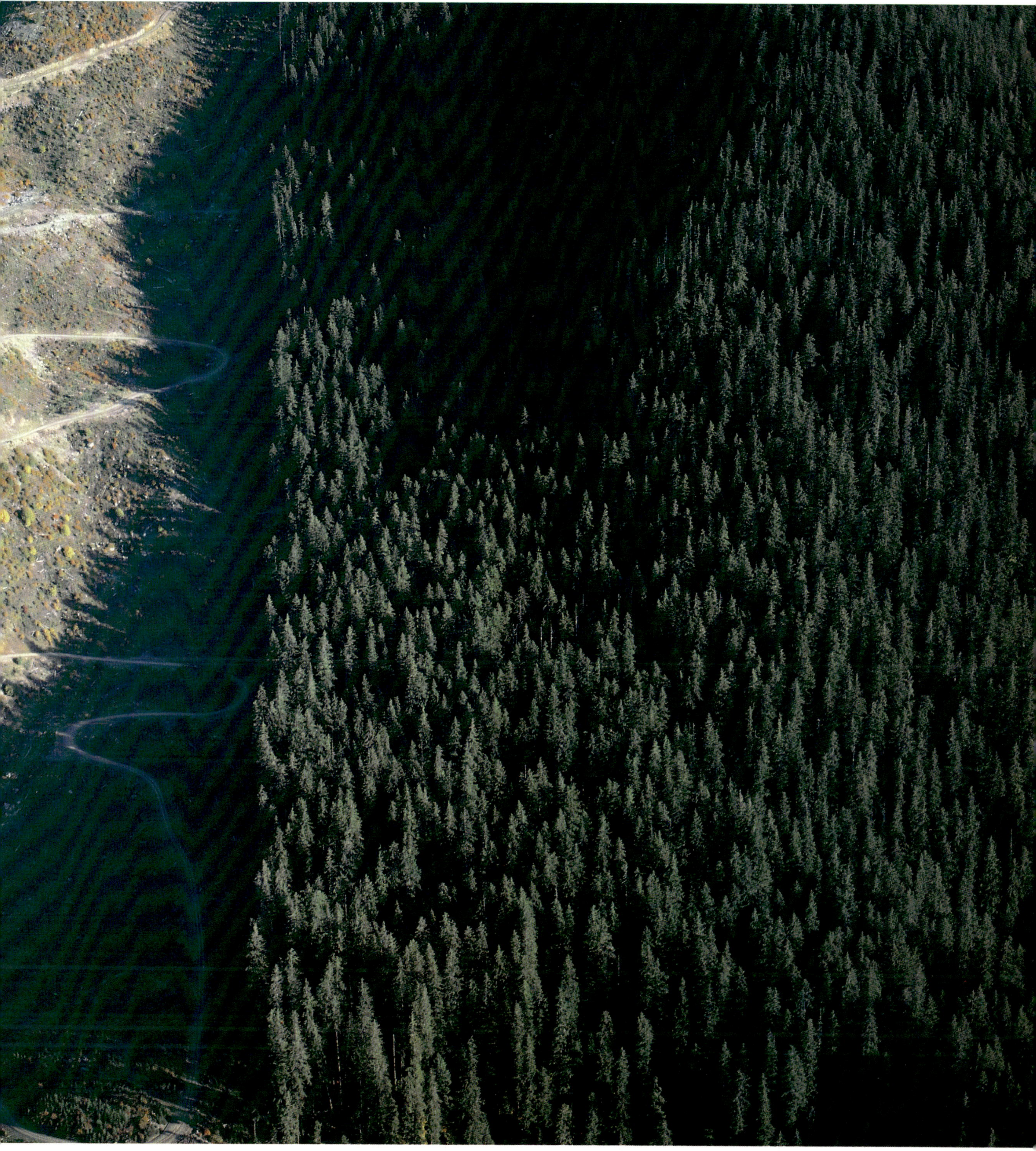

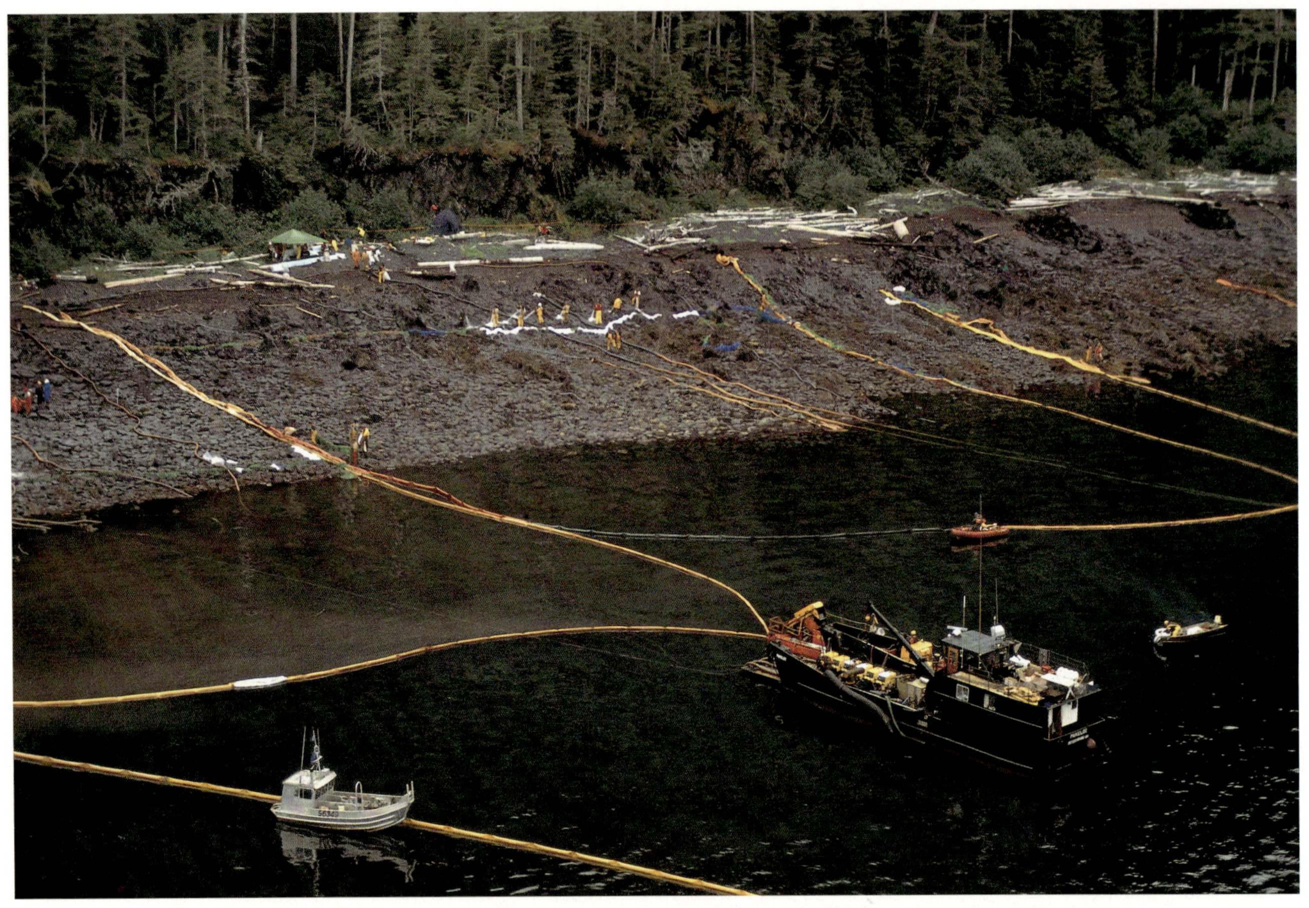

Ken Graham, *Maxi barge task force scours oil from Snug Harbor Beach, Prince William Sound, Alaska*, 1989

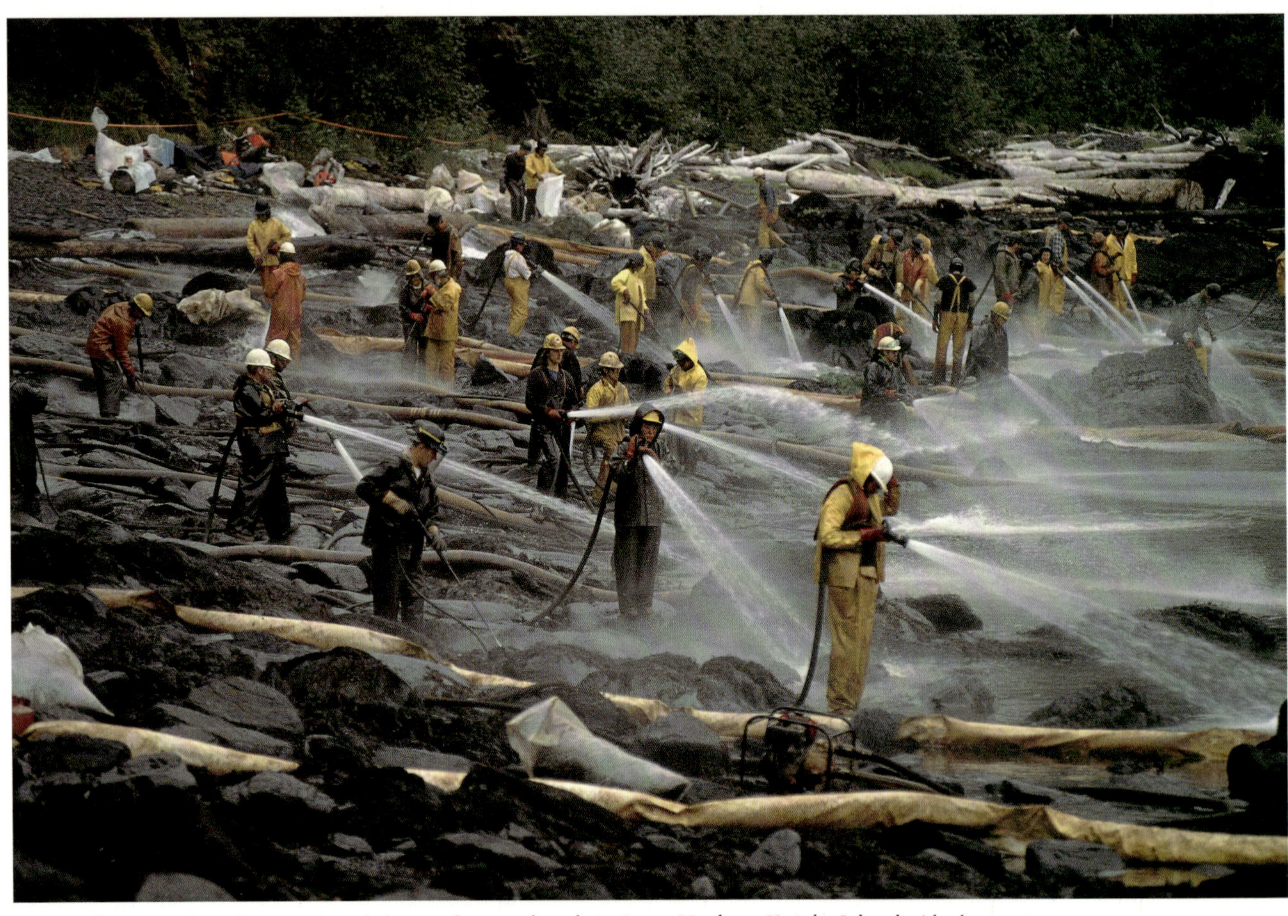

Ken Graham, *Multitude armed with hoses cleans a beach in Snug Harbor, Knight Island, Alaska*, 1989

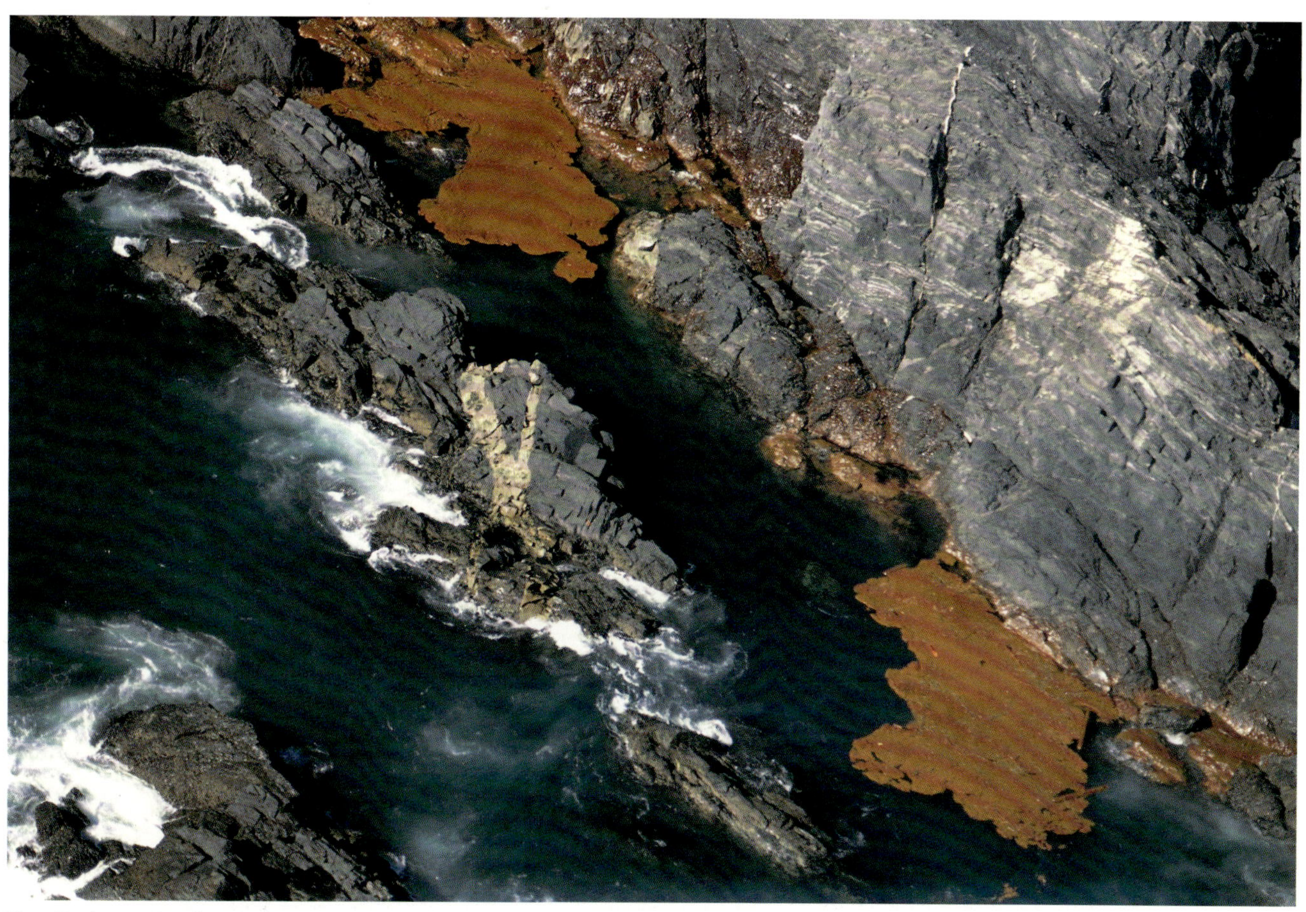

Ken Graham, *Crude oil clings to vertical coastline, Kenai Fjords, Alaska,* 1989

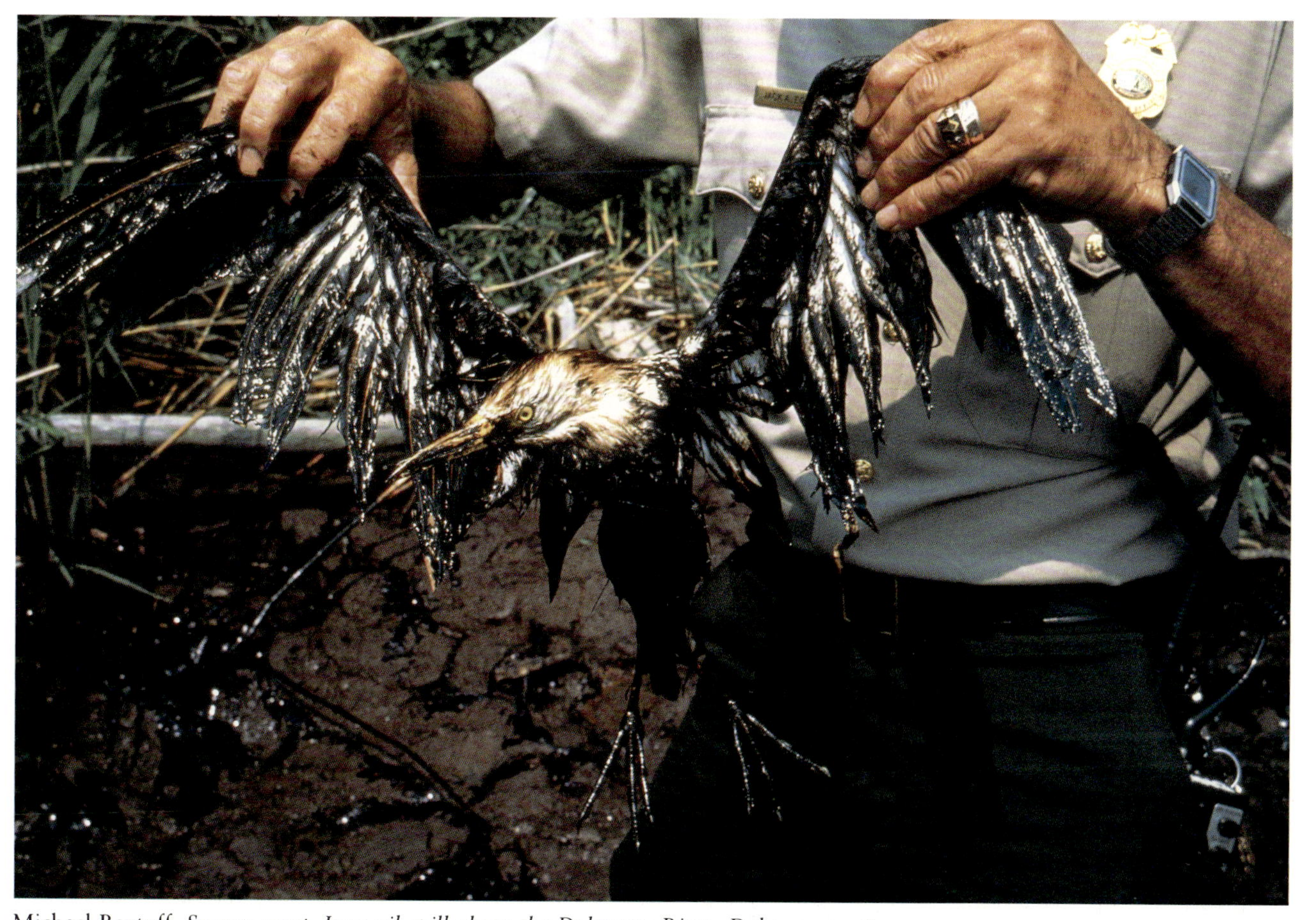

Michael Baytoff, *Snowy egret, June oil spill along the Delaware River, Delaware,* 1989

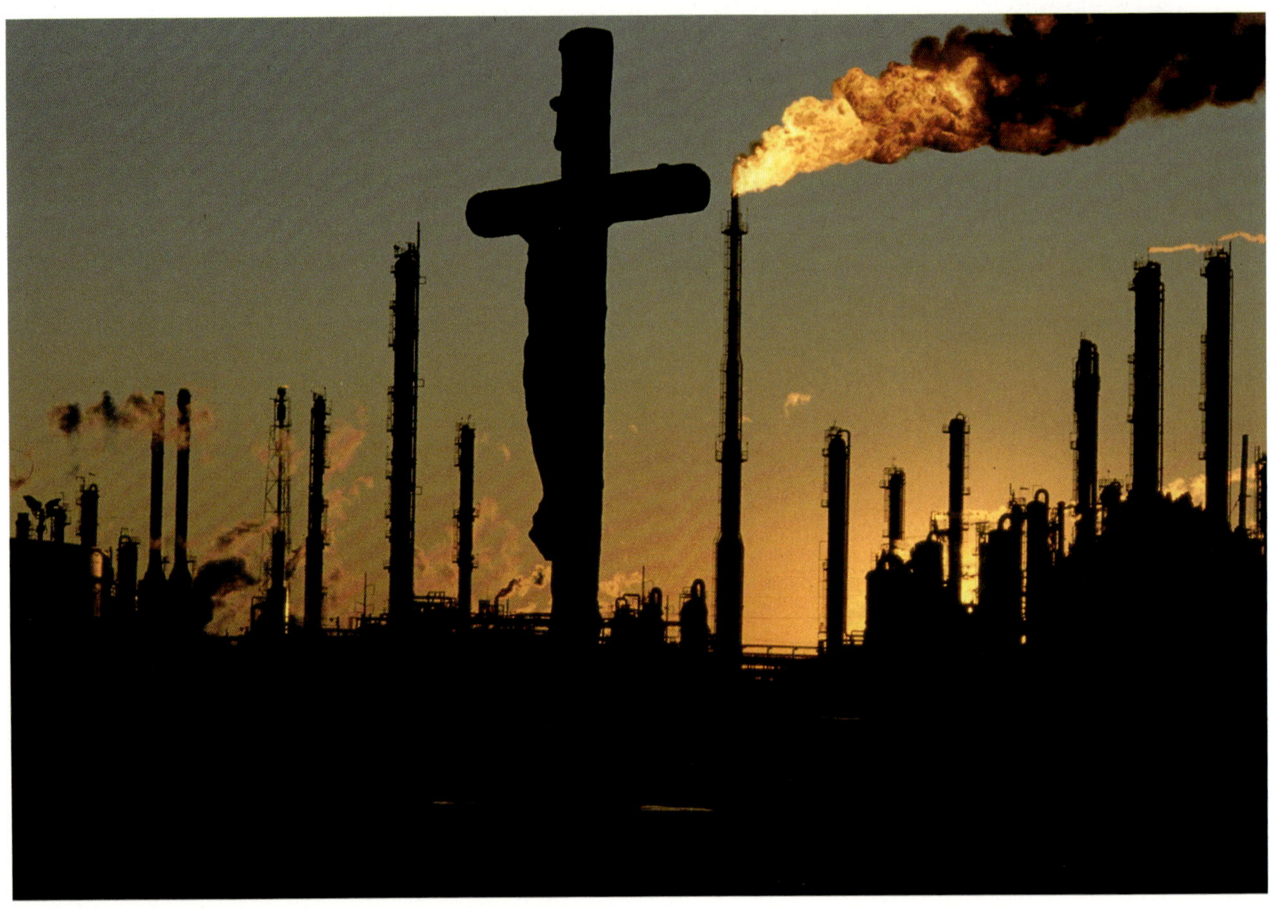

Sam Kittner, *Graveyard and Chemical Plant, Louisiana,* 1989

of the National Audubon Society, has been to nationalize and even internationalize key battles. "Visual images are the key for us," says Evans. "They've kept ancient forests standing and oil rigs out of the Arctic Refuge." Cameras connect the global village. Viewers thousands of miles away can watch pictures of thousand-year-old Sitka spruce trees falling under a logger's chain saw. They can see oil-covered otters being lifted from Prince William Sound. They can feel the fear of those on a Greenpeace zodiac boat as Soviet whalers fire a harpoon over its bow to mortally wound one of the world's largest marine mammals. Such pictures can generate thousands of words in citizen anger, enough to sway Congress or force the new president of Brazil to name an environmentalist to his cabinet.

When the *Exxon Valdez* fouled Prince William Sound, it disrupted a slick campaign aimed at persuading Congress to allow oil drilling in Alaska's Arctic National Wildlife Refuge. Oil lobbyists had effectively argued the necessity of reducing dependence on foreign petroleum. Environmentalists had been unable to sway the public with pretty pictures of caribou. But images of oil-soaked beaches, birds, and seals triggered outrage. Alaska Senator Ted Stevens put it best: the *Exxon Valdez* spill had set drilling back at least two years. Asked when it would resurface, he replied: "When the oil spill is no longer news."

Direct action has proven a potent way to focus the camera on environmental events. "The Fox" was its prophet. This anonymous ecological saboteur stalked Chicago in the late 1960s. He never showed his face, but publicized his deeds with calls to TV stations and explained his outrage to columnist Mike Royko. Refineries found their outfalls plugged. Banners were hung from smokestacks. The Fox even invaded the executive offices of a steel company to dump smelly effluent on its carpets.

Over twenty years later, the Fox is frequently copied. Greenpeace protestors recently decorated a stack at the Longview Fiber Company pulp mill in Washington, on the Columbia River. When the press arrived, the activists were ready with documentation of dioxin dumping into one of North America's great rivers.

Direct action is sometimes condemned by mainstream environmentalists who stress action through Congress and the courts. But confrontations can purchase time. In rain forests along the Northwest coast, the radical environmental group Earth First! has plunked down protesters in ancient trees marked for logging. When hauled down and arrested, they've given such names as "Doug Fir" and "Bobcat." These tree-ins have generated nationwide attention and slowed the pace of logging.

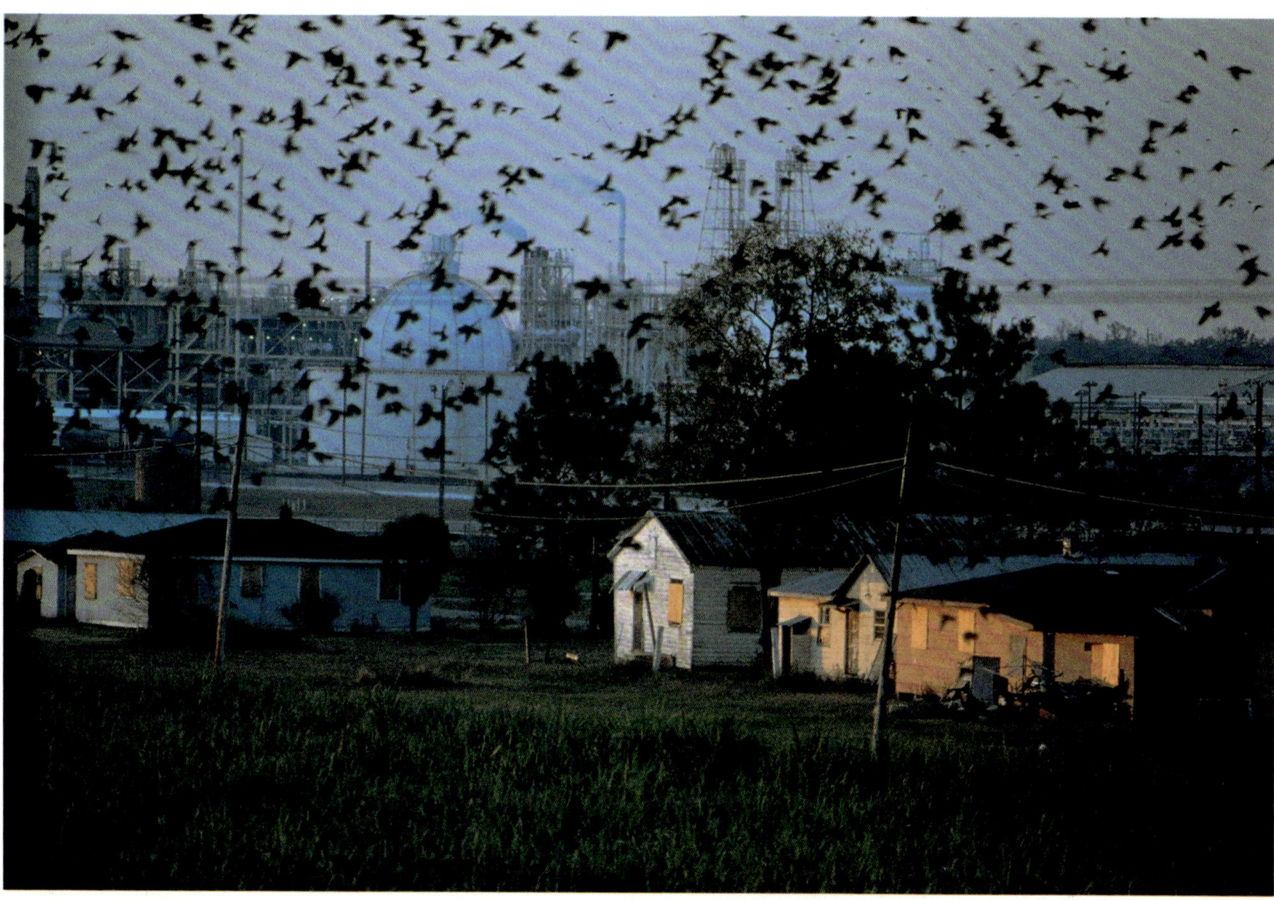

Sam Kittner, *Reveilletown, Louisiana*, 1988

A daring, filmed protest can focus attention on activities that some might wish to remain unnoticed. The Greenpeace Foundation was formed in Vancouver, British Columbia, in 1971, an outgrowth of protests aimed at planned U.S. nuclear tests in Alaska's Aleutian Islands. In 1973 Greenpeace began stalking bigger game—atmospheric nuclear tests being conducted by the French. Greenpeace vessels were boarded by the French navy, and crew members beaten. But the protesters kept sailing into test zones, and kept arguing that radiation posed a danger to peoples of the South Pacific. In 1986 French commandos sank a Greenpeace ship as it prepared to sail from a New Zealand harbor. One crew member was killed. The resulting uproar strained French relations with New Zealand, drove the French defense minister to resign, and cast France in the role of international outlaw.

Greenpeace has chosen the camera lens as its weapon for a variety of environmental crusades. "We go to the scene of a crime and bring back images of what's going on," says Alan Reichman, ocean ecology director for Greenpeace International. "In that way we mobilize public concern and pressure. We're not talking abstractions and descriptions. We're showing a factory ship which cuts up whales. We're showing marine mammals trapped in nets. We're showing what comes out of pulp mills." Reichman has helped create memorable images.

He was part of a flotilla of zodiac boats that tried to stop a supertanker test run up the Strait of Juan de Fuca between British Columbia and Washington. Airborne photographers had a field day as the tiny craft buzzed around the 185,000-ton oil ship. A maneuverability test by the U.S. Coast Guard was turned into a political confrontation over whether to permit supertankers in sensitive West Coast estuaries.

A Greenpeace photo service makes pictures available to news sources, and engages in visual lobbying on Capitol Hill. Members of Congress, aides, and press gathered in a Longworth Building office last year to watch films of dolphins and birds entangled in the thick mesh of driftnet fishing lines. The seventy-mile-long driftnets are set on the North Pacific by Japanese and Taiwanese fishermen, supposedly to catch tuna and squid. In real life, they snare thousands of birds, marine mammals, and salmon. Congress has since pressed a reluctant Bush administration to support a worldwide ban on driftnet fishing.

The media savvy of such groups as Greenpeace has reached the environmental mainstream. The Natural Resources Defense Council has generally stayed far removed from visual imagery: its battles have been fought in court, notably with suits that have forced the U.S. Department of Energy to abide by the nation's environmental laws in operating its nuclear weapons plants. On February 26, 1989, though, NRDC entered the

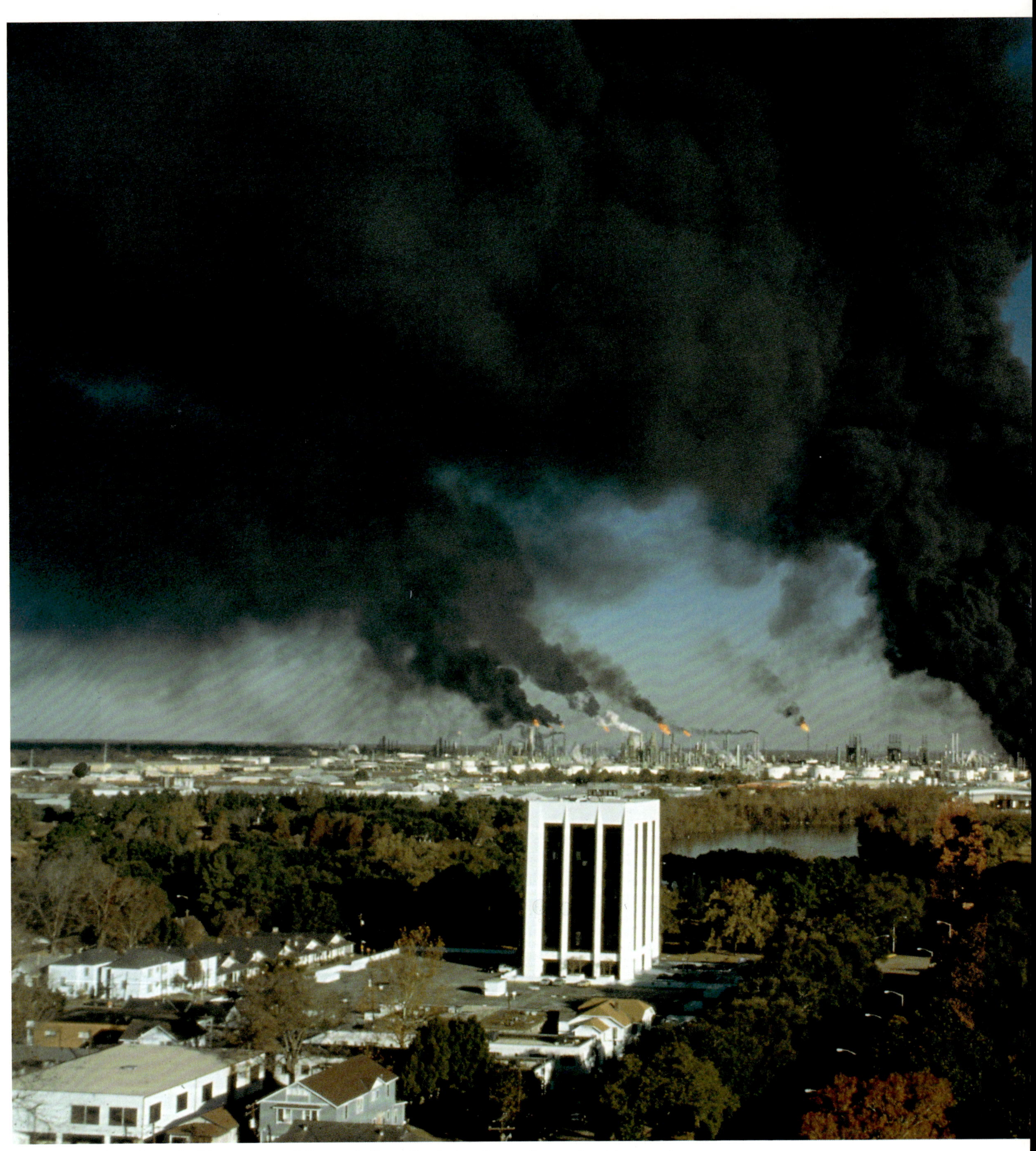

Sam Kittner, *State Capitol of Louisiana and Exxon Refinery Explosion, Baton Rouge, Louisiana,* 1989

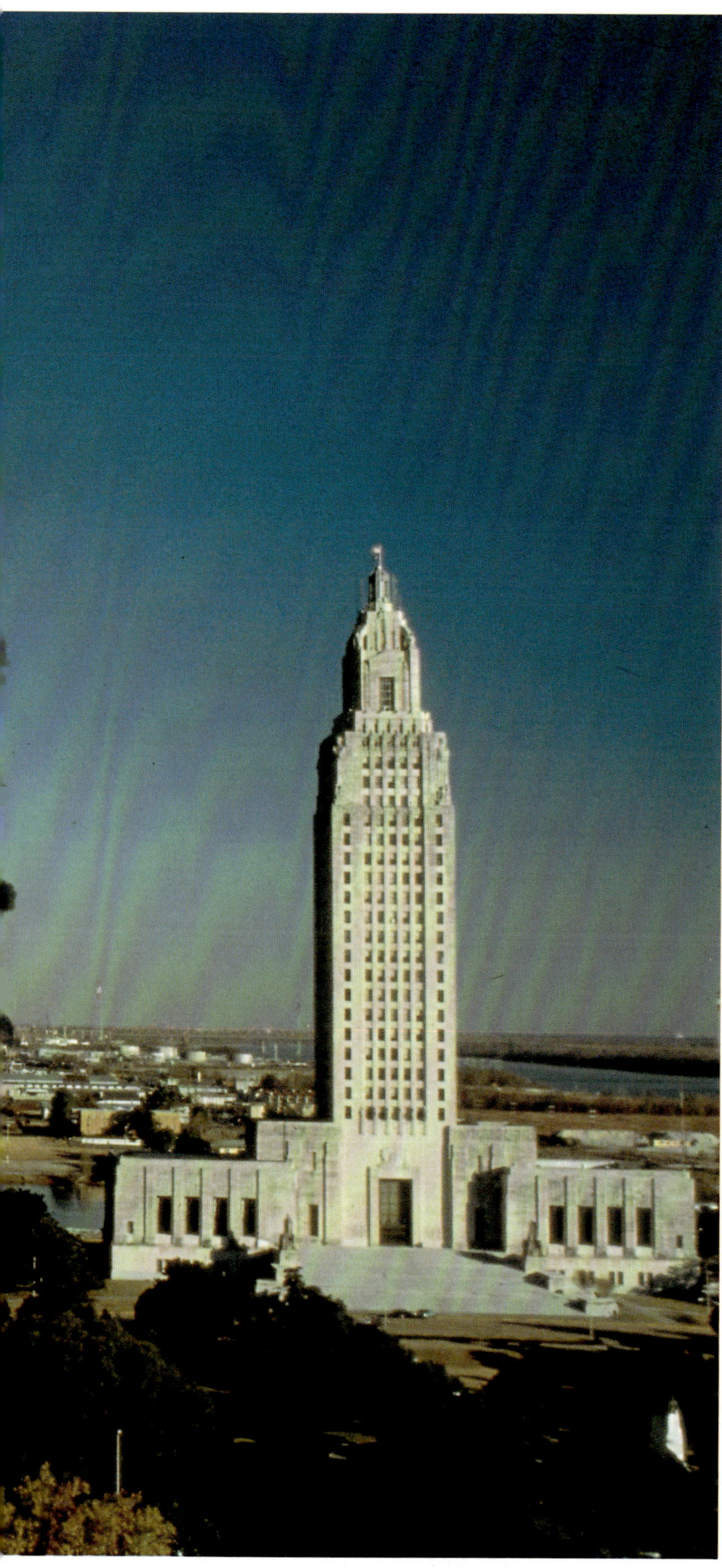

court of public opinion. It gave CBS's "60 Minutes" a study entitled "Intolerable Risk: Pesticides in Our Children's Food." One of the pesticides in the report was daminozide (trade name Alar), a chemical sprayed on apples to improve their color, crispness, and shelf life. In its study, NRDC predicted that Alar might cause one case of cancer for every 4,200 preschool children—a rate of risk 240 times the standard considered acceptable by the Environmental Protection Agency.

Although written by scientists, "Intolerable Risk" translated well to the TV screen. "60 Minutes" focused on Alar. Americans saw apples being sprayed in fields. They watched those apples going into baby food. And a day later, Oscar-winning actress (and parent) Meryl Streep went before a Senate hearing to argue the case for a ban on Alar. During the week following the "60 Minutes" report, apple sales fell fourteen percent, and industry losses were estimated at over $100 million. A few months later, Uniroyal Chemical, Inc., announced it was taking the product off the market.

The media determines what is seen, and often what is saved. Photographs taken in a remote corner of northwest Wyoming helped create Yellowstone National Park over a century ago. Pictures can also lift politicians' sights up from ledger sheets. The U.S. Forest Service urged a veto of 1976 legislation creating a 393,000-acre Alpine Lakes Wilderness Area in Washington, arguing that it would cost too much to acquire private lands. Washington Governor Dan Evans, an avid backpacker, carried a picture book into an Oval Office meeting with President Gerald Ford. Evans turned to photos of the Enchantment Lakes region and told of guiding his three young sons over rugged, 7,800-foot Aasgard Pass during a violent storm. "Dan, we've got to save it," said Ford. He signed the bill.

As a writer I hate to admit it, but the camera's lens can be more powerful than the writer's pen. A physical confrontation convinced me. The state had let a logging contract on one of the few stands of old-growth trees left on Whidbey Island in Washington's scenic Puget Sound. Island environmentalists vowed to block the logging. I stood at the end of a narrow logging track with Mark Anderson, a young photographer with KING-TV in Seattle. A logging rig rumbled into view; protesters sat down in its path, and Anderson began filming. The truck stopped. After much waving of arms, the loggers retreated. A few hours later, KING carried an unforgettable film of trucks and bodies. It followed up with a film of the undisturbed forest. Birds chirped and sunlight wafted through 500-year-old trees. Anderson grew up in a logging town and knew the difference between a natural scene and a "working forest." Logging plans were promptly suspended.

The lawyering over Whidbey's forest was long and tedious. Not long ago, however, I enjoyed a walk among those same ancient trees, now—thanks at least in part to the powerful images presented by KING-TV and others—part of South Whidbey State Park.　　□

Out of the Garden

National parks embody a central paradox in cultural attitudes toward the land: in theory intended to remain forever wild, unsullied by human presence, they are also a government service, and every citizen is assumed to have the implicit right to have access to them and to their restorative powers, whether physical or spiritual.

The debate over the proper balance between access and isolation, between the rights of the public and the rights of the land, has resulted in an awkward but probably inevitable amalgam. The spectacularly scenic landscapes of the national parks are framed by contradictory cultural attitudes toward wilderness. In effect many of them have become theme parks, wilderness Disneylands, allowing steady streams of tourists a chance to glimpse natural wonders through the fly-specked windshields of their overcrowded cars as they pass through on their way to somewhere else. The theory behind such development is to allow controlled access in order to avert uncontrolled development; the result is a denatured nature, much like a silk rose on a diner table.

The parks recreate, on a grand scale, the romantic gardens of 19th-century Europe, where nature was returned to an artificial and picturesque wildness, as a counterbalance to the spread of industrialism. They offer places where people can go to contemplate their own insignificance in the face of Nature—which by definition excludes them. But the result too often is a crowd of individuals, all attempting to enjoy the wilderness experience from the parking lot outside the gift shop.

It is just this dual role that Len Jenshel addresses in his photographs of national parks. The gently curving highway that leads to the breathtaking butte, the traffic-control cones that sit in front of the sunset backdrop, the cattle guard that disrupts the dreamy pastel landscape—all testify to the human presence in the land, all suggest the carefully controlled and predetermined quality of the scenic landscape of the national parks.

Welcome to Wildernessland.　　　□

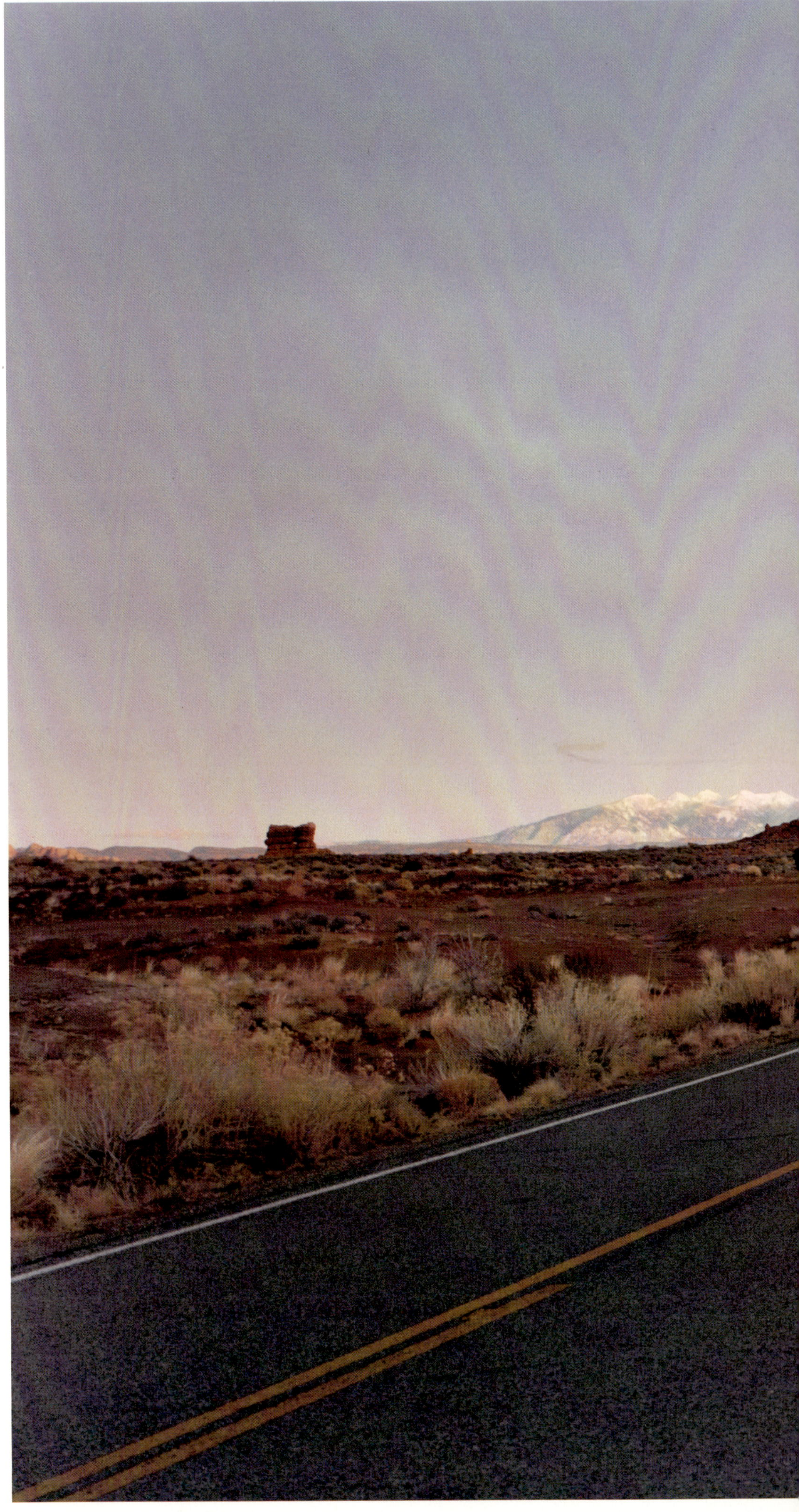

Len Jenshel, *Arches National Park, Utah*, 1985

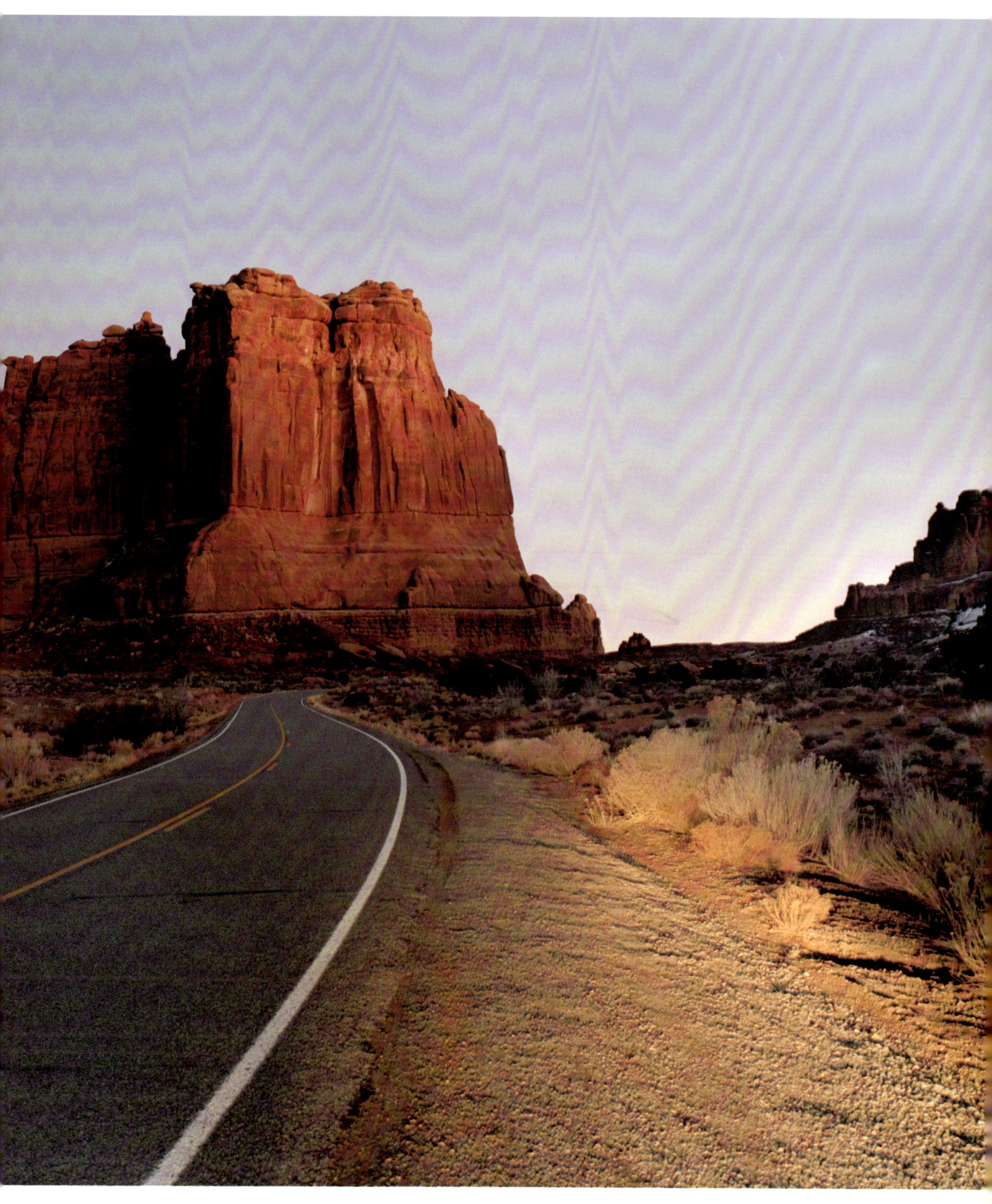

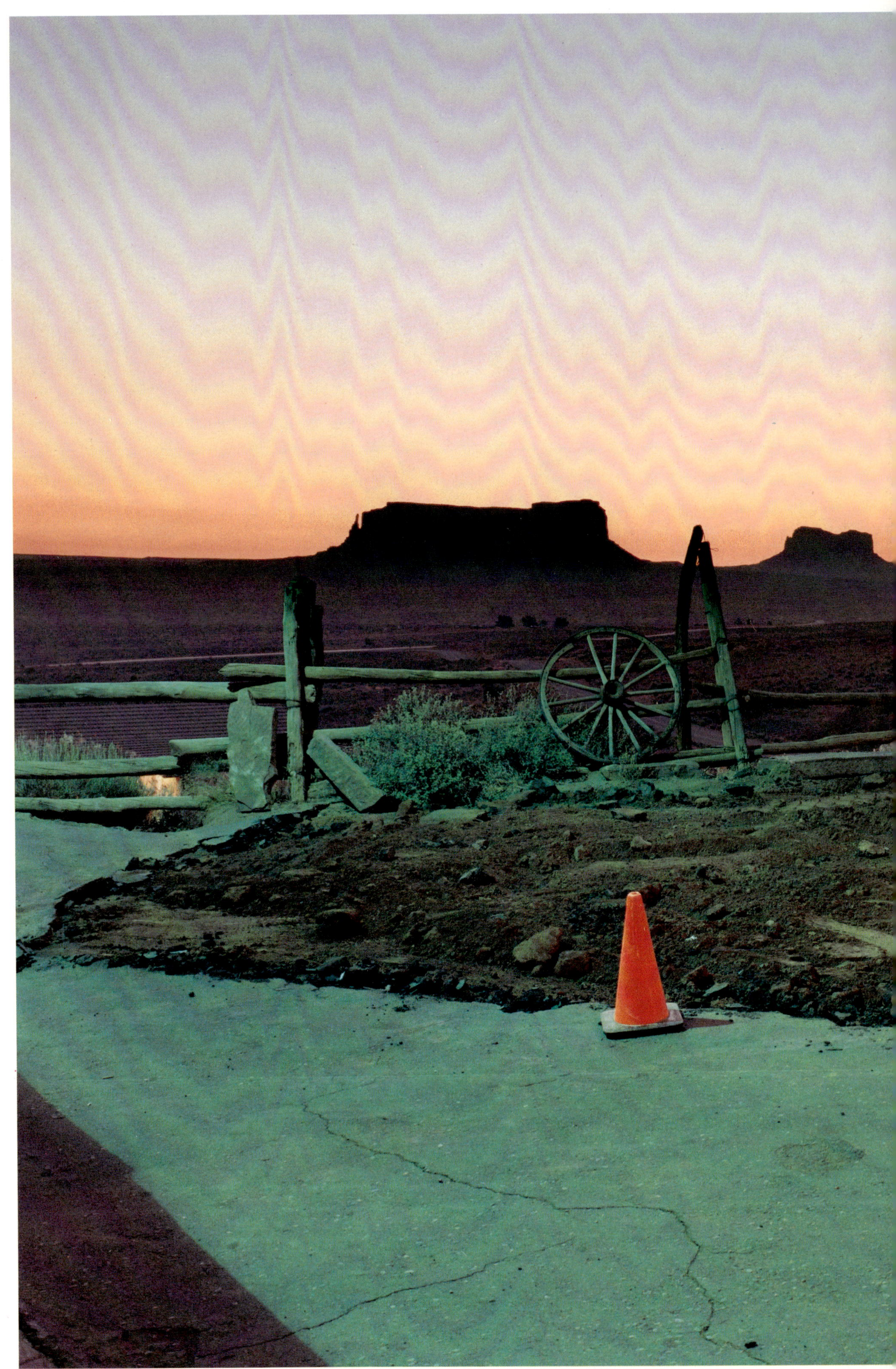

Len Jenshel,
Goulding's Lodge,
Monument Valley,
Utah, 1987

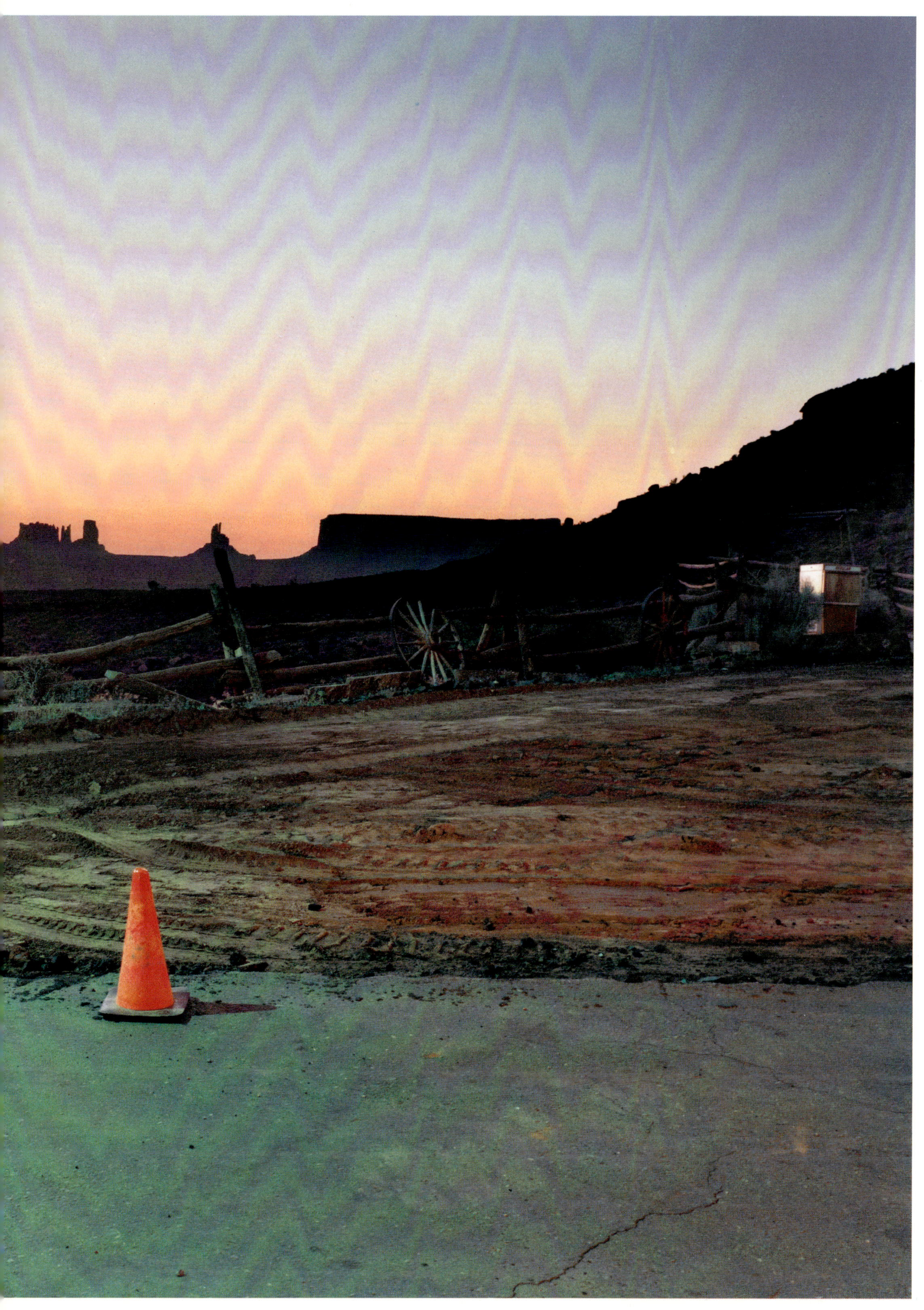

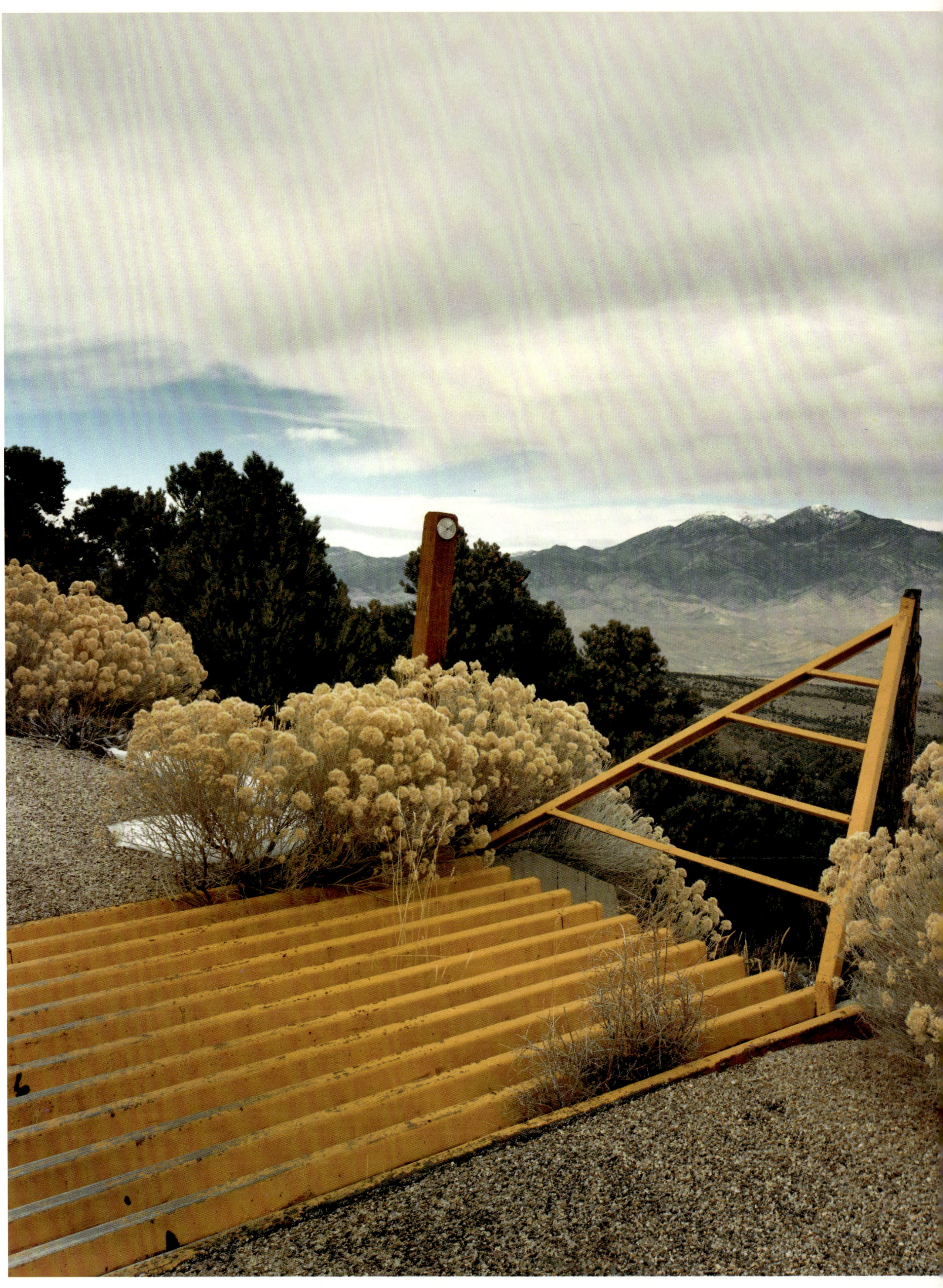

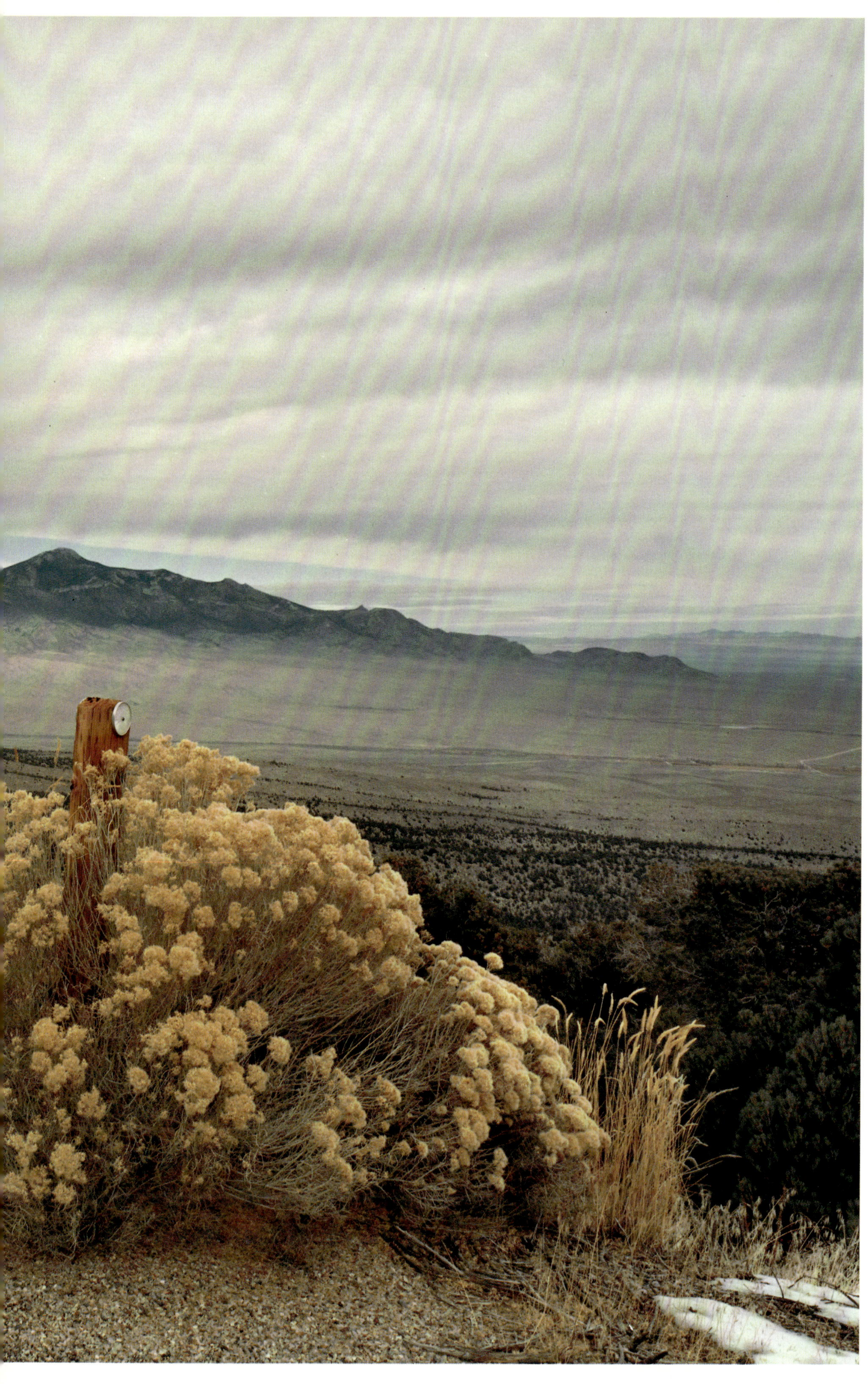

Len Jenshel,
*Great Basin
National Park,
Nevada*, 1987

Wilderness as Saint

By Wes Jackson

Since the roots of our trouble are so largely religious, whether we call it that or not, we must rethink and refeel our nature and destiny.

LYNN WHITE, JR., "The Historical Roots of
Our Ecological Crisis," *Science*, 1967

The notion of the saint in Roman Catholicism calls upon the faithful to stand or kneel before a statue, light a candle, meditate, think, and perhaps whisper some words before departure. Some of these faithful go in peace thinking, "Well, that's covered," and carry on more or less as before. This "isolation of virtue" approach is also found in the attitudes of countless wilderness advocates, who want to set wilderness aside for similar reasons. Pristine wilderness is a prime candidate for ecological sainthood. More than a few wilderness enthusiasts have noted, along with John Muir, that the spiritual uplift that comes from standing in a forest wilderness, soaking up the silences of a holy natural cathedral, is a religious experience of the highest order.

Those who walk out of these wilderness refuges, where *nature's economy* rules, to rejoin civilization, where the *human economy* dominates, are among the most likely to send a check to their favorite defenders of nature's arrangements, such as the Sierra Club, the Wilderness Society, or Earth First! Many of these same devotees, though, say little to protest the spread of lethal farm chemicals over more than half a million square miles of the best agricultural land in the world, in the American Midwest. Soil erosion may be of no concern to these people, either. To have a designated holy land and ignore the rest—to treat our wilderness as saint and Iowa farmland, or for that matter an East Saint Louis slum, otherwise—is a form of schizophrenia. Either the whole thing is holy or it isn't.

How many devout eco-fundamentalists would be as interested in cleaning up the poverty and industrial blight of East Saint Louis, or in defending a farmer's soil conservation efforts or use of such good farming techniques as crop rotation without chemicals, with the fervor with which he or she will spike a tree or put sugar in the fuel tank of a bulldozer?

The secular and religious pilgrims who travel over Interstate 70 to the Colorado wilderness every summer are familiar to many Kansans. Our state's economic-development people are constantly devising little lures to get these people—whom they call tourists—to stay a while. Too many of them, though, shoot by at night through a 400-mile-long dark tunnel on their way to the parks of the Rockies, whether to consume their beauty or to pay homage to them. If it is daylight during the western Kansas–eastern Colorado leg, most of these tourists simply *en-*

dure our agricultural landscape. If I wanted to pout about it, I'd talk about all of those jaded souls greedy for dramatic beauty but unable to experience the deeper and subtler beauty of our gently undulating landscape. They are too busy exceeding the 65-mile-an-hour speed limit in order to reach the mountains as soon as possible and see what in their minds is the real wilderness. But another sad reality is that the wilderness they seek is now as much an artifact of civilization as a gilded Christian saint in a cathedral, as much an artifact as the agricultural landscape.

Without civilization, wilderness is doomed. This is part of the modern tragedy. I say modern, for it hasn't always been that way. In the early days of agriculture, wilderness stood ready to reclaim a neglected field and restore it to a vegetative structure similar to that of its virgin surroundings. Even if civilization, acting through public policy, were to step in and halt further destruction, we may have gone too far already in our cutting and plowing for restoration to any original condition to take place on its own. I hope not. I expect not. None of us can really know, though, because it's too close a call. But we can say this. If we don't save agriculture—and by this I mean saving soil and farmers and farm communities, and keeping ground water and soil from being overloaded with chemicals— then we will eventually lose our wilderness. That is the history of civilization, the history of earth abuse. That is how nearly all Eastern and Western civilizations have lost their reference points, and is perhaps why we Americans have drifted toward bestowing sainthood on our own wildernesses.

At the Land Institute, in Salina, Kansas, we look to the never-plowed prairie wilderness as a model in our attempts to build a sustainable agriculture. In other words, nature is our standard or measure. More than a decade ago, just as we were starting our research, Terry Evans began to photograph these prairies in both color and black and white. Her book, *Prairie: Images of Ground and Sky* (University Press of Kansas, 1986), carries some of her best efforts to help us all *see* our prairie wilderness. The pictures on these pages depict both prairie and formerly prairie land now used for till agriculture.

In our research efforts we bounce back and forth between nature's prairie and agriculture. Like the prairie, we feature perennials in mixtures, but breed them to produce seeds as substitutes for annual monocultures of grain. At diverse sites over our hundred-acre, never-plowed native prairie, our ecologist, Dr. Jon Piper, and Land Institute interns clip and sort aboveground plant material into families of grasses, legumes, sunflowers, and others. By knowing how the various ratios of these major plant families differ across soil types and in wet

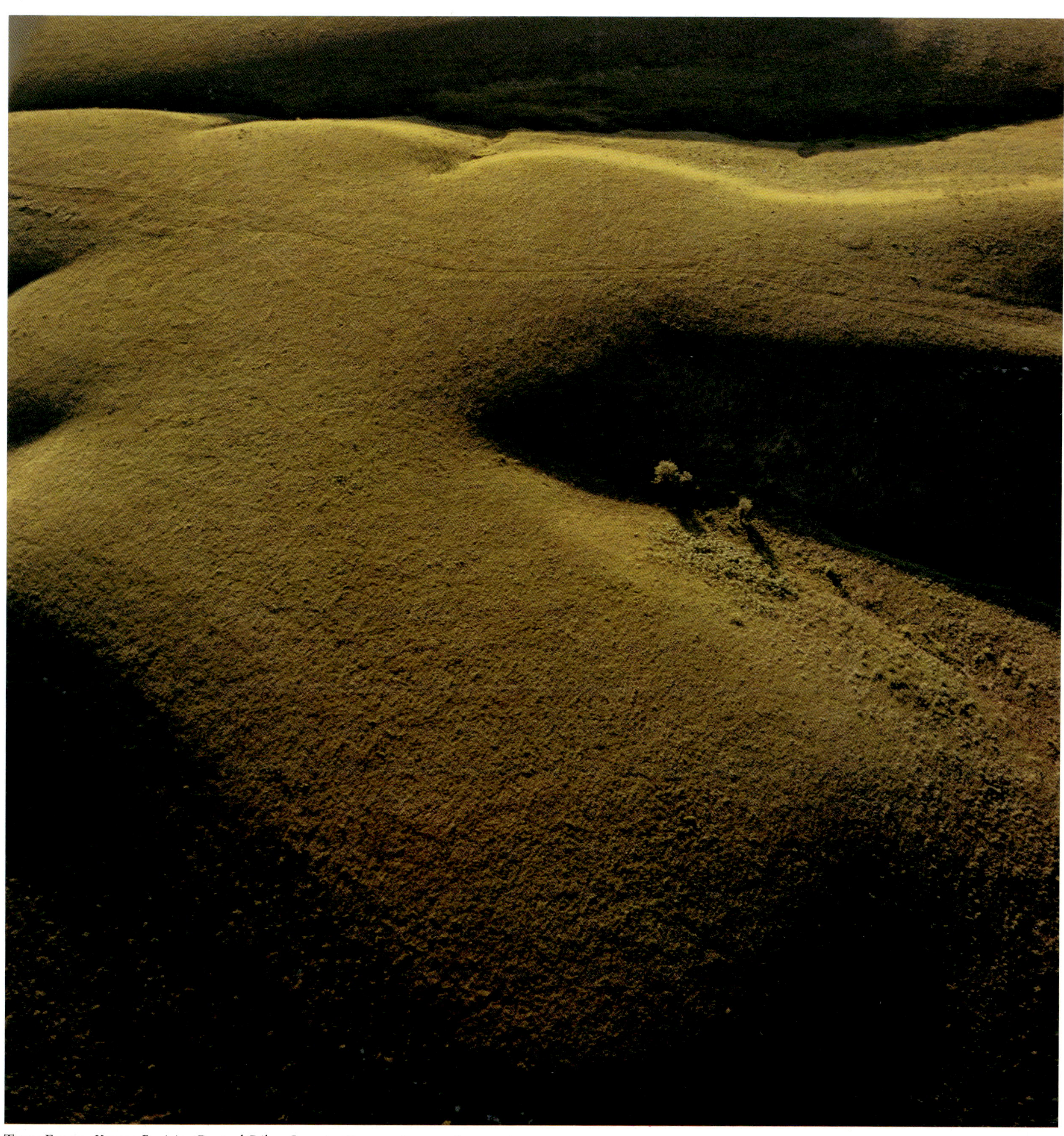

Terry Evans, *Konza Prairie, Central Riley County, Kansas,* June 1982

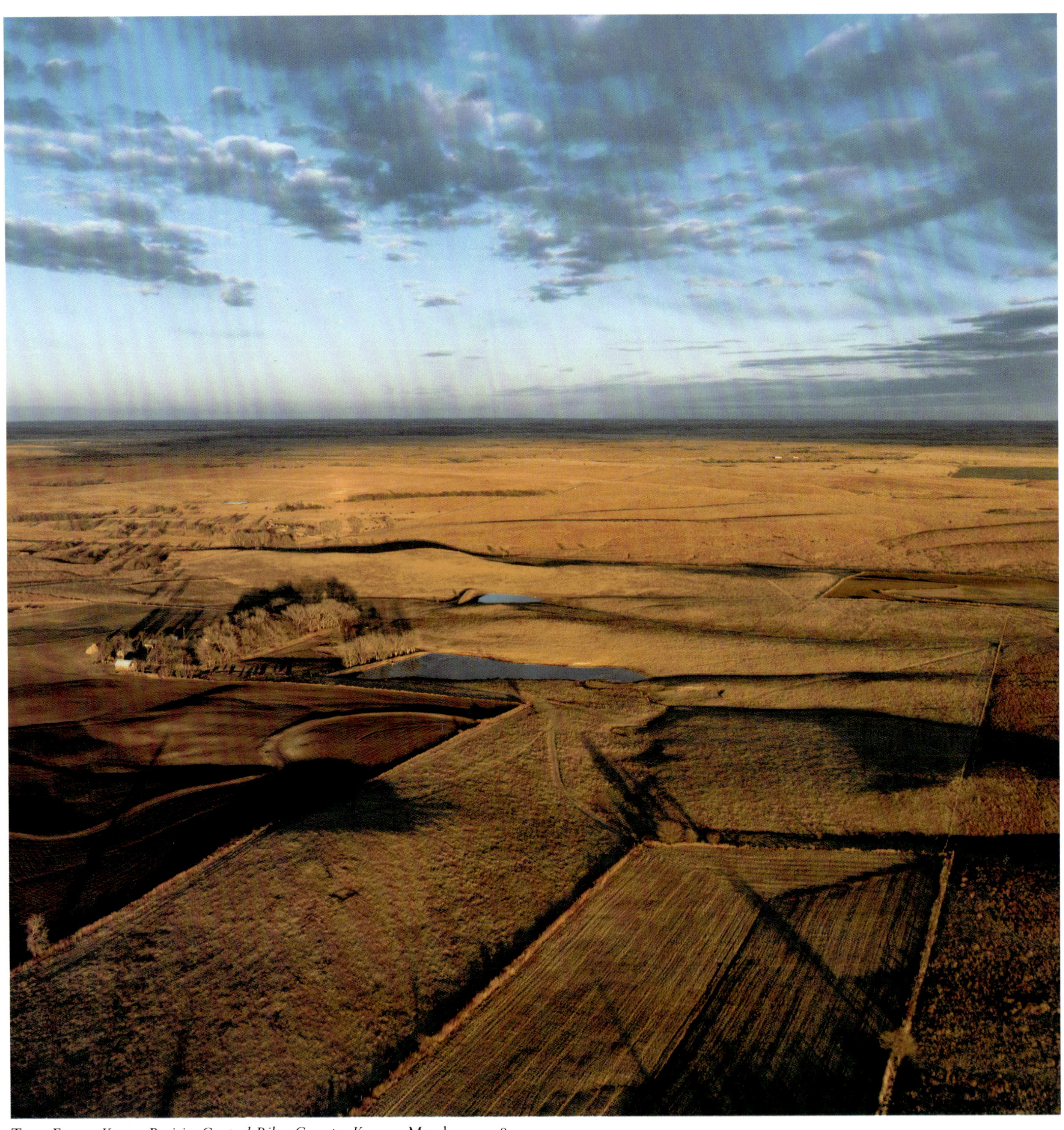

Terry Evans, *Konza Prairie, Central Riley County, Kansas*, March 13, 1985

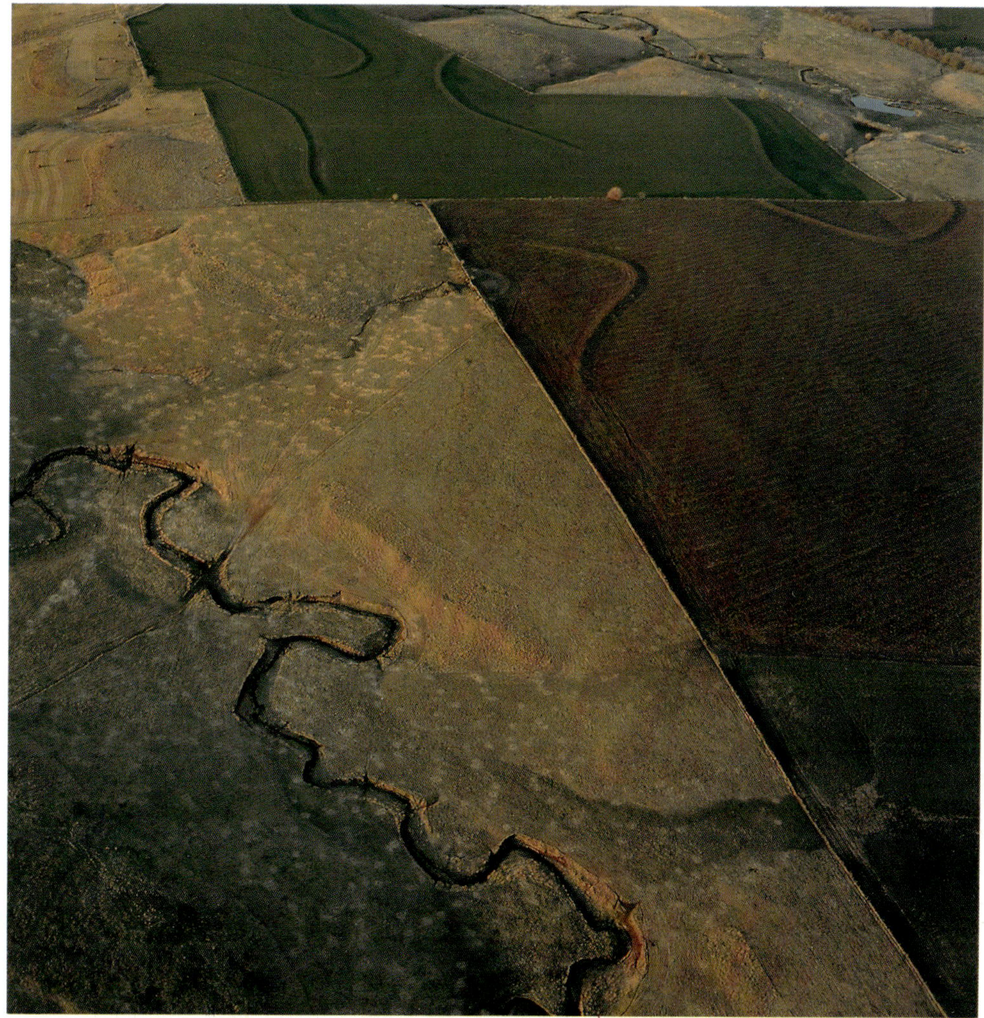

Terry Evans, *Fields with Ponds and Sky, Central Ottawa County, Kansas*, November 20, 1989

and dry years, in combination with our data derived from soil-root interactions, we are ready to reasonably mimic the native structure with four of our selected perennials. These species are still undergoing germ plasm evaluation as we breed for high seed yield and resistance to seed shatter and pests.

We're not alone on this "mimicking nature" front. Dr. Jack Ewel and his colleagues at the University of Florida have mimicked native succession in the tropics. By substituting vine for vine, tree for tree, shrub for shrub, using only plants in the mimic that require human intervention, Ewel concludes that nearly always, when the structure is supplied, the function is granted: high productivity, responsiveness to pests, and good protection of the soil.

The "mimic approach" employed by the Land Institute and Jack Ewel represents the most extreme category of attempts to use nature as a standard. Other workers, such as Dr. Steve Gliessman of the University of California at Santa Cruz, employ ecological principles, but with little intention of trying to imitate nature's structure precisely. Nevertheless the principles have been elucidated from countless studies conducted on natural ecosystems over many decades. This approach offers the promise of a better agriculture, for by featuring species diversity, maintaining ground cover, and relying on internal sources of nutrients, such methods result in better control of weeds, diseases, and insects. Incidently, nearly all of the good examples of traditional agriculture have employed what we now recognize as sound ecological principles.

If humanity is to be successful in this venture to place agriculture back on its biological feet by looking to nature, to wilderness, as the dominant model, and away from the industrial world, we will have to work on several fronts at once. To set up sustainable agriculture as a saint would be as bad as treating wilderness as a saint. A sustainable agriculture must fit into the economy of a sustainable culture. So we have to work to build a sustainable society that includes agriculture.

We can begin this long journey by acknowledging that we are first and foremost land animals, and that in a sunshine future we will have to look more to the land. This means that our agricultural landscape will require more people loving it, loving it as much as it deserves, as much as John Muir loved the Sierra. And I don't mean just farmers. City people, those who reside at the very core of civilization, must love our agricultural lands, too. How can that come about? That's a tough one, but here is a small suggestion.

Many of these tourists who whiz by—typically in one of those loaded-down station wagons with a luggage carrier on

53

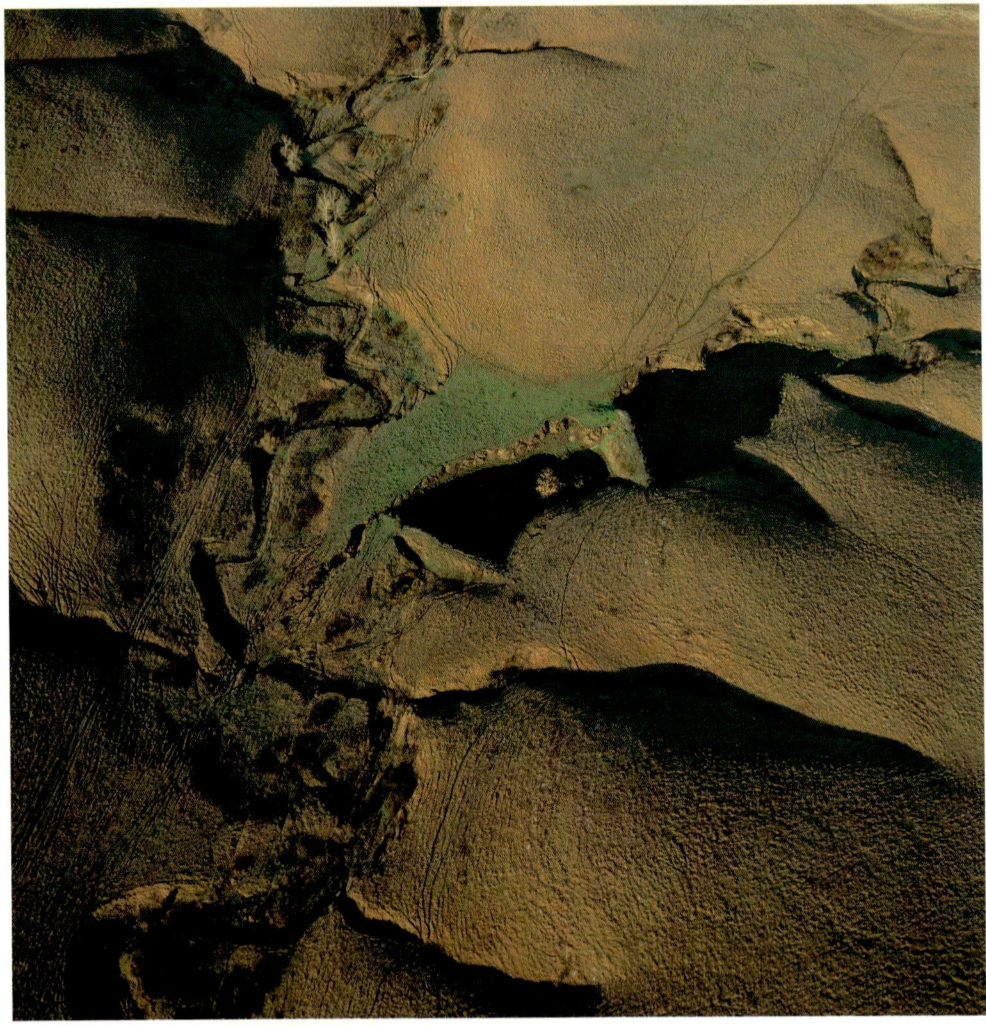

Terry Evans, *The Edge of the Prairie, Northern Geary County, Kansas*, March 6, 1985

the roof, with kids bored and quarreling in the back—must be wondering how they might make their next trip more pleasant. I suggest that the next time, in preparing for their journey, they study maps and some of the history of the regions through which they will pass. What if they learned the drainages of rivers and streams, and required the children to learn them, too? Parents could let the children know before the trip that they could expect to be quizzed about such topics as where the water that falls on the passing countryside eventually goes. Parents should make themselves mentally ready to pull off the Interstate, at any time, and find the small cafes the locals frequent. I would encourage eavesdropping and asking questions. Find out about the agricultural economy, about agrichemicals, about farm debt, about the size of the town now and twenty years ago, about where the kids who leave town go. (One has to be careful how this is done, for rural people become sensitive when the overly loquacious ask too many questions, and know how to clam up.) The kids should examine the local crops up close, finger the soil, and be prepared to say something intelligent about it. (More home study on soils before the trip.) Any parent or grandparent who loves America will prepare for the trip by getting area maps from the U.S. or state geological survey. Anybody headed for the mountains should study up ahead of time so they know such things as the period of the Rocky Mountain uplift and why the land tilts toward Kansas City seven feet per mile from Denver. Kids should know when the Cretaceous seas covered the area, depositing limestone, and how that limestone now figures in the good rich soils of central Kansas. Check the fossils in the limestone. The kids will like that.

This is a small suggestion, and only one example. What I am after is for more of us to make it our plan to become *travelers* rather than *tourists*. Tourists visit Pikes Peak. Travelers will find the peak that divides the Arkansas and Missouri watersheds. If we can develop the gumption to endure our children's protests now, and if necessary even to suffer, the payoff will come twenty years from now. We will beam with pride as we observe our children's love for the agricultural and natural American landscape, and as they carry the tradition on to our grandchildren. Too many families remember only how their children devoted too much of their creative energy on long trips to things like drawing imaginary dividing lines in the back seat, daring any sibling to cross them by as much as one millimeter. We can do better than that, with ourselves and our children. We must do better than that. Nothing less than the American landscape and our future are on the line. □

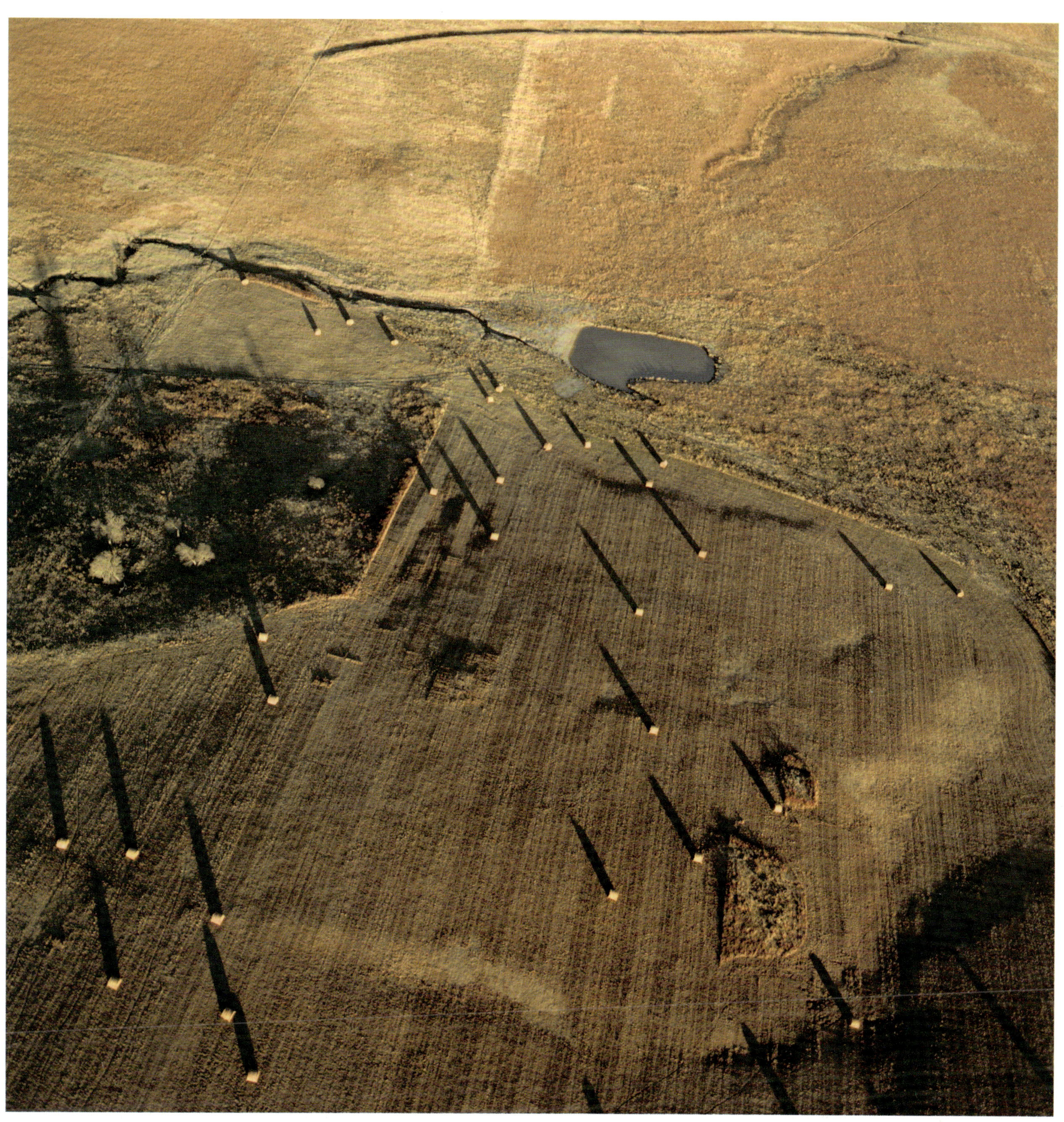

Terry Evans, *Hay Bales, Northwest Saline County, Kansas*, November 28, 1989

Water in the West

By Gerald Haslam

Squinting across the seared, supine surface of California's Great Central Valley in 1863, William Henry Brewer and other members of the state's geological survey party found themselves traveling "a plain of absolute desolation." Hands cupped over their eyes, they could perceive no mountains, no trees, no relief, only heat so thick it swerved light. The young men rode south "upward of thirty miles without any tree or bush—except once a single small willow was visible for two hours. . . . It was like the ocean but it depressed the spirits more."

That same parched vale is now the richest farming region in the world. Last year alone it produced nearly $15 billion in agriculture—more than the value of all the gold mined in the history of the Golden State. How was that possible? Historian W. H. Hutchinson says there were three principal reasons: "Water, water, and more water."

The control and manipulation of water in the arid West has been the key to everything from economics to politics here. There would be few Idaho potatoes without water projects, little Arizona cotton, no Utah alfalfa. There would also be no Phoenix, no Las Vegas, and no Los Angeles—not as we know them, anyway. There would be no Reno or El Paso or Albuquerque, either, because they too have grown in desiccated areas.

The American West is, in the main, arid to semi-arid land. But the beauty and value of arid lands have rarely been apparent to people whose ancestors migrated from green Europe, so enormous amounts of money have been spent and rapacious bureaucracies created in an effort "to make the desert bloom." Despite these efforts, only a tiny portion of the land has so far been "developed," but that has bloomed abundantly.

Unfortunately, these efforts have also produced the seeds of their own doom—problems such as soil salinization, compaction, and subsidence; the leaching and concentrating of natural toxins from previously dry earth; the overuse of agricultural chemicals that in turn concentrate in the environment; and the devastation of once huge aquifers in order to flood-irrigate crops better suited for other climates in other places. These developments now seem to have placed Westerners on the path once trod by Assyrians, Mesopotamians, and Aztecs, desert peoples who also challenged nature—and failed.

In the past year, ten photographers—Laurie Brown, Greg Coniff, Robert Dawson, Terry Evans, Frank Gohlke, Peter Goin, Wanda Hammerbeck, Mark Klett, Meridel Rubenstein, and Martin Stupich— along with curator Ellen Manchester, have embarked on a project to dramatize this long-ignored environmental crisis. "We've been managing water as an abstract legal right or a commodity," points out Dawson, the Californian who initiated the endeavor, "rather than the most basic physical source of life. We believe that water is misused nationwide. We're focusing on the arid West because development here stands in high relief against the vast, open landscape. It's here that the impact of technology, government, and human ambition is most visible." Many major water-policy decisions remain to be made, and only an informed public can do that.

Nowhere are the gains and losses associated with water manipulation more obvious than in Dawson's home region, the Great Central Valley of California—450 miles long, up to 75 miles wide, about the size of England—the physical and economic core of our richest state. All significant cities there, the state's heartland, grew near watercourses: an oasis civilization.

But it isn't the existence of cities that makes this area vital. No, it is the fact that a stunning twenty-five percent of *all* table food produced in the United States is grown in this single, incredibly fertile valley.

The climate here seems close to perfect for farming: following a short, splendid spring, an extended summer develops—

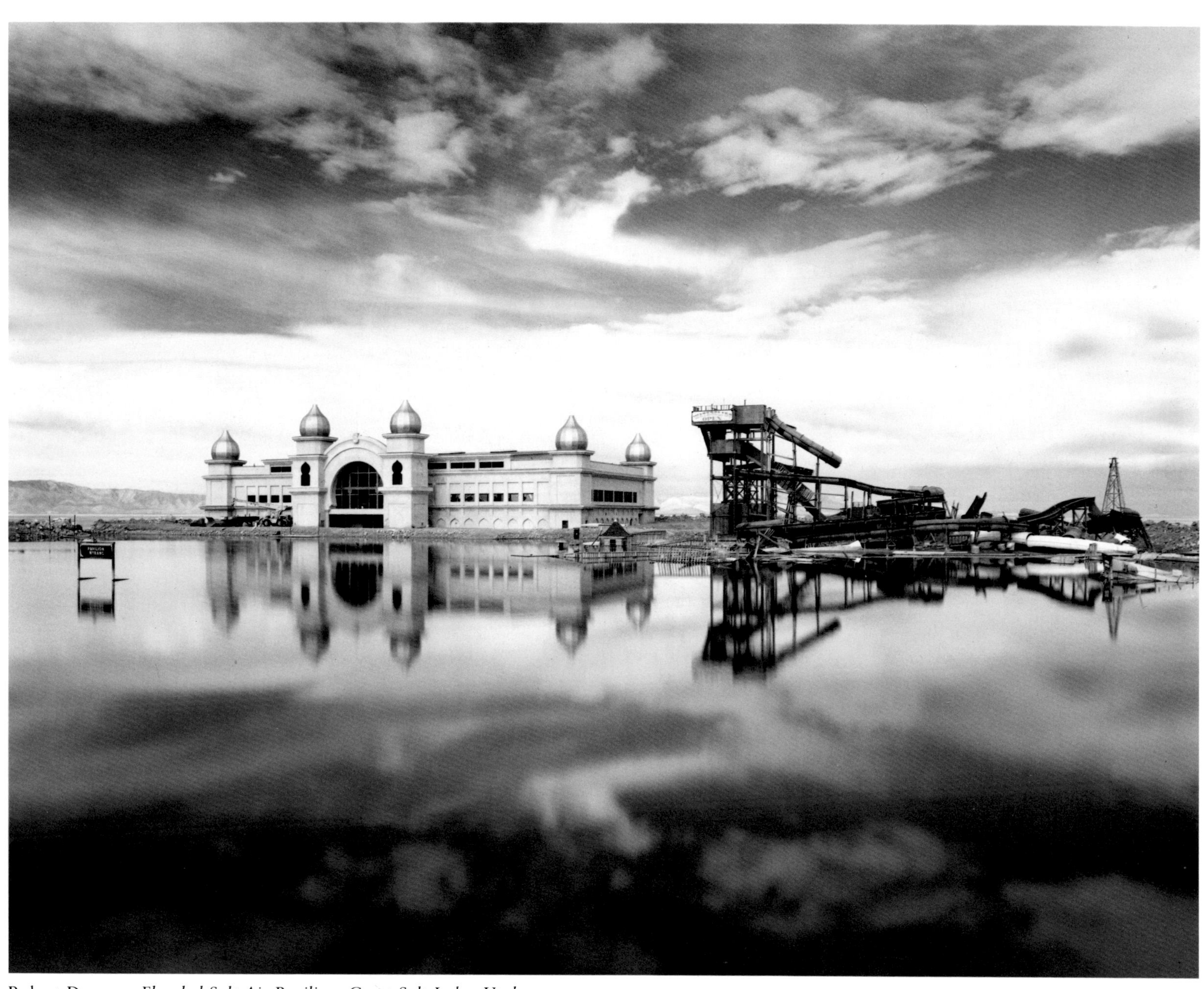

Robert Dawson, *Flooded Salt Air Pavilion, Great Salt Lake, Utah,*
from the "Water in the West Project," 1985

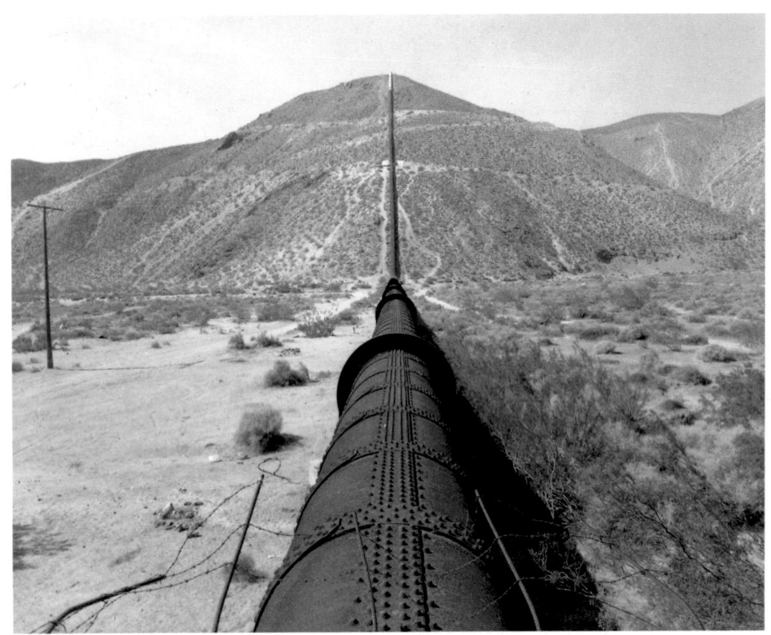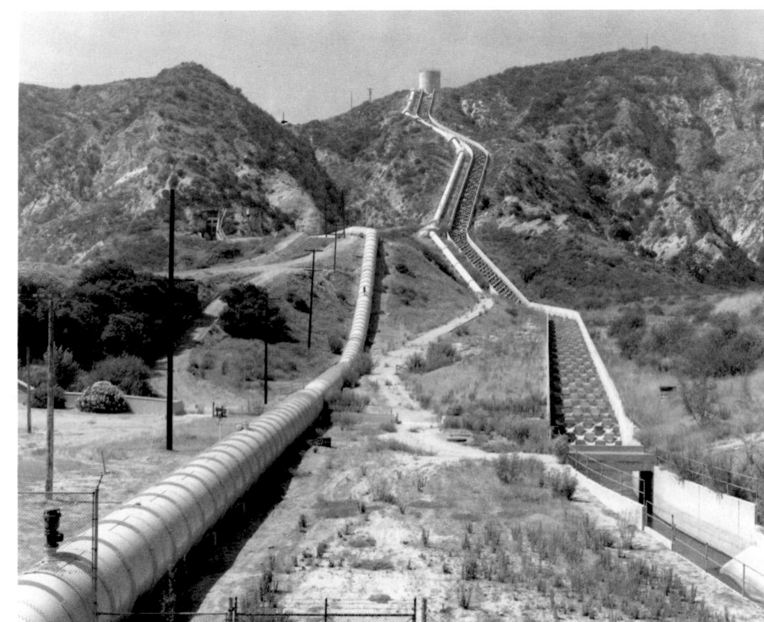

Robert Dawson, *Owens Valley Water Leaving Owens Valley and Entering Los Angeles, Los Angeles, California,* from the "Water in the West Project," 1989

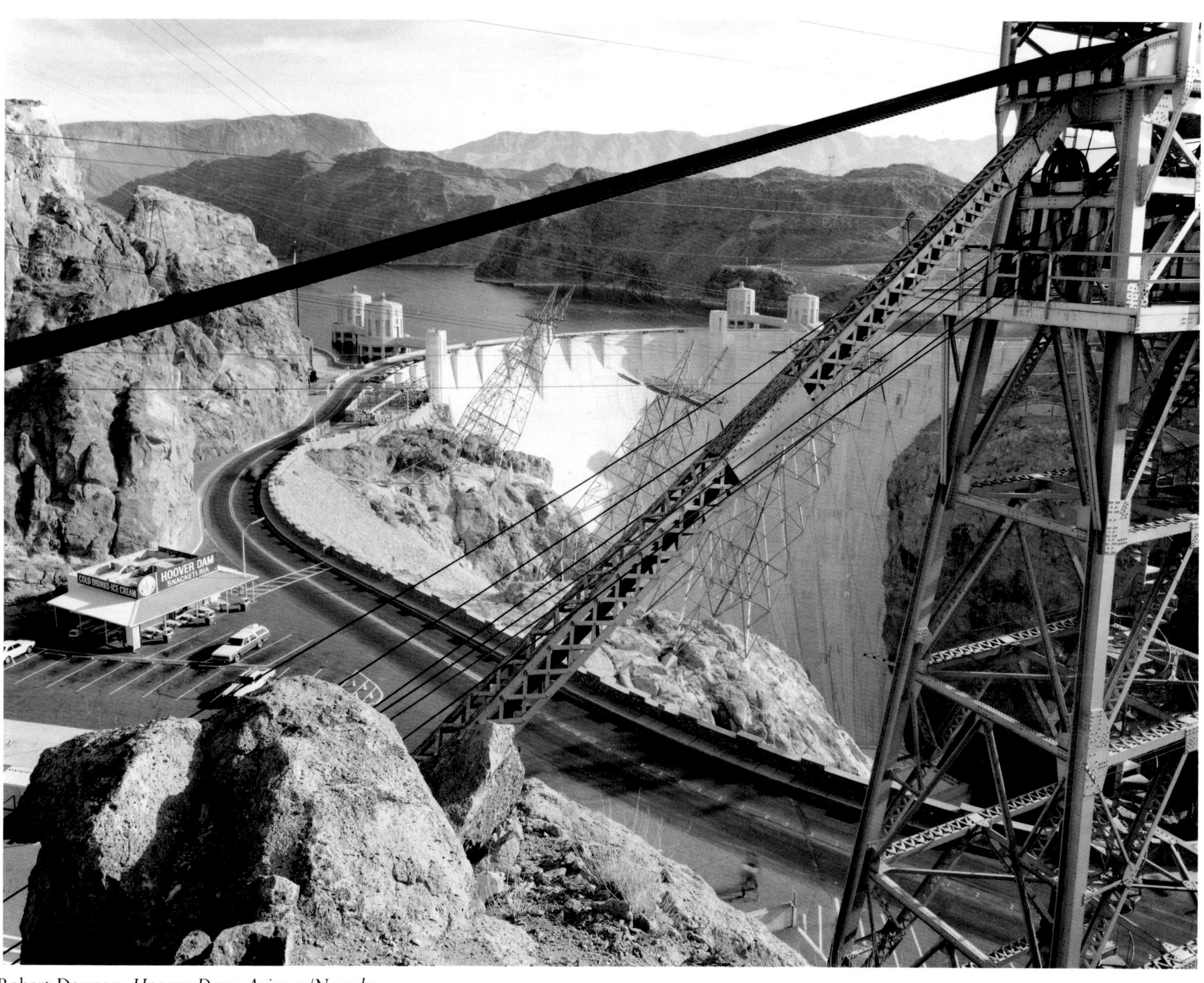

Robert Dawson, *Hoover Dam, Arizona/Nevada,*
from the "Water in the West Project," 1987

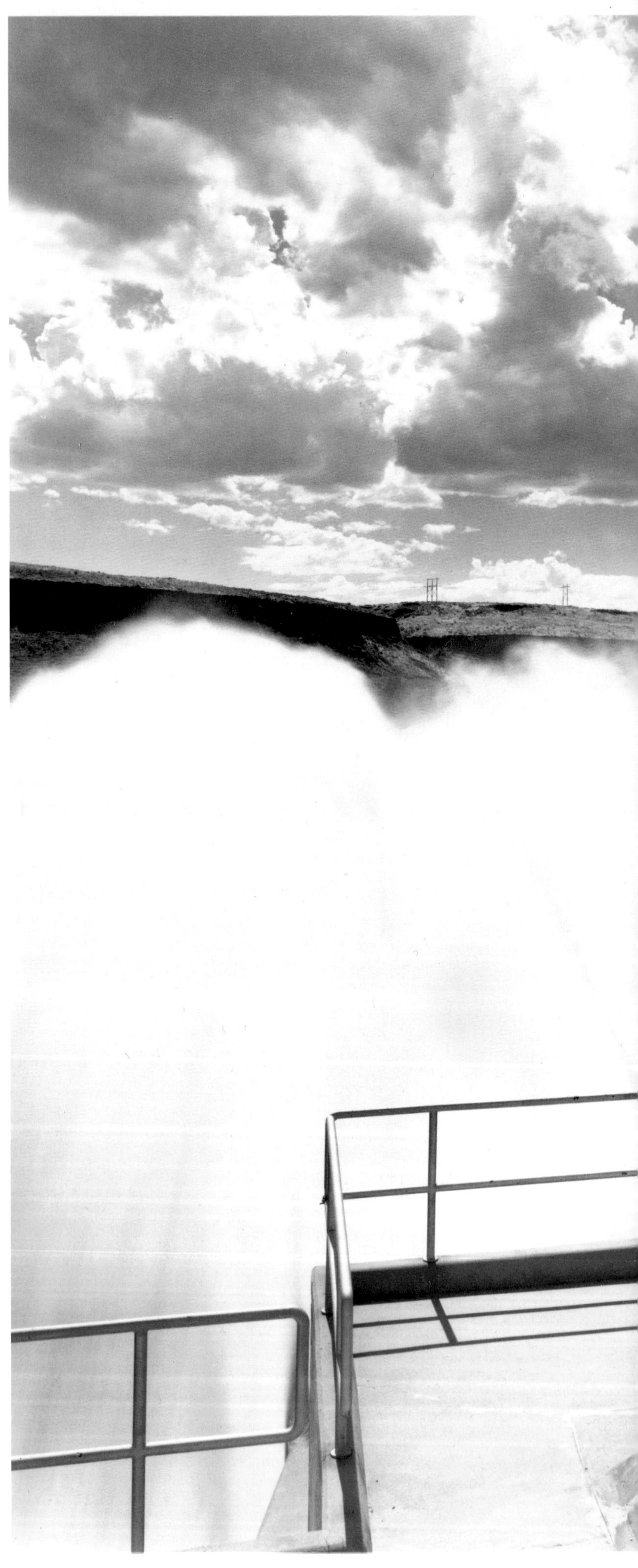

providing over 300 growing days a year. Sun prevails and the horizon seems to expand: the earth itself appears to be sweating. Thanks to water pumped or imported, the list of crops grown in this natural hothouse is continually expanding as new varieties are planted: exotic herbs and condiments this year, kiwi fruit and frost-free berries the next. Meanwhile, native plants are rare, and native animals—pronghorns, grizzlies, and condors—stand stuffed in local museums.

Here, too, a largely Hispanic work force toils on great farms owned by corporations, because this remains a place where the poor of any background can at least try to escape the cycle of poverty, one generation laboring that another might take advantage of the region's rich promise. But it isn't an easy climb, because there also has tended to be a direct link between centralized irrigation systems and centralized political and economic power, and that in turn has created a paternalistic, class-ridden society with nonwhites on the bottom.

Modern agribusiness is competitive, and Valley farmers and ranchers have been notably creative, inventing such agricultural devices as the combine harvester, the Fresno scraper, the Stockton gang-plow, the Randall harrow, special adaptations of the clamshell dredge, peach defuzzers, olive pitters, wind machines to fight frost, hydraulic platforms for pruning, pneumatic tree-shakers for bringing down the fruit and nuts—a technological nascence of amazing creativity. But none of them would mean much without imported or pumped water.

Many farmers date their entry into Valley agriculture to the period just after World War I when the unregulated pumping of ground water allowed fields to burgeon. Eventually farmers were pumping more and more from wells that had to be drilled deeper and deeper into unreplenishable aquifers. When the Central Valley Project and the California State Water Project— the two largest and most complex irrigation systems on earth— were completed, it seemed that, at last, the tapping of irreplaceable ground water locally could cease.

Today, over 1,200 dams have been built and thousands of miles of canals cross this one-time desert; eighty-five percent of *all* water channeled in California is used to irrigate farms. Even that hasn't stopped subsurface pumping; it has actually expanded since those huge stores of surface water became available. Pumping now exceeds replenishment by a over a half *trillion* gallons annually, while ecosystems hundreds of miles to the north are threatened by the diversion of their rivers and creeks.

Writer Wallace Stegner has suggested that this areas's—and, by analogy, the West's—agriculture may have "to shrink back to something like the old, original scale, and maybe less than the original scale because there isn't the ground water there

Robert Dawson, *Lucky Peak Dam, near Boise, Idaho*, 1984

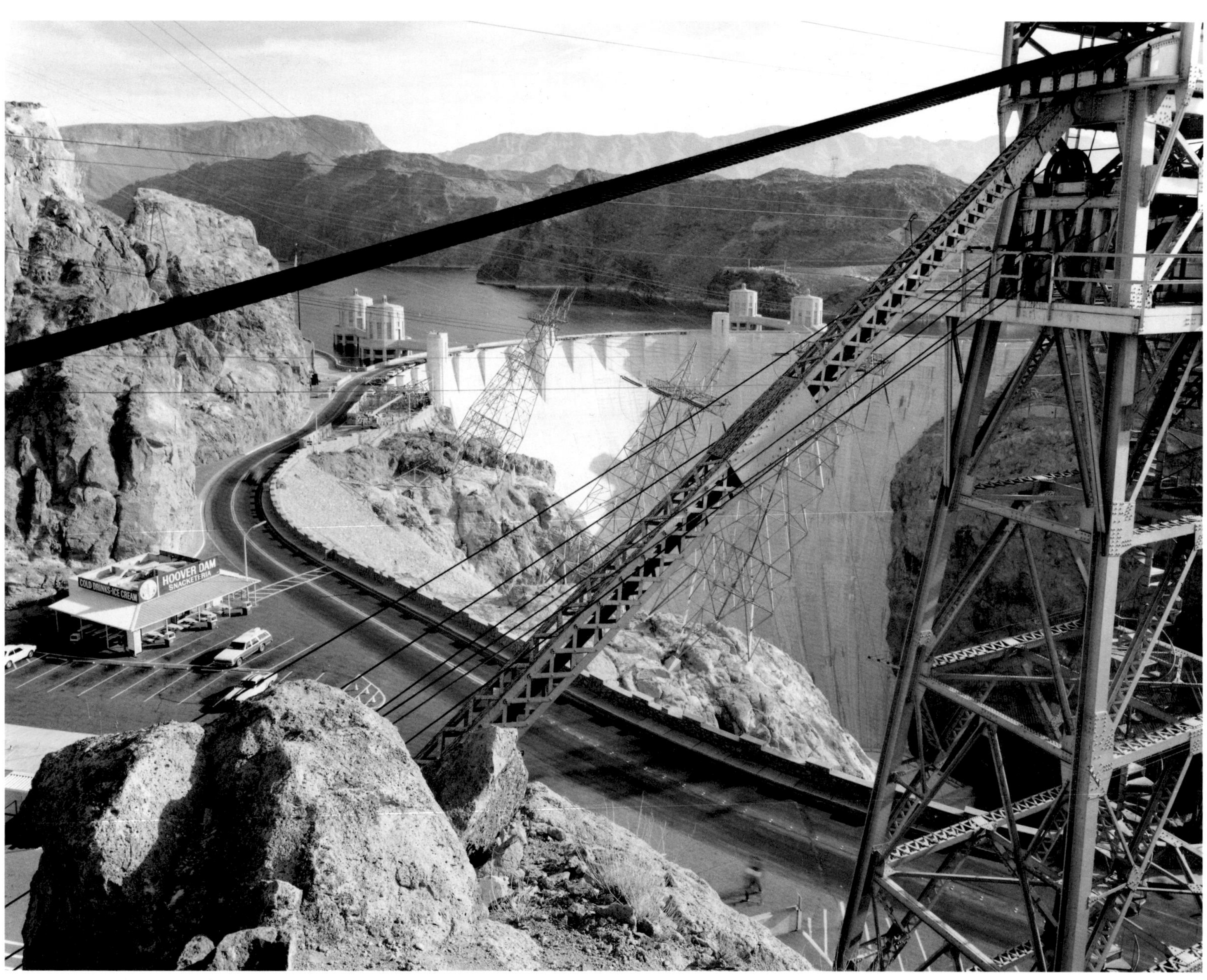

Robert Dawson, *Hoover Dam, Arizona/Nevada,*
from the "Water in the West Project," 1987

providing over 300 growing days a year. Sun prevails and the horizon seems to expand: the earth itself appears to be sweating. Thanks to water pumped or imported, the list of crops grown in this natural hothouse is continually expanding as new varieties are planted: exotic herbs and condiments this year, kiwi fruit and frost-free berries the next. Meanwhile, native plants are rare, and native animals—pronghorns, grizzlies, and condors—stand stuffed in local museums.

Here, too, a largely Hispanic work force toils on great farms owned by corporations, because this remains a place where the poor of any background can at least try to escape the cycle of poverty, one generation laboring that another might take advantage of the region's rich promise. But it isn't an easy climb, because there also has tended to be a direct link between centralized irrigation systems and centralized political and economic power, and that in turn has created a paternalistic, class-ridden society with nonwhites on the bottom.

Modern agribusiness is competitive, and Valley farmers and ranchers have been notably creative, inventing such agricultural devices as the combine harvester, the Fresno scraper, the Stockton gang-plow, the Randall harrow, special adaptations of the clamshell dredge, peach defuzzers, olive pitters, wind machines to fight frost, hydraulic platforms for pruning, pneumatic tree-shakers for bringing down the fruit and nuts—a technological nascence of amazing creativity. But none of them would mean much without imported or pumped water.

Many farmers date their entry into Valley agriculture to the period just after World War I when the unregulated pumping of ground water allowed fields to burgeon. Eventually farmers were pumping more and more from wells that had to be drilled deeper and deeper into unreplenishable aquifers. When the Central Valley Project and the California State Water Project—the two largest and most complex irrigation systems on earth—were completed, it seemed that, at last, the tapping of irreplaceable ground water locally could cease.

Today, over 1,200 dams have been built and thousands of miles of canals cross this one-time desert; eighty-five percent of *all* water channeled in California is used to irrigate farms. Even that hasn't stopped subsurface pumping; it has actually expanded since those huge stores of surface water became available. Pumping now exceeds replenishment by a over a half *trillion* gallons annually, while ecosystems hundreds of miles to the north are threatened by the diversion of their rivers and creeks.

Writer Wallace Stegner has suggested that this areas's—and, by analogy, the West's—agriculture may have "to shrink back to something like the old, original scale, and maybe less than the original scale because there isn't the ground water there

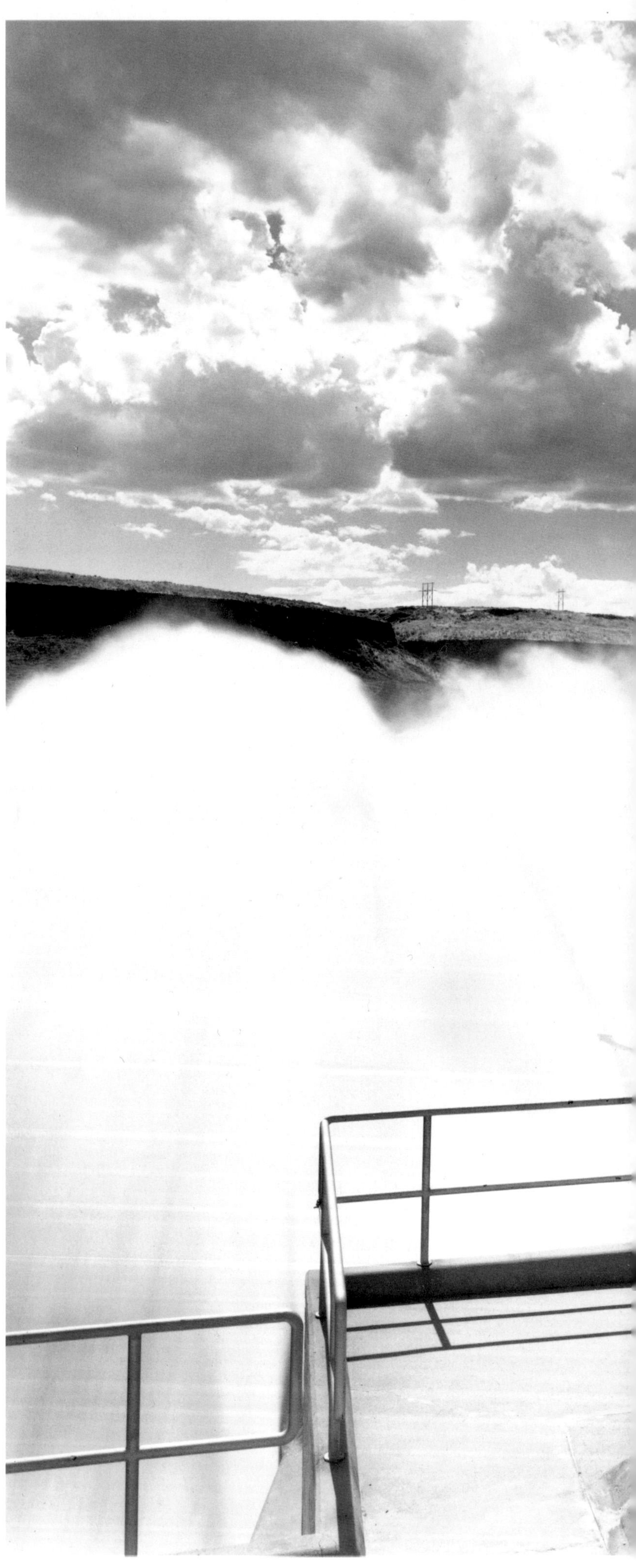

Robert Dawson, *Lucky Peak Dam, near Boise, Idaho,* 1984

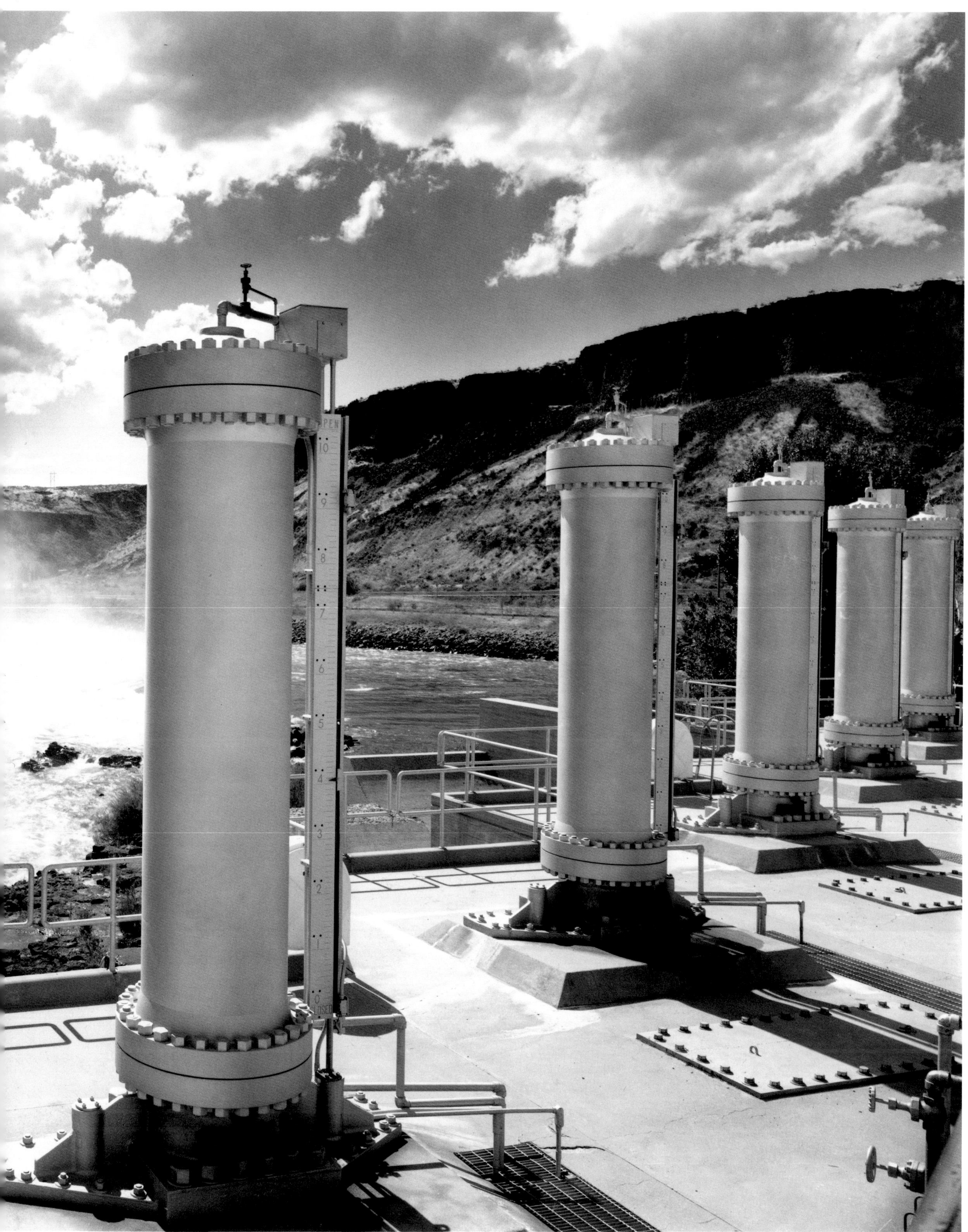
OPEN
10
9
8
7
6
5
4
3
2
1
0
CLOSED

anymore. It's actually more desert than it was when people first began to move in." Hutchinson adds, "We have to stop pretending we're frontiersmen dealing with unlimited water. There's too damn many of us and too damned little of *it*."

Thanks to the faceless, powerful bureaucracy that manipulates Western resources for profit and power, giant agribusinesses in the Valley can buy that water for under ten dollars per acre-foot, while northern California householders have paid well over a thousand dollars for the same acre-foot—with the difference subsidized by taxpayers. It seems to critics that such water is too cheap to use wisely and that both hubris and ignorance are manifest in the illusion that moisture unused by humans is somehow squandered, the natural world be damned—and dammed. Ironically, most people—including most Westerners—seem to choose not to be aware of all this, lest salads and beef suddenly become more expensive.

Irrigation in this valley and in the West is big business, and both the vast water projects in California were justified, in part at least, as measures that would save existing family farms and perhaps increase the number of acres cultivated by small farmers. Both have, in fact, led to more and more acres under cultivation by huge corporations—Chevron U.S.A., Prudential Insurance Company, Shell Oil Company, Southern Pacific Railroad, J.G. Boswell Company, and Getty Oil, among others.

How has the quest for water changed the West? Last year, driving through the Central Valley, I decided to show my son what was once the largest body of fresh water west of the Great Lakes. We crossed the California Aqueduct, the state's longest "river," a man-made, 444-mile-long cement channel, and then I stopped the car at a vista point. An immense agricultural panorama opened before us, cultivated fields of various hues extending as far as vision.

"Where's the lake?" Garth asked. "I don't see any water."

"There," I said. "It's all fields now."

Tulare Lake once covered 468,000 acres, but its water and land was coveted, so today it is a grid of agricultural patches. All its tributary streams have been diverted and its bed is now dry so, ironically, it must be irrigated. As we gazed at this scene a hawk wheeled overhead, riding a thermal. Far ahead a yellow tractor shimmered through heat waves like a crawdad creeping across the old lake's floor. We saw no dwellings, few trees.

"Where're the farmhouses, Dad? Where're the *people*?"

"In San Francisco," I replied, "in corporate boardrooms."

That hawk swung far over a green field where tiny fingers of water from elsewhere glistened through rows and a lone brown man, an irrigator, leaned on a shovel.

Welcome to the real West—where water brokers and agribusiness have replaced cowboys and Indians as the principal players. ☐

Robert Dawson, *Private Property, Lake Tahoe, California,* 1988

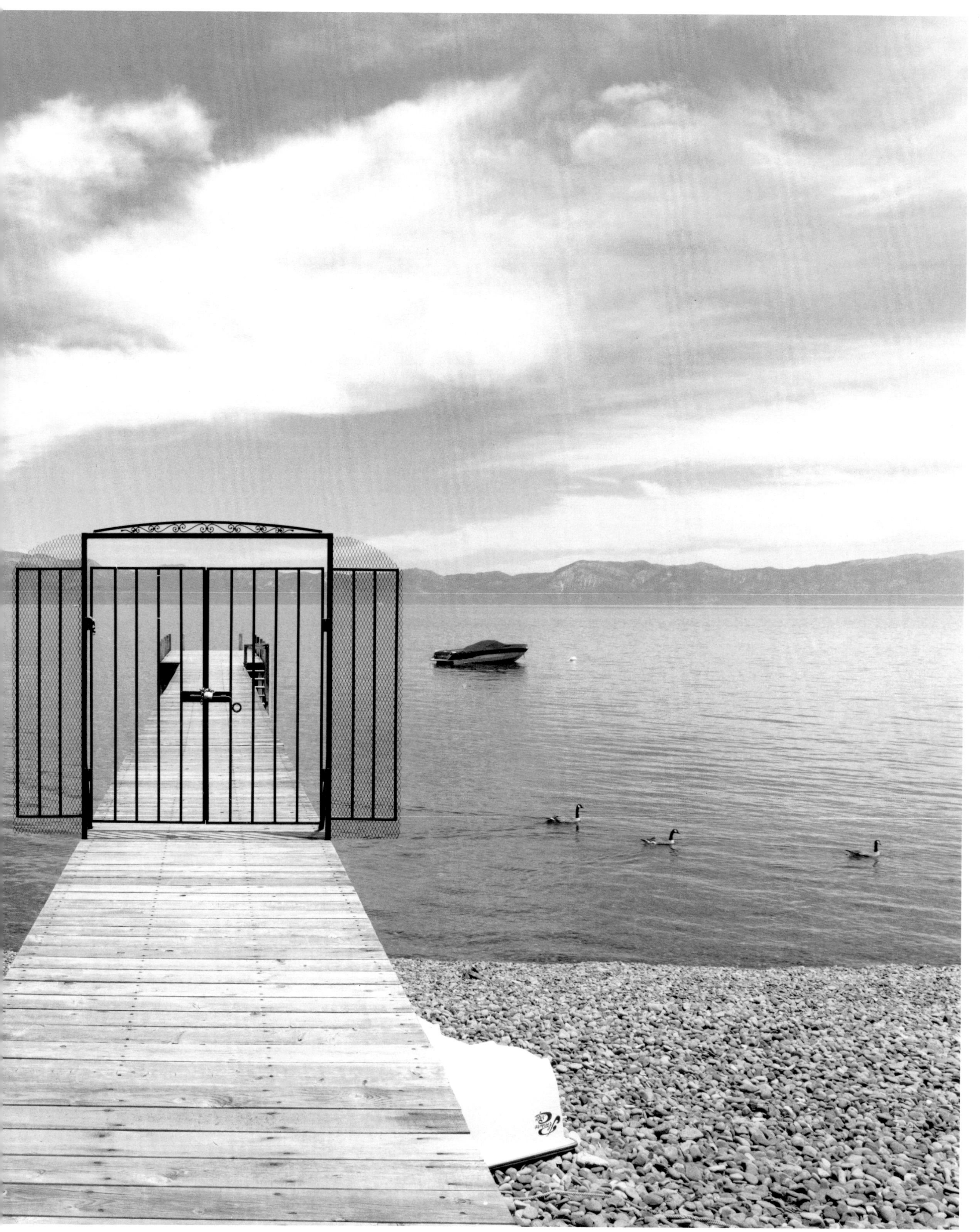

Of Houses and Highways

By J. B. Jackson

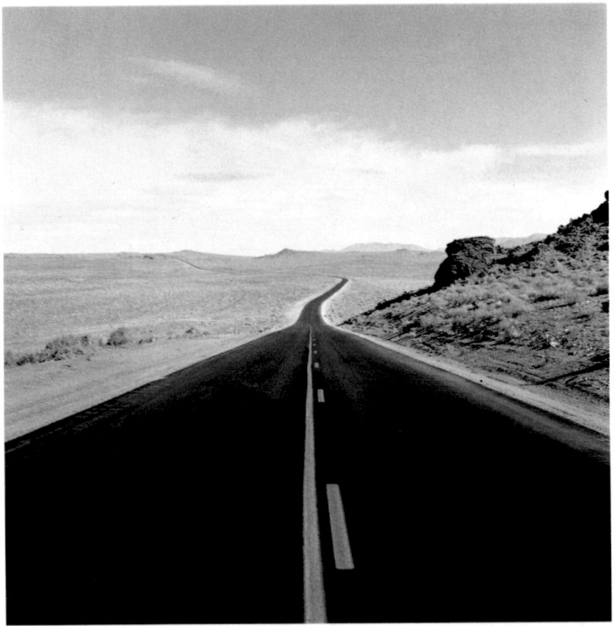

Peter deLory, *Two-Lane Blacktop, Pyramid Lake Indian Reservation, Nevada,* 1989

Landscape and scenery are not the same. A landscape is not a plantlike, organic entity that grows and develops and dies according to immutable natural laws, as some environmentalists would have it: it is a man-made composition of structures and spaces designed to serve the needs of its inhabitants, and when those needs—economic, social, ideological—change, then the landscape changes, not always to everyone's satisfaction.

It happens that those changes often occur before we are aware of the forces that triggered them; the landscape shows symptoms before we recognize the cause. A case in point is the radical shift taking place in the American landscape in the relationship between those spaces devoted to movement and communication on the one hand, and those devoted to permanence and autonomy on the other; or, to put it more simply, the relationship between the road and the house. It is easy to see that in the formation or re-formation of our landscape the street or road or highway or track now has the upper hand. But why should this be the case?

In the past, these two kinds of space seemed to be in balance. It was possible to argue about which was the more essential in the functioning of a landscape: the house or the road. House,

of course, stood for family and continuity and sense of place and identity. Yet it was the road that brought us together and made a unit out of a collection of fragments and gave us a sense of history. The issue was essentially a matter of how we perceived a given landscape: was it a territory with its own unique characteristics, or was it merely the outcome of a group of people living and working together?

In any case, the existence of one of those two spaces or structures presupposes the existence of the other. House and road are meant to interact, and without their interaction and mutual adjustment there can never be a landscape—nothing but trackless solitude, an expanse of scenery. So when we speculate about the growing dominance of the road, we are speculating about the nature of our American landscape, and about our response to it.

In the traditional pretechnological landscape of Europe and colonial America, the road had one elementary purpose: to serve the house, to link it with the small world where the family could satisfy its daily needs. Aside from remnants of roads built by Romans and an occasional "King's Highway" meant for commerce and the movement of troops, the average country road until well into the eighteenth century was primitive and

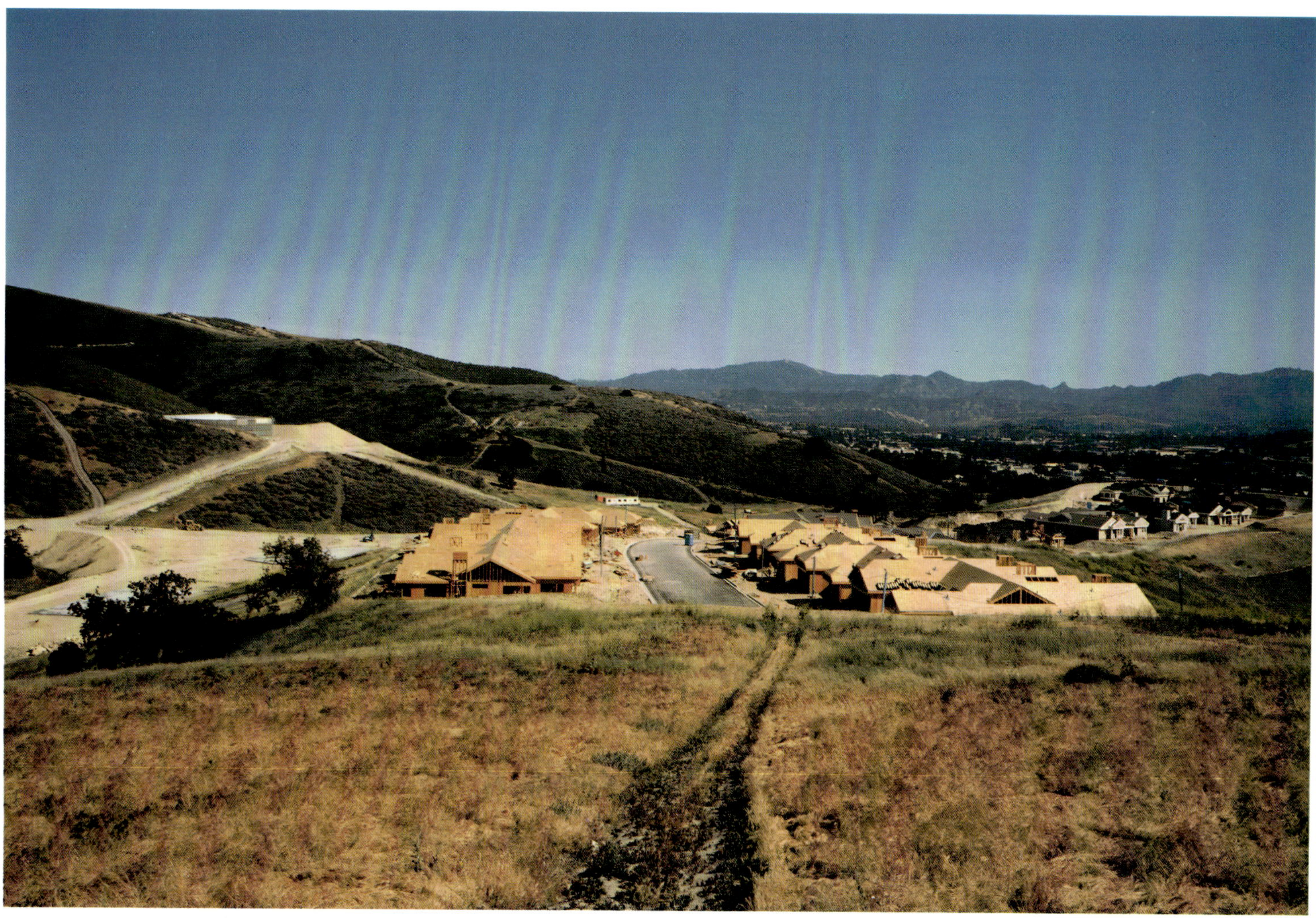

John Ganis, *Housing Development, Southern California,* 1989

bad: narrow, rough, twisting, and unpredictable. When it became ruinous it was abandoned. No local authority built it or maintained it. It was beaten into existence by the tread of farmers and peddlers and churchgoers and neighbors, by the passage of cows and sheep driven to pasture and home again. Far from providing access to the outside world, it led no further than a few miles to the village mill, the parish church, the manor house, and the tavern. A traveler wanting to reach the nearest town had to grope his way through uncharted lanes and paths and temporary rights of way, and though no household could do without it, the road was treated with disdain: a place to dump rubbish, to dig for sand and gravel, to turn pigs loose to forage. Seasonal mud would bog down through traffic of freight wagons, and even the neighboring farmers dared not raise certain crops for fear of not getting them to market on time.

Nevertheless, the traditional country road had its merits. No farm, however remote, was ever left unvisited: for it went from house to house like a friendly dog, hoping for a welcome. In its meanderings it was always respectful of the integrity of private property and made great detours to avoid trespassing. This was also the case in America. On a presidential tour of New England, Washington complained of losing his way because, as he said, the roads were laid out to suit the convenience of the farmer, and not the traveling public. Furthermore, this policy of serving the house allowed the road to participate in daily existence. The traveler saw men in the fields, houses being built, gardens planted, and families celebrating. The labyrinthine road, by discouraging the presence of transients, helped reinforce the image of the landscape as a closed community.

Modern lovers of rural picturesqueness are haunted by the memory of the old-style landscape where house had priority over road. The layout of many prosperous suburbs, with curving streets, no sidewalks, and spacious lawns, is our way of conferring status on the house. Nevertheless it is clear that the contemporary workaday road—or street, or highway—has departed from that medieval tradition. In fact, a new and very different kind of road made its appearance in the latter decades

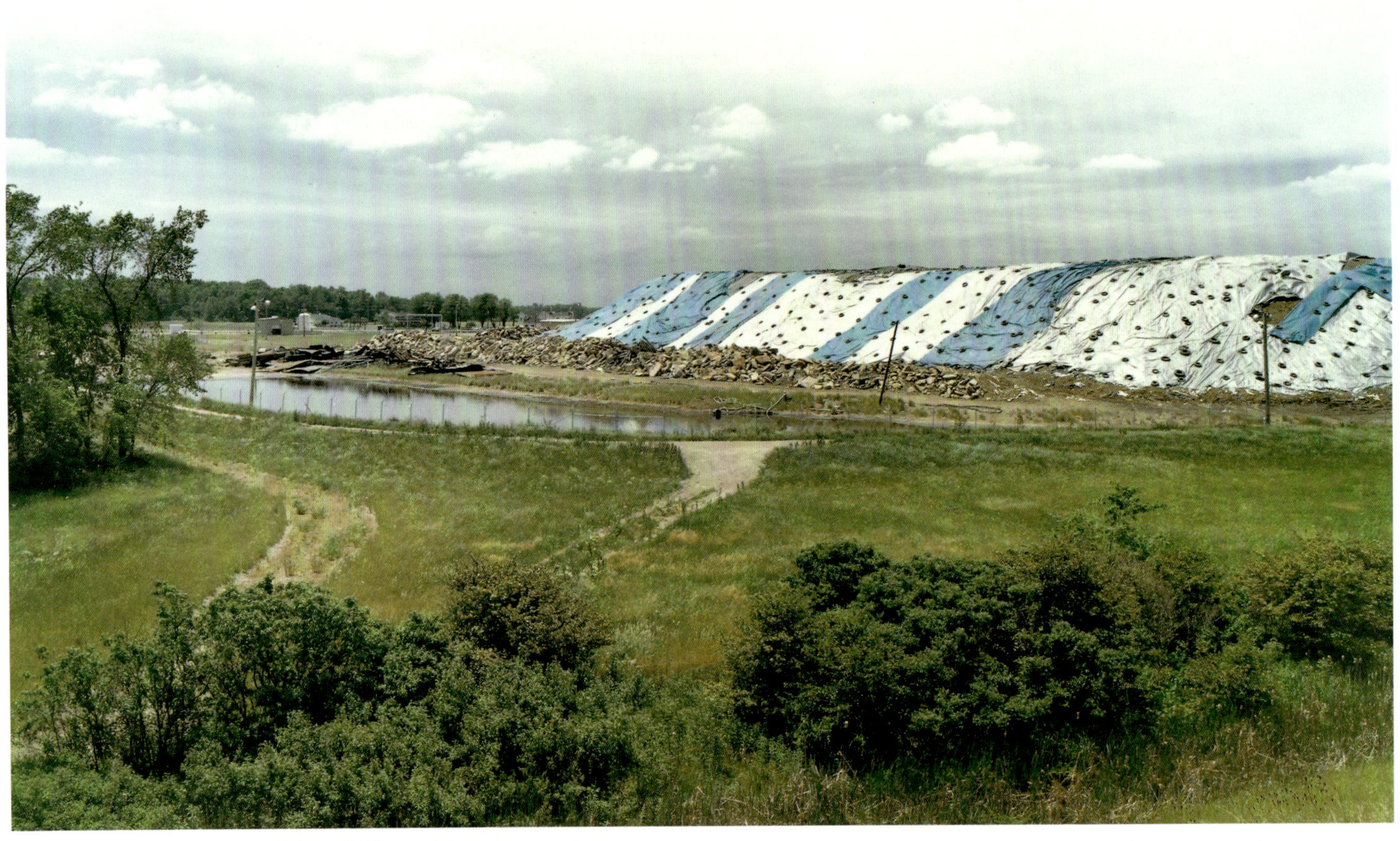

John Ganis, *Waste Disposal Site, Ohio*, 1988

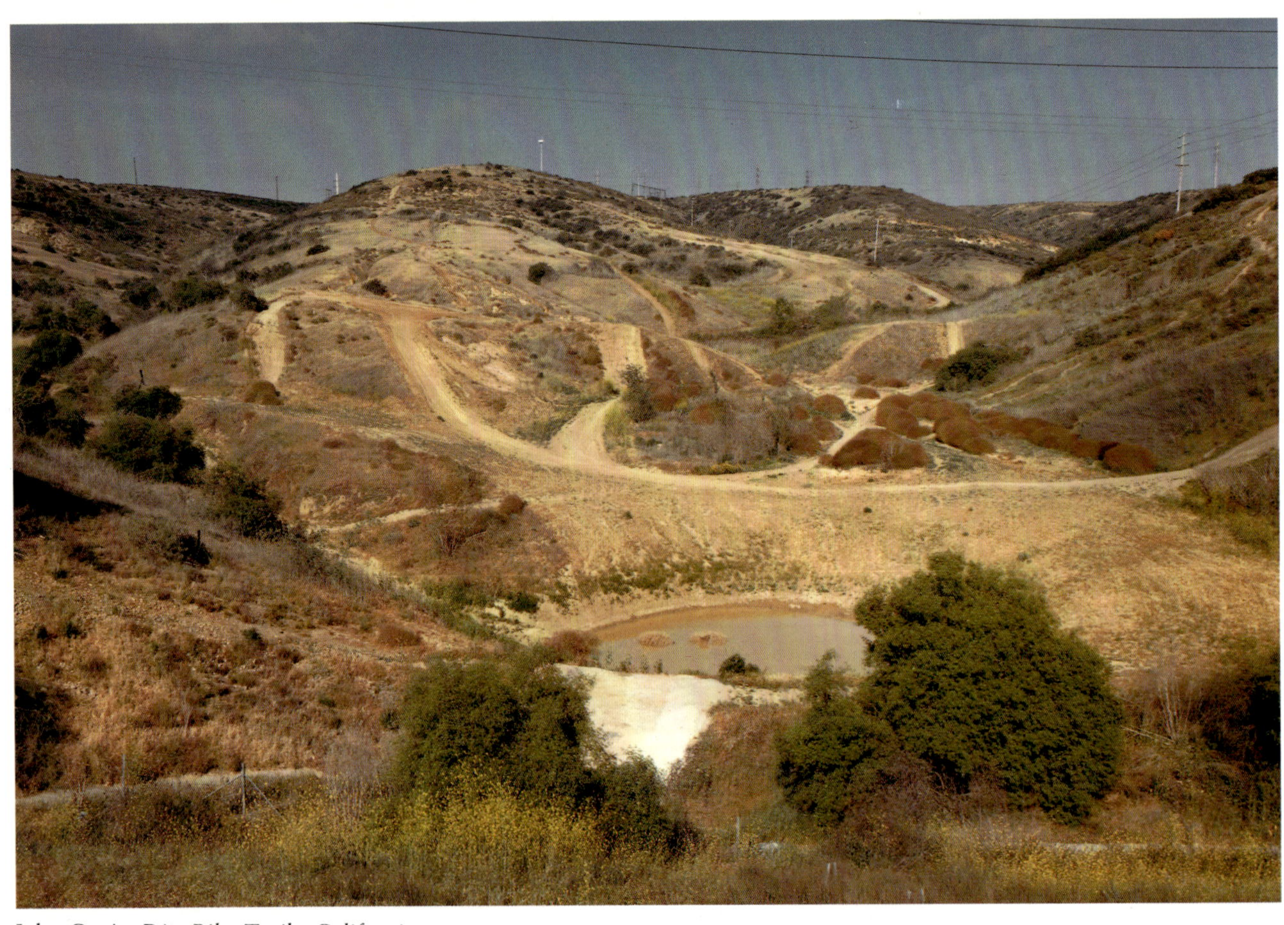

John Ganis, *Dirt Bike Trails, California*, 1989

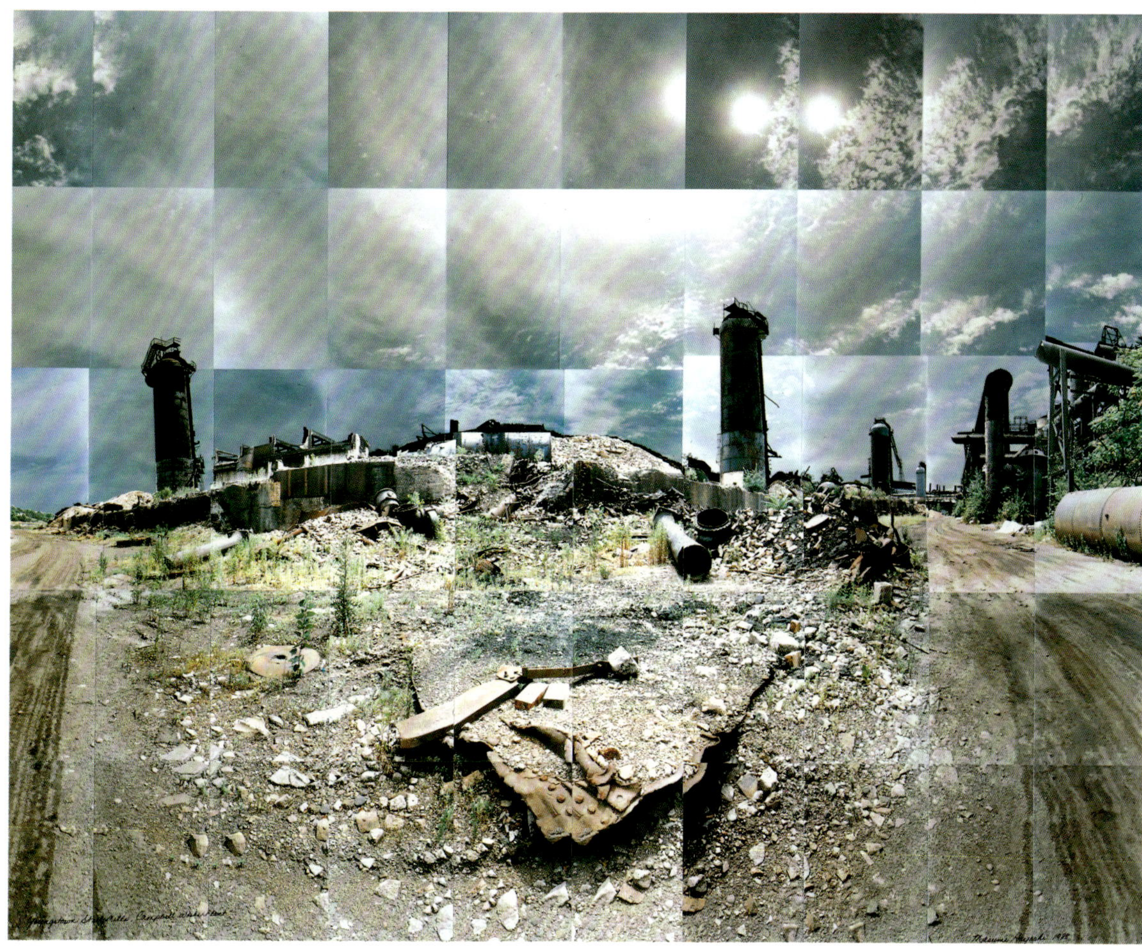

Masumi Hayashi, *Campbell Works Plant,* 1988

of the eighteenth century. That was the beginning of a long period of radical political and economic change which historians have, of course, amply chronicled. Still, historical explanations are less persuasive than visual evidence, and one glance is often enough to convince us that the modern road is, both in appearance and function, unlike the old house-oriented road. Whatever its technical definition, the modern road is a highway: broad and smooth, expertly engineered with the safety and comfort of the traveler in mind, designed for fast, uninterrupted long-range travel. In terms of impact on the landscape—whether urban or rural—the contrast between the two kinds of road is even more striking. Whereas the old road was careful to respect the integrity of every place it contacted, the modern road is oblivious of all local peculiarities, and demands direct access to wherever it wants to go. The topography suffers, boundaries and frontiers are destroyed, small-scale territories along with their history and associations are roughly bulldozed out of the way, and a uniform landscape is often the consequence. That is one reason, and a valid one, for resisting the arrogance and destructiveness of our highway programs.

To many observers the highway has become the locus of a dangerous and lawless cult of speed and competition and ostentatious behavior, a cult spreading further and further along the highway margins in the form of strip developments, junkyards, billboards, and abandoned farmland. Conservative reaction has been predictable: city traffic jams could be put up with, annoying though they were, but through traffic on country roads was to be resisted, for it brought in outsiders bent on destroying the established rural order and on defiling the landscape. To many environmental activists, the highway has become the symbol of a monstrous culture without any discernible goal, hooked like an addict, clamoring for unlimited supplies of goods and cheap energy and more and more highways. The solution they propose is drastically simple: we are to return to the landscape of a much older day, where our way of life was more in tune with the natural environment.

That is why to a large group of Americans, most of them prosperous, well educated, and aesthetically sensitive, the current environmental movement means reclaiming a *private* experience of nature, specifically the experience of the wilderness where nature has been untouched by man; where there is solitude, and where roads—even trails—are outlawed.

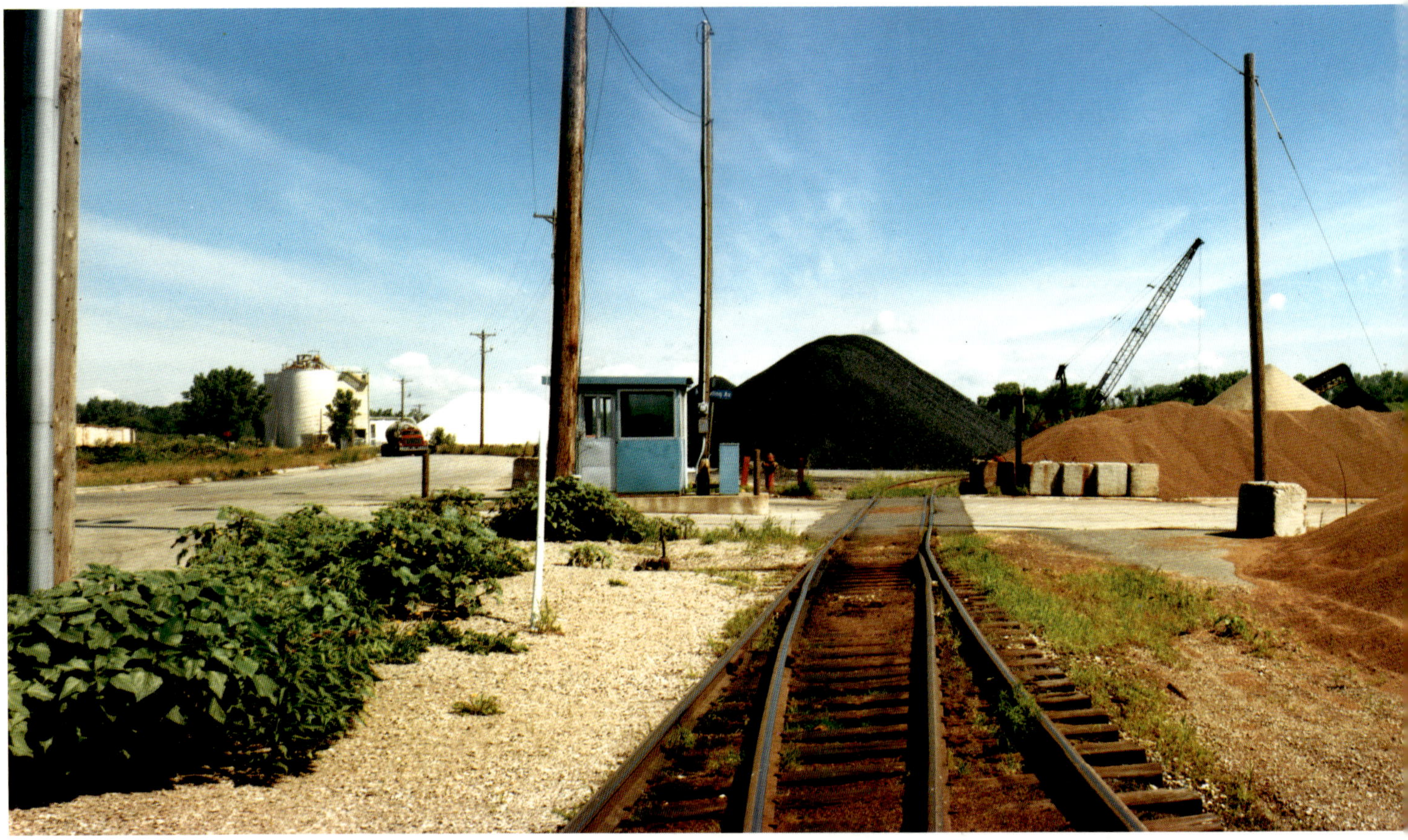

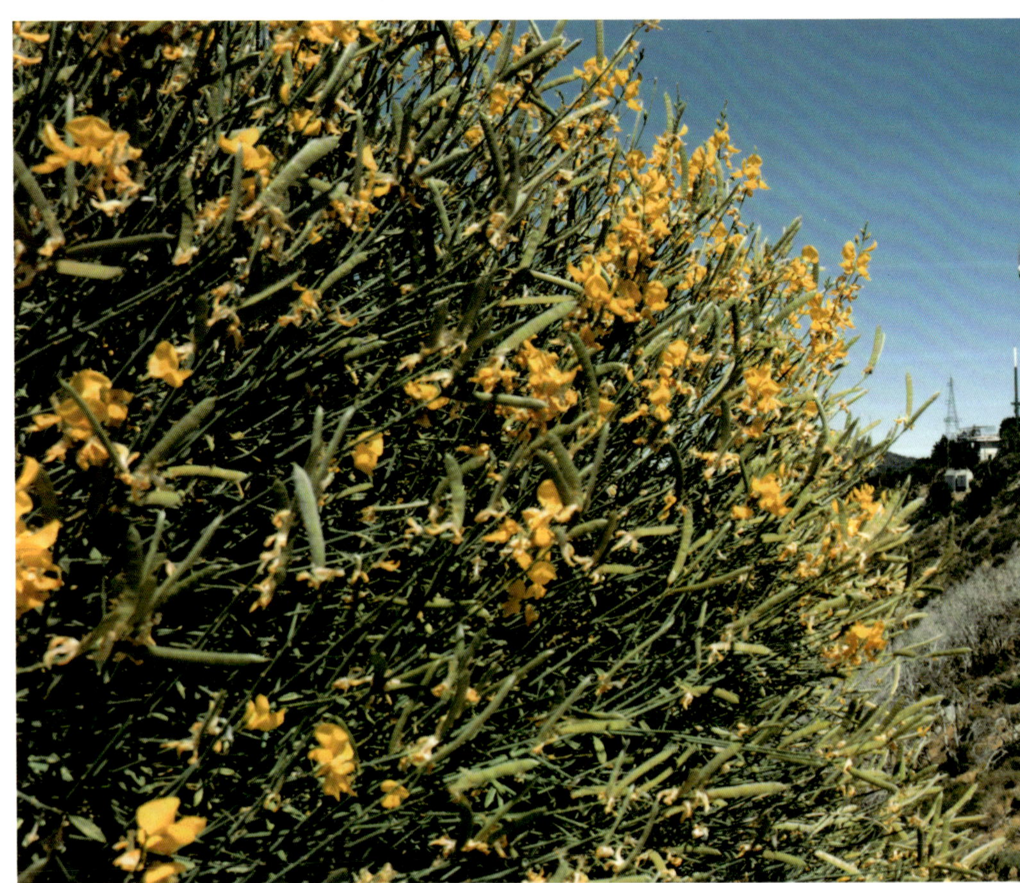

Stuart Klipper, above: *Materials Depot, Port of Minneapolis, Minnesota*, from "The World in a Few States," 1986; right: *Broadcasting Antennas, Mount Wilson, Los Angeles County, California*, from "The World in a Few States," 1988

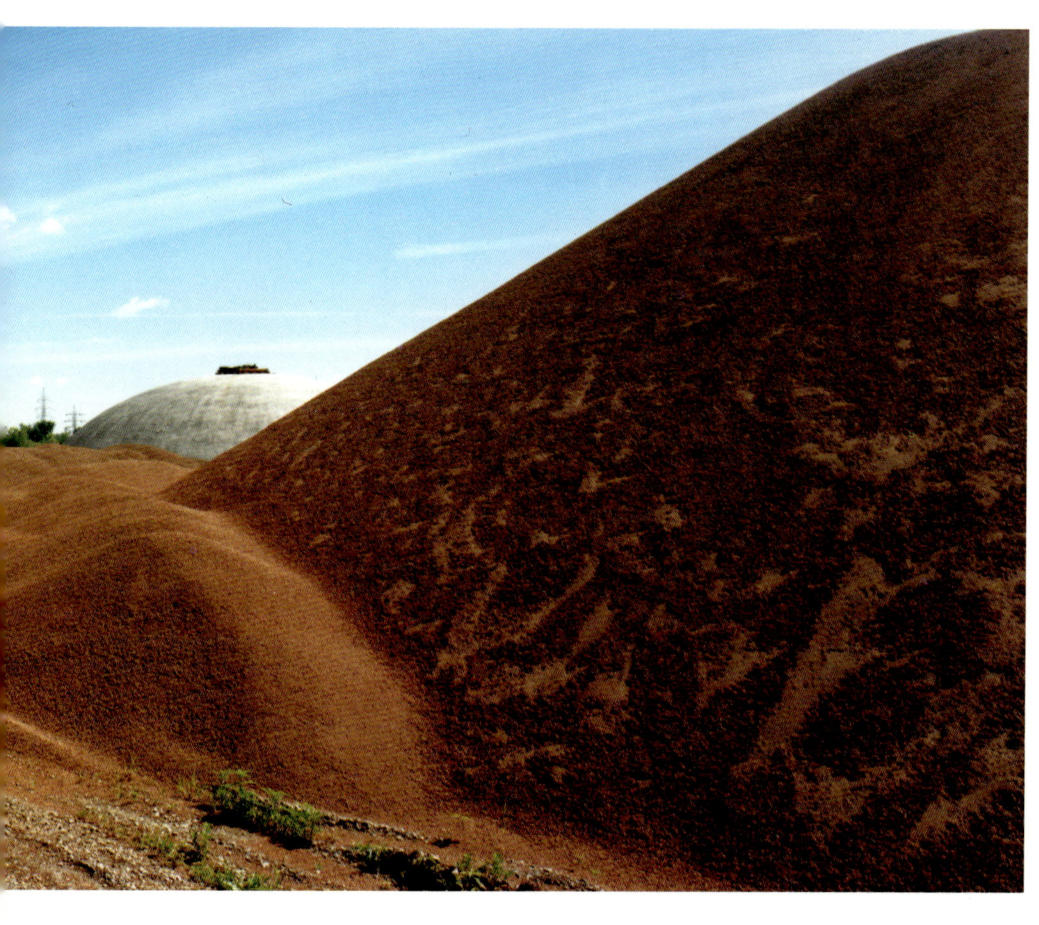

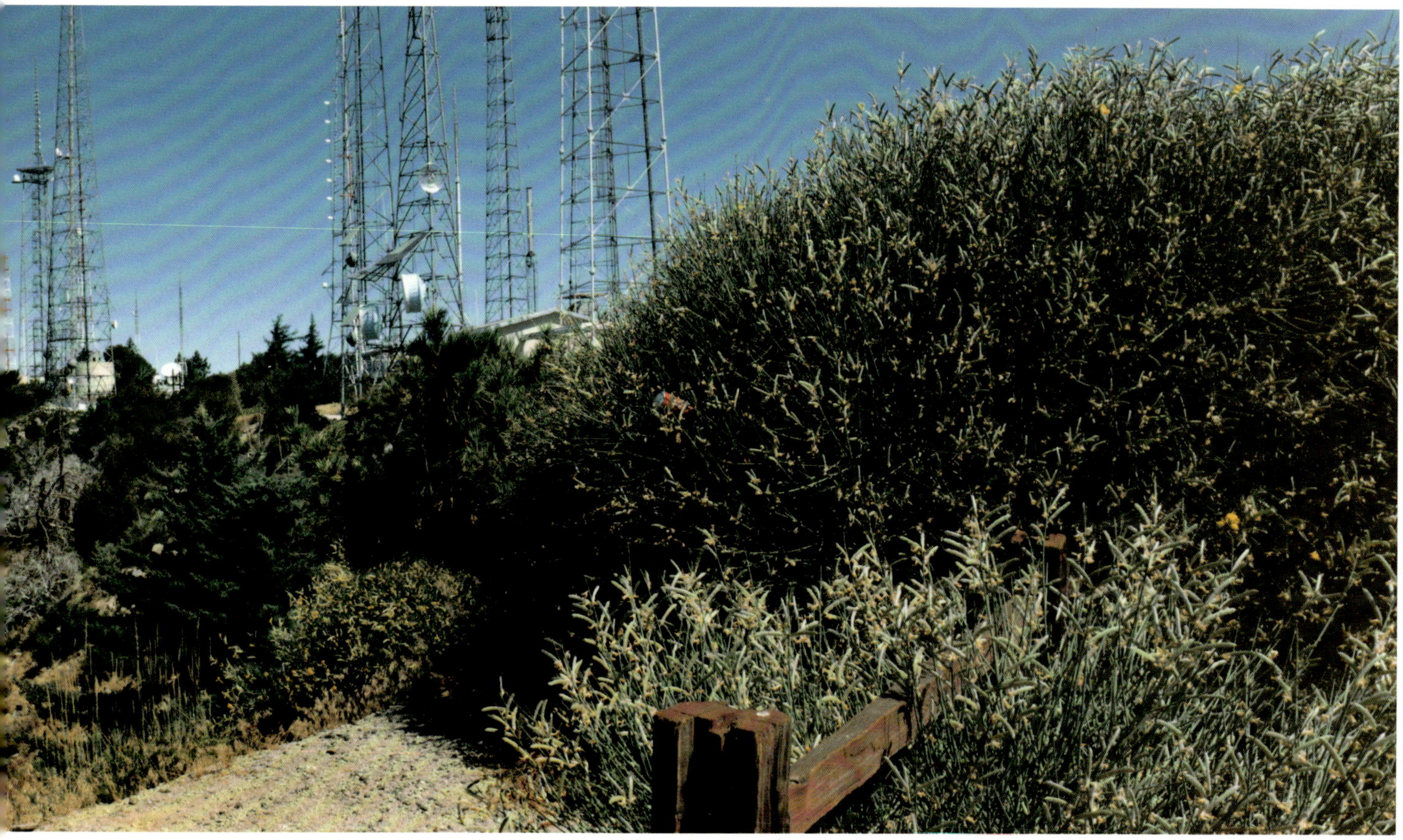

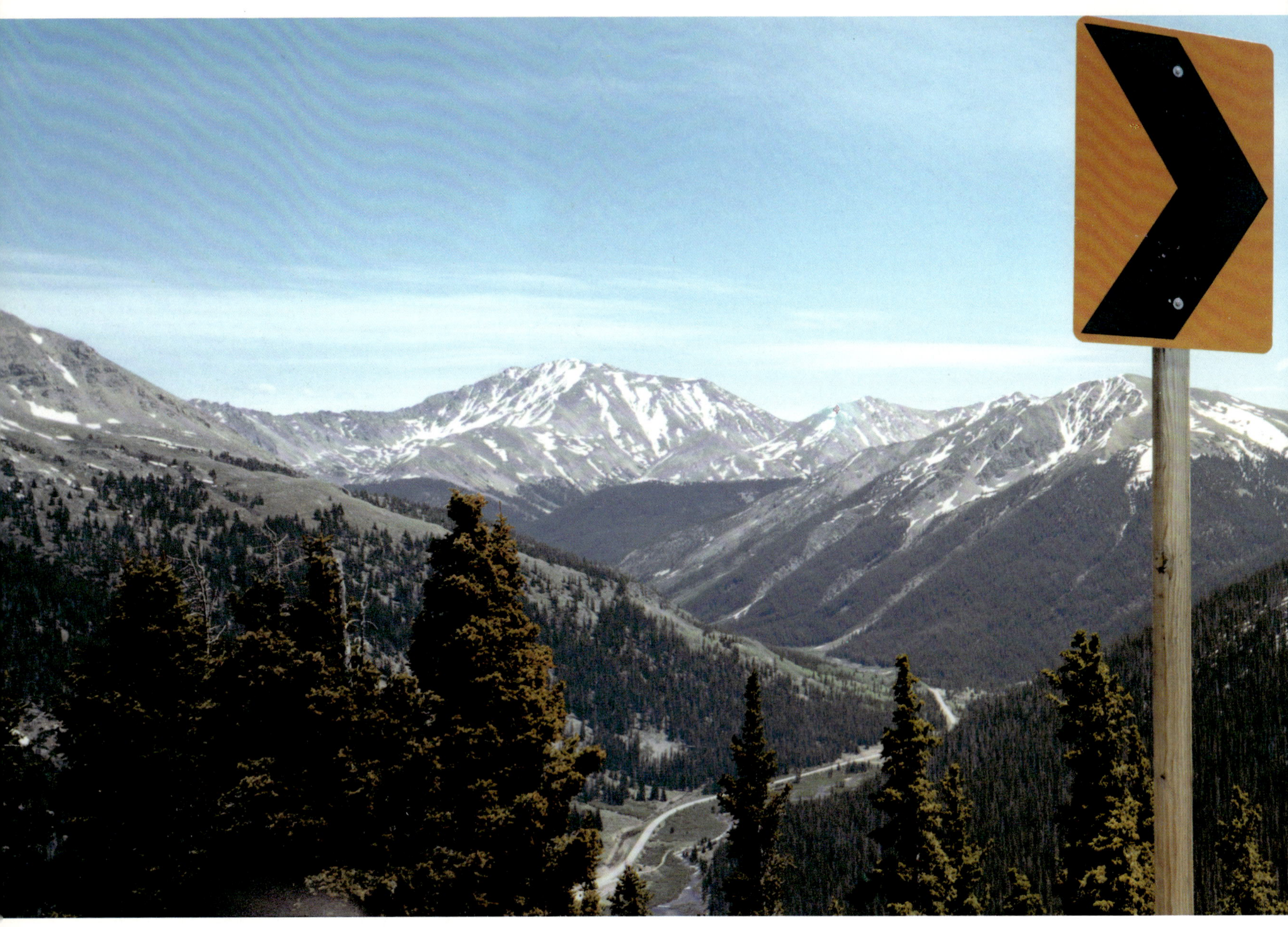

Stuart Klipper, *Independence Pass, Pitkin County, Colorado,* from "The World in a Few States," 1983

But to most Americans the environmental movement has a much more prosaic, and at the same time more important, goal. It aims at restoring our environment to the point where it is once again safe and healthy and livable; what worries us are the dangers lurking in toxic wastes, pesticides, polluted air and water. These are not only evil in themselves, they prevent our having direct contact with the therapeutic powers of the natural environment; they make us fearful of the world and of others.

That is where the highway comes into the picture: it allows us to escape our polluted urban environment and briefly to enjoy contact with the countryside. There is nothing mystical in the experience: popular notions of hygiene and diet and medicine have long since suppressed any lingering sense of "oneness with nature." We turn to the natural environment much as we turn to the physician or specialist: not to be transformed or converted, but for help in leading our daily existence. The highway five days a week, is crowded with commuters and trucks and men and women going about their mundane business. On weekends it is scarcely less crowded with families in search of health and strength and relaxation. They are not looking for wilderness; they are looking for fresh air, clean water, sunlight, and greenery. They lie on the grass, they swim, they get a suntan; they jog, sleep, and make friends with strangers. For that too is one of the benefits of this kind of contact with nature: it is never solitary. It creates its own ephemeral society—gregarious, noncompetitive, and totally lacking in a sense of territoriality.

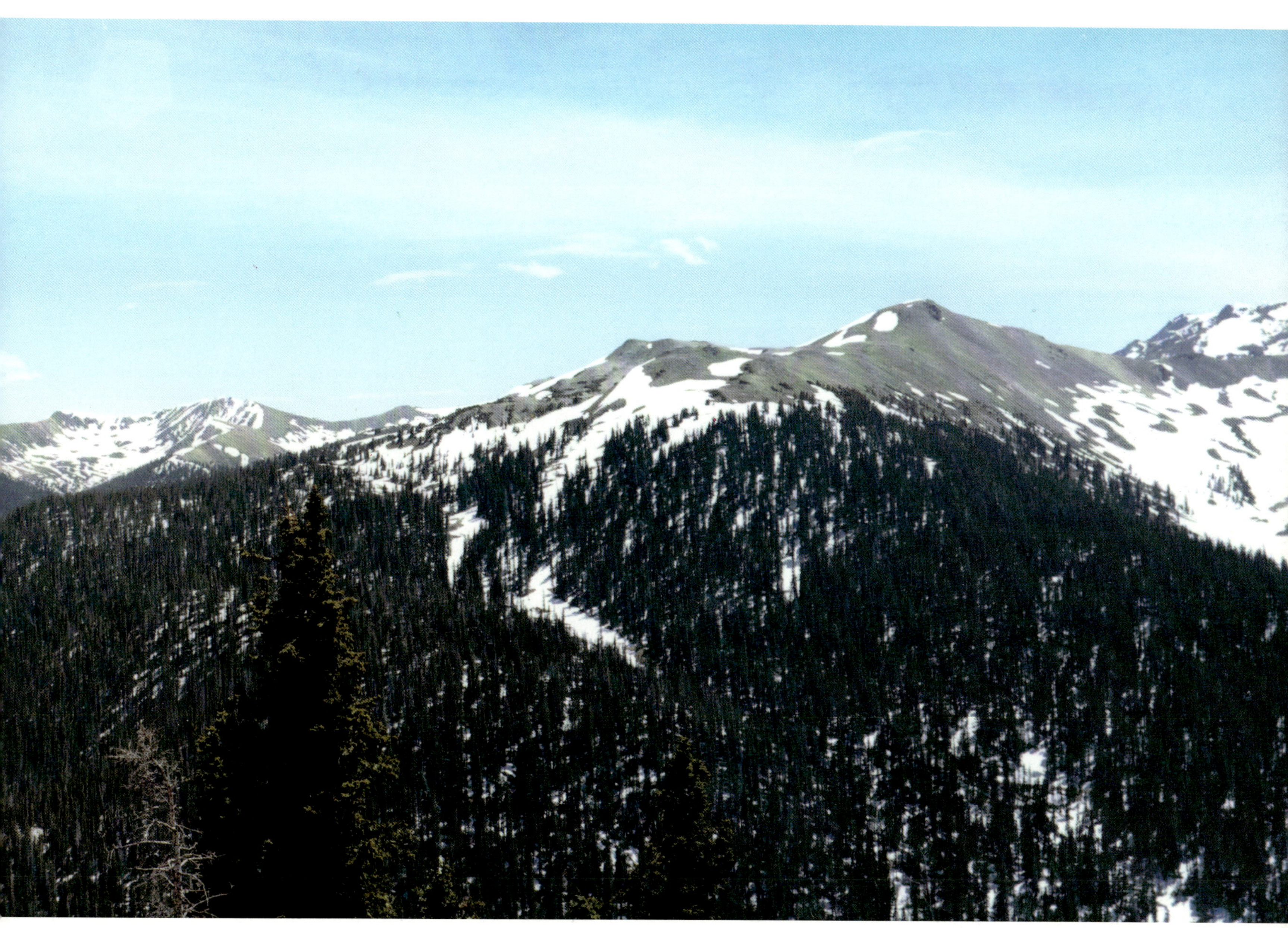

What the highway, and the automobile, have done in the way of creating informal public places and informal contacts—games, roadside sales, recreation areas, holiday facilities, and outdoor gathering places, urban as well as rural—is a topic in itself. It can merely be said that the road—or street, or highway—has at least two accomplishments to its credit, two contributions to the evolving American landscape: it has brought into being many new public spaces and much public interaction, and it has provided an opportunity for many of us to reestablish our dependency on nature; to recognize it again as something we can love without possessing, something we can share.

In discussing a much earlier transition, Mircea Eliade had this to say (in *The Forge and the Crucible,* 1962): "It is useful to remember that the only revolution comparable to it in the past history of humanity, that is, the discovery of agriculture, provided upheavals and spiritual breakdowns whose magnitude the modern mind finds it well-nigh impossible to conceive. . . . Thousands and thousands of years were to elapse before the final lamentations of the Old World died away, forever doomed by the advent of agriculture. One must also suppose that the profound spiritual crisis aroused by man's decision to *call a halt and bind himself to the soil* must have taken many hundreds of years to become completely integrated. . . . The technical discoveries of the modern world, its conquest of 'Time and Space,' represent a revolution of similar proportions, the consequences of which are still very far from having become part of us."

People and Ideas

THE LEGACY OF ANSEL ADAMS:
DEBTS AND BURDENS
By Mark Klett

In our era of environmental awareness, Ansel Adams has become the most recognized American landscape photographer. His enormous influence on the photographic world continues even after his death, and there now appears to be a long list of potential successors to his position of influence and fame. But, as one of hundreds who now re-explores the landscape with a camera, I wonder if we really expect, or even want, one individual to emerge as the next photographer/legend. I raise the issue because I am increasingly uncomfortable with the idea of legend building, and when it comes to the legacy of my predecessors, including Ansel Adams, I have felt both a debt and a burden.

So many photographers can credit Adams with raising their appreciation of the natural world that it is not surprising that his life as well as his work have become models. Adams embodied the traditions of two centuries. He was a master at the equipment and techniques of large-format photography, the tools and crafts first used, and still used predominantly, in the large spaces of the American West. And like the geographical survey photographers less than a hundred years before him, he concentrated his efforts on the West's monumental places, photographing some of the same territory. Still, there were important differences between his approach and that of the nineteenth-century photographers, whose work he respected but did not consider art. Adams viewed their work as topographical, and for his work that was not enough. His was a faith in a working process, in the ability of beautifully made photographs to inspire awe and reaffirm the ennobling powers of the natural world.

Considering what we actually find out in the land today, Adams's pictures seem an expression of our best hopes that the lessons of wilderness will preserve us. Perhaps that explains the still growing list of his work's publications—the most recent of which is *Ansel Adams: The American Wilderness* (Little Brown and Company). Although he may have not sought it, I believe that after his death Adams fully achieved the role of Western hero. Unlike in Western movies, this hero carried a camera instead of a gun. Like mythical heroes he was an individual who faced a great threat (the loss of wilderness) and fought from a position of moral strength.

It may be argued that we need heroes now more than ever, but the problem with this model for photographers today is that in reality a hero's battles are seldom fought alone. Moral values are not isolated, either. The movements of an era are the product of shared goals and pursuits, however much one person may seem to embody them. To be seen as the leader, one must compete for the title and attempt to win the equivalent of a long-distance foot race. Often this has more to do with career-building than a commitment to goals.

The virtue of Adams's combination of notoriety and longevity was that it helped raise an environmental consciousness about the land. His depopulated scenes suggest that the landscape does best without our presence, and that wilderness is an entity defined by our absence. However, anyone who has visited the site of one of Adams's photographs knows that the romance of his landscapes is often best experienced in the photographs themselves. The reality of place is quite different. Parking lots of tour buses now intersect the trails to his favorite Yosemite vantage points. The natural beauty of the land is still there to be seen, but you will not see it alone.

As Adams's photographs became more popular, so did the wilderness he photographed. Now we must reserve some national park campgrounds in advance, and as a convenience we may do so at any Ticketron outlet. Could it be that Adams's photographs contributed to the crowding of parks like Yosemite? Did his photographs exploit as well as preserve the places he loved? (Consider the bitter feelings of the environmentalist Colin Fletcher about the effects of his writings on an appreciative public, as quoted in Roderick Nash's *Wilderness and the American Mind:* "The woods are overrun, and sons of bitches like me are half the problem.") It seems ironic that Adams's photographs, while inspirational, may also engender feelings of great loss, and a sense of remorse for the land's passage from wilderness to occupied territory.

If those of us who live in the West find this notion a little troubling, it is probably because the landscape, for better and worse, has become our home. Seen without the make-over of skillful camera work, it is no longer exotic territory. The effects of population increases, the need for recreation, the choices between environment or material growth, and the battles for water and resources are only a few of the more obvious issues. Not that the land has ceased to offer solace, or awe, or romance; but it is becoming more of a struggle to reconcile the older ways of seeing the West with the realities of daily life. The landscape is not so much a paradise to long for (some say a paradise to be lost) as it is a mirror that reflects our own cultural image. We now view landscape photographs, both past

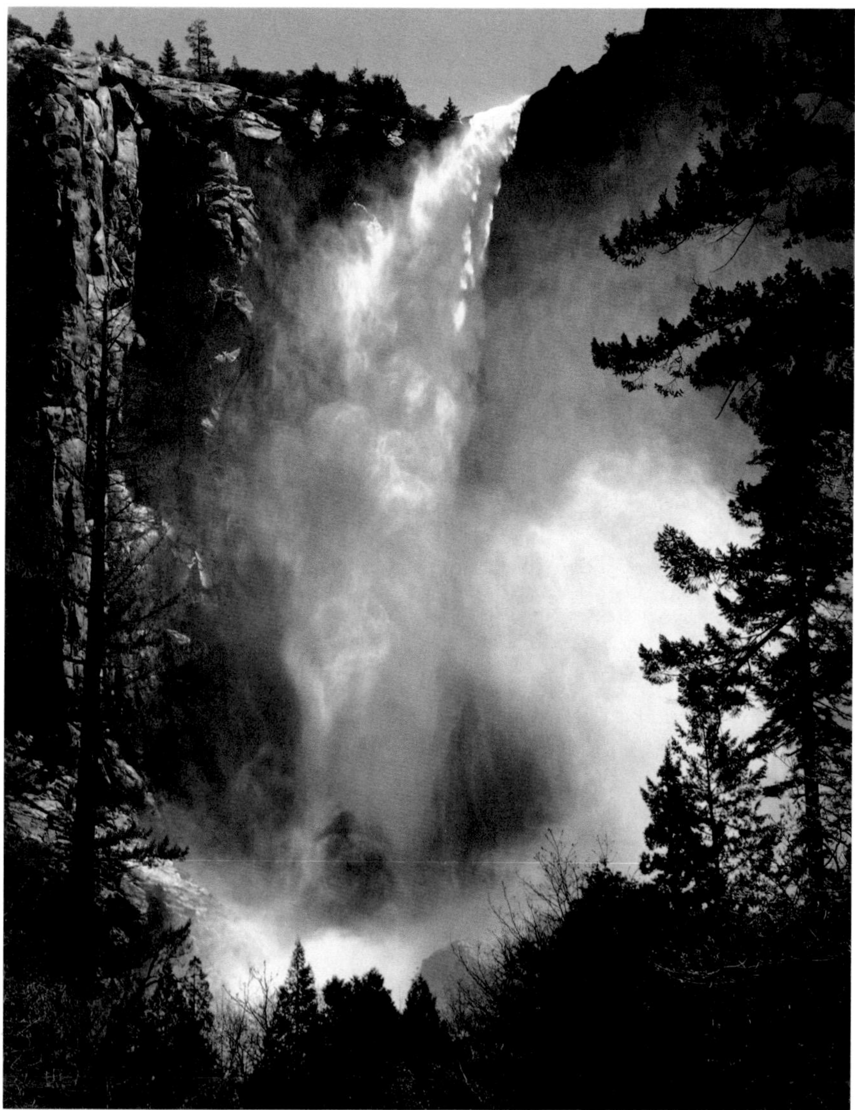

Ansel Adams, *Bridal Veil Fall, Yosemite National Park, California*, 1927

and present, much like the shadows on the walls of Plato's cave. They are artifacts of what we think we know about the land, and how we have come to know it—the language of an individual's experience in his or her time, and at their best a form of commentary.

Seen through today's postmodern eyes, Adams's photographs may seem anachronistic. It is hard to retain his optimism about wilderness and photography; harder still not to be cynical or dogmatic in opposition to the many forces of our abuse to the land. Yet how difficult it is, instead, to praise what is left to enjoy—to find, for example, significance in quiet, less monumental landscapes, and to appreciate them in spite of our human presence, to see that we have a place on the land, and that the land is not a commodity separate from ourselves; or simply to experience a basic connection with place, and to realize that this feeling is not the result of a cultural construct.

These are formidable pursuits for photographers; so if in our time we find ourselves looking for a new hero, we might stop and reconsider. The small contributions of many people working with clarity and conviction may make a greater difference than any singular vision. We might, in fact, be suspicious of any individual who seeks to inherit the Adams legacy. The real challenge for landscape photographers today is not to discover new wilderness places, but to explore new wilderness values. For that effort we must concede that no one works alone, and that every voice counts.

TOPOGRAPHIC TRANSLATIONS
By Nan Richardson

Paysages Photographiques: En France Les Années Quatre-Vingt, by the Mission Photographique de la DATAR (Délégation à l'Aménagement du territoire et à l'Action Régionale). Published by Éditions Hazan, Paris, 1989.

Billing itself as "the most important photographic commission in history," the *Mission Photographique* draws its historic precedents from the Second Empire's *Mission Héliographique* of 1851, and, more directly, from the Farm Security Administration (FSA) documentation of New Deal America. In a paradoxical quid pro quo, this survey began its documentation of twentieth-century France under one premise, codified by Walker Evans as "a clear fact stated clearly," and ended, almost inevitably, by accepting the highly inflected, interpretive collection of artists' impressions that define the best of this body of work.

In France in 1851 the Commission on Historic Monuments of the Department of Fine Arts commissioned five prominent photographers to document monuments in connection with a program of government-sponsored restoration. While Hippolyte Bayard used albumen-coated glass plates; Gustave Le Gray, Henri Le Secq, Edouard Denis Baldus, and Olivier Mestral chose to venture into the new technique of the calotype. Their decision may have had to do with the intention of the Commission to maximize the availability of the studies to those working with architecture, though judging by the sparse references in architectural histories of the time, the effort at democratized dissemination appears to have failed.

The FSA, in marked contrast, was a massive mobilization of social documentation at a critical political moment in American history. The FSA's images of a country in the grip of massive unemployment, rampant social ills, and widespread poverty have had a lasting and universal impact, due both to the large-scale publicity given the program as well as to the memorable images created by its gifted photographers, especially Walker Evans and Dorothea Lange.

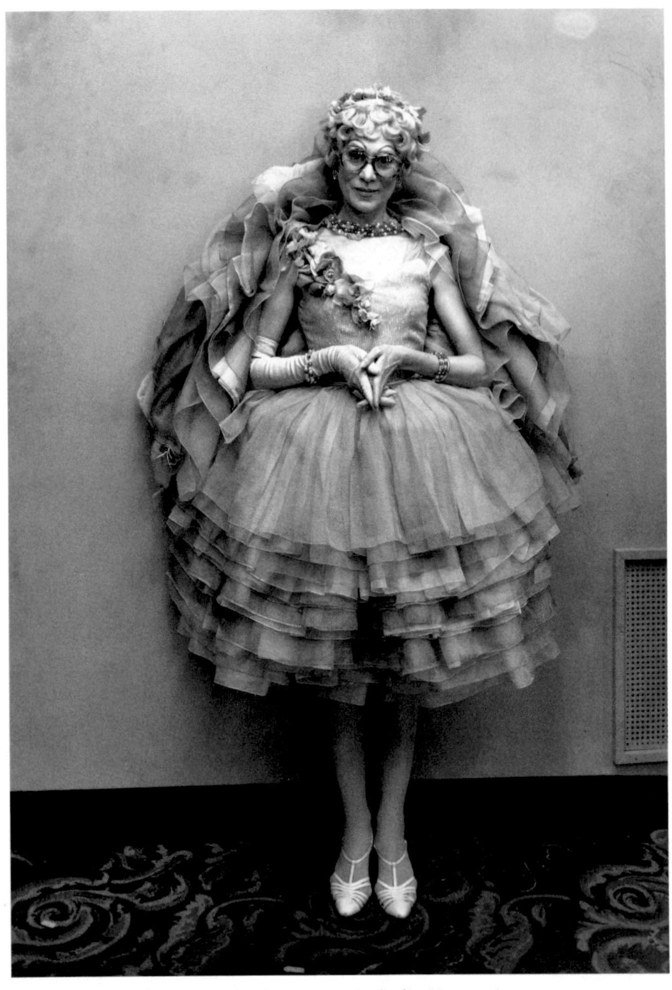

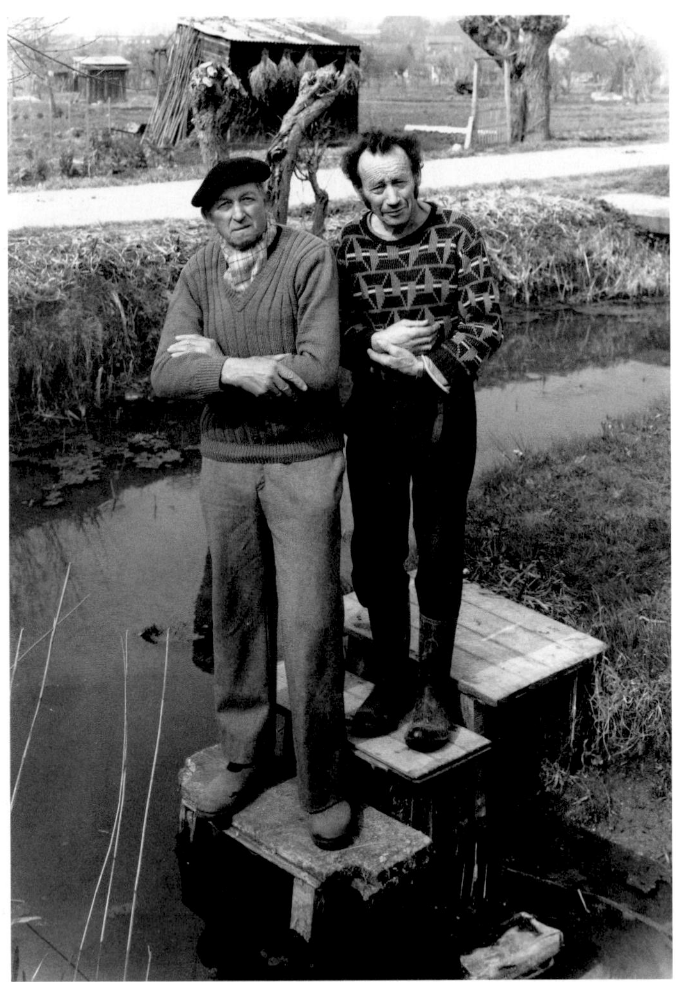

François Despatin and Christian Gobeli, *Portrait*   François Despatin and Christian Gobeli, *Portrait*

Evans's definition of "plain style," unadorned and direct, has come to be regarded not as the objectivity he willed it to be, but as a subjective metaphor for that intention, and in itself a style.

In both its ideas and its choice of photographers, the present Mission seems unclear about which predecessor to follow. The final 700-page volume documenting the project owes much to the work of the American "New Topographics" landscape photographers of the 1970s, among them Frank Gohlke, Richard Misrach, Mark Klett, and Lewis Baltz. As a group, these photographers drew a direct line from Evans, acknowledging an aesthetic in which photographs are simultaneously records, artifacts, and art objects. Using conventions of art, they made evident the political and social effects of human actions upon the landscape. Their works referred to the now-classic topographic surveys of frontier America by Timothy O'Sullivan, Carleton Watkins, William Henry Jackson, and others, as well as to the modernist landscapes of Ansel Adams, Paul Strand, and Edward Weston. Into a formal style, which seemed clinical and detached, they injected a subtext of political portent.

But while the landscape lineage has been unbroken in America, landscape as a tradition has been all but lost in France since Eugène Atget—a lacuna of fifty years. Atget was himself indebted to the era of Camille Pissarro, Camille Corot, and Claude Monet, the Barbizon and Impressionist painters whose influence can be seen in his first major series, entitled "Landscapes/Documents"; twenty years later he returned to the subject with new vigor and deliberate experimentation. Atget's seminal contribution was finally recognized—but by the Surrealists, and for qualities other than those Evans named, in an article written five years after Atget's death, in Lincoln Kirstein's magazine, *Hound and Horn:* "The latter half of the 19th century offers that fantastic figure, the art photographer, really an unsuccessful painter. . . . Eugène Atget worked right through this period of utter decadence in photography . . . his general note is lyrical understanding of the street, trained observation, special feeling for patina, eye for revealing detail." It was a perception not shared by Atget's contemporaries, and this direct line, from Atget, to Evans, to recent American landscape photography as the dominant force in the genre, is one that the Mission borrows from without acknowledgment.

If the Mission's ambitions seem close to those of the FSA, its net effect will probably resemble that of the *Mission Héliographique.* In the massive volume that presents the results of this five-year survey, where nearly thirty photographers chose subjects and/or geographic areas of concentration for their individ-

74

ual "reports," directors François Hers and Bernard Latarget describe the group's intent to confront "the challenge of locating forms and visual themes adequate to describe the profound social transformations occurring in modern France." (DATAR is the equivalent of an Industrial Action Board, whose raison d'être is to preserve the national culture through land management and rural and industrial development control, so this subject matter is their essential province.)

Hers and Latarget's introductory essay describes the theory that propelled the choices of photographers, and the editorial choices that define this collection. They are reacting against "work that emphasizes psychological reactions to events (à la Bresson)" as an outmoded genre. They speak of "encouraging photographers to evolve a style to reveal the effects of nuclear waste, factory sprawl . . . a political effort to awaken people to what is happening to their landscape." They offer the disclaimer that the net results "hardly constitute an inventory or survey," but have gone to pains to make clear demarcations of subject matter between the individual projects, from suburbs, beauty spots, mountains, seashores, factories, offices, watering holes, and more, all in search of a *"paysage raisonné,"* as the organizers call it, borrowing (somewhat outmodedly) from Poussin or Cézanne.

The most successful works come from unexpected sources: Sophie Ristelhueber found in mountain ranges *"une froide nécessité* (a cold necessity)" where the nostalgic return to Burgundy, to the paternal homestead of *Depardon, Antoine, Fermier* (Depardon, Antoine, Farmer), by son Raymond, *"Chasseur d'images # 23393"* (Hunter of images # 23393), (as his amateur photographer's discount card dubbed him) offers undiluted nostalgic charm in details like a polished stone floor below a simple wooden table covered with waxed cloth, and outside, the soulful eyes of snowy Limousin cattle in a muddy farmyard. Moroccan Alain Ceccaroli's velvety industrial wastelands turn sinister, while the seaside resorts in Italian Gabriele Basilico's pictures have the wintry abandoned feeling of the off-season carnival. Classic

studies of fields and hills by Pierre de Fenöyl contrast with the brilliant organic blobs of cyan, magenta, and gold dancing across the surfaces of Czech-born Tom Drahos's "new cities" like some irradiated fantasy; the truncated divisions of a labyrinthine Marseilles is described by German Holger Trülzsch in a layout that adds considerable visual interest. Every format is given play, including several dark and brooding panoramics of northern factories by Josef Koudelka, squared-off fields and flowers by Gohlke, and stacked blocks of arid wastelands by Baltz.

Robert Doisneau has called the Mission "the most direct witness possible to the way we live now," and curiously, it is in the startling contemporaneity of his work, where black-and-white images he took forty years ago are juxtaposed with astonishingly bold and assured color, that the effect is to see anew, and to ask the fundamental question—of what landscape is, as John Ruskin put it, but "human passions and human hopes."

EVANS IN THE NIGHT OF PHOTOGRAPHY
By Edmundo Desnoes

Walker Evans: Havana 1933, essay by Gilles Mora, sequence by John T. Hill. Published by Pantheon Books, New York, and Contrejour, Paris, 1989 ($35.00).

No matter how powerful or subtle a photo may be, there is always something absent, missing. If it is a powerful document, the referent is always hovering under or above it; if a subtle statement of beauty, you seem to slide off its surface, unable to hold on to the porous nature of the aesthetic experience.

Gilles Mora's *Walker Evans: Havana 1933,* rescued from the shadow of lost negatives, is both powerful and subtle—yet you perceive the ghost, the missing bodies, as you slide off the open surface of seventy rediscovered images.

Evans arrived in Havana in May of 1933 with two cameras, a tripod, light summer cotton and linen outfits, a featherweight Panama hat—but no previous

experience or knowledge of Cuba. But his eyes had experience and knowledge his mind ignored. In two weeks roaming through the streets and barrios of the city and nearby pueblos, he saw, tore off, and rescued a coherent vision of Havana no one before had ever recorded, much less created. Only a portfolio of thirty-one photographs was used to illustrate *The Crime of Cuba,* Carleton Beals's radical and rhetorical analysis of the times of dictator Machado in Cuba. Beals's essay has faded, but Evans's photos are still throbbing with the physical light of absence.

They—the ones published then and those now rediscovered—continue to throb because the intelligence of Evans's eyes captured an urban labyrinth without the need to explain anything, without being pornographic or didactic. Evans, under the influence of James Joyce, believed in the virtue of detachment. His images record the concreteness of the world with a slanted indifference and involvement one has to wait another twenty years to find in Robert Frank's vision of America.

In *The Crime of Cuba,* surrounded by the didactic discourse of Beals, Evans's photos were seen as an extension of the

Walker Evans, *Interior, Barber Shop,* 1933

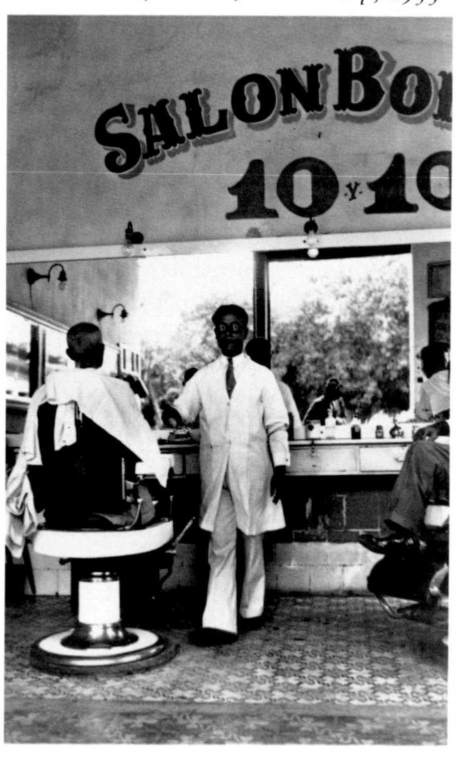

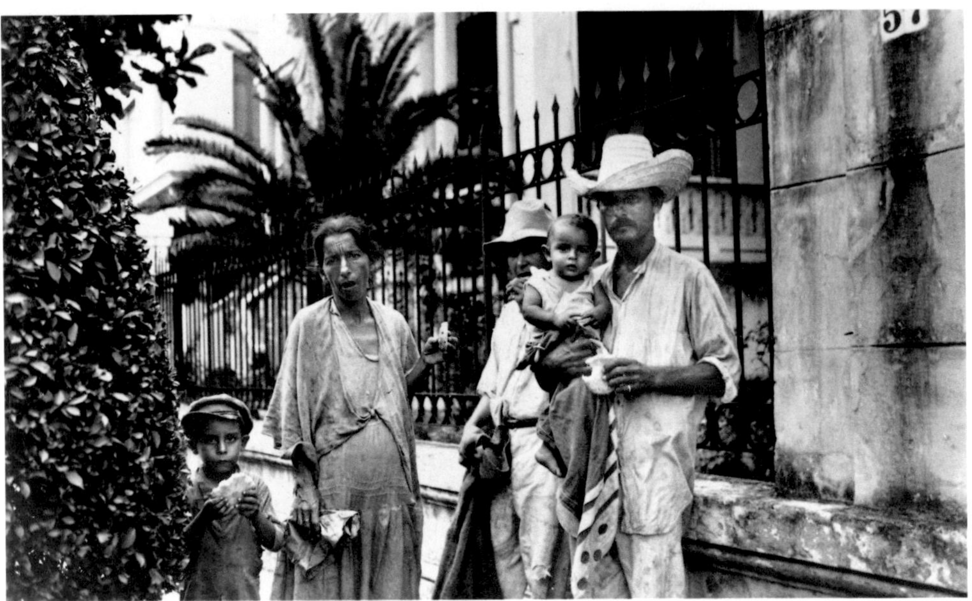

Walker Evans, *Havana Country Family*, 1933

political indictment against a Latin American dictatorship. Now, in a book by themselves, the Cuban photos of Walker Evans have a cold objectivity, a friendly detachment, a vision that remains a valid metaphor for many Third World countries as the century comes to a close. No theatrical dramatization of underdevelopment, such as Sebastiao Salgado's coffee-table books on Brazil, can compete with the cruel warmth of Evans's vision.

Yet something is absent from these photos. One always knows photos are ghosts—they stand for something that has departed. Or else, when they attempt to achieve the textural density of painting, they seem plastic, nonporous. Photography, I feel, has failed to achieve the legitimacy, the broad acceptance, of traditional art. While cinema, in spite of its grounding in the physical and material, has managed to be fully accepted as art, as artifice, as dream, photography is still contaminated with the referent, still wet from the stream of so-called physical and social reality. After Susan Sontag and Roland Barthes brought photography into the realm of a rigorous intellectual discourse, it seemed photos would occupy a space equal to that of painting and sculpture—but this has yet to happen. Even "Photography Until Now," the recent exhibit at the Museum of Modern Art, was a document, a visual record—a shadow more than a sub-

stance. Maybe photography will always be more a bridge than a destination. And therein lies its power and its specificity— its ability to sell both reality, in the printed media, and dreams, in books, galleries, and museums.

In *Walker Evans: Havana 1933*, the streets, the buildings, the people of the Cuban capital hover and haunt these images. On the other hand, the style, the way Evans saw the place and, in doing so rescued it from the dissolution of time, will always be a testimony of a visual language as human as the written word.

Thirty years ago, when I discovered these photos in a second-hand bookstore in downtown Havana—where I had been born three years before Evans's visit—I felt I had rediscovered my adolescence. The city did not begin to change drastically until after World War II: the streets, the *Parque Central*, the people in Evans's pictures were no different from those I discovered when I left the enclosure of my house, the patio surrounding it, and began to discover the mystery, the dangers, and the pleasures of a cosmopolitan Caribbean city rotting and growing under the sun.

Now not only time and the ravages of aging, but also the Revolution of 1959, separates me, us, from these photos. Light-years seem to place these photos in the night that photography dots with light.

It wasn't art, it was first and foremost memory; it wasn't a painter's interpretation, it was a photographer's selection— ripping off reality. The cobblestones, the peeling, crumbling facade of the buildings, the extended hands of beggars, the surface of park benches, the bodies of women, the eyes of the whores were remembered by my own body; my feet, my limbs, my skin remembered.

I remember how a slice of childhood came back to me when John T. Hill showed me the photos in the hope that I might identify where and what was going on in them and I discovered a train— not a trolley, a train—I had taken with my aunt Julia to the seaside after being sick with whooping cough. I even remembered how the wicker seats had to be turned around at the end of the line.

Moving through these photos, traveling over and over through the Havana streets, I discovered the Proustian catalyst of photos. Unlike in painting or literature, recognizing a pattern on a tile floor or a street corner in a photo releases a cascade of memories. On page 43 of this book, my eyes dropped from the woman in white to the tiled floor where geometric and floral patterns broke loose a string of memories: the smooth cold relief of walking barefooted in the tropics, after getting out of bed; my mother's sharp, fragile voice; the sound of falling cutlery and bouncing marbles; the urinal under my bed; flying cockroaches; mud, and nude bodies. It happened again on page 49: I could almost feel the barber's cold scissors and the monstrous sadness of lumps of hair strewn on the patterns of the tile floor. Maybe music and a certain smell can do the same, but never other visual art forms.

The formal beauty, the aesthetic impact of photography seems to lie in its frozen stillness, in its arbitrary cutting and tearing off of accepted perceptions of reality. A photo stops us precisely because reality flows, never stops. There is the enchantment of ghosts, the fascination of mortality in photos. And the photos of Walker Evans have captured the banality of Havana in the summer of 1933, forced us to contemplate with a poignant and indifferent eye the poverty, the flow of quotidian existence.

CONTRIBUTORS

JOEL CONNELLY is the National Correspondent for the *Seattle Post-Intelligencer.*

EDMUNDO DESNOES is a Cuban-born novelist and the author of *Memories of Underdevelopment* (NAL).

GERALD HASLAM's most recent books are *California Stories* (University of Nevada Press) and *Coming of Age in California* (Devil Mountain Books), both of which will be published this spring.

J. B. JACKSON is the author of *The Necessity for Ruins* (University of California Press), among other books. He edited *Landscape* for the first seventeen years of its existence, and now lives in Santa Fe, New Mexico.

WES JACKSON is the President of the Land Institute, a nonprofit educational/research organization devoted to the search for sustainable alternatives in agriculture and earth stewardship, in Salina, Kansas. His work includes *New Roots for Agriculture* (University of Nebraska Press), co-edited with Wendell Berry and Bruce Colman; *Meeting the Expectations of the Land* (North Point Press); and *Altars of Unhewn Stone* (North Point Press).

MARK KLETT is a photographer living in Arizona whose work is concerned with issues of the evolving landscape. He is the co-author of *Headlands: Marin Coast at the Golden Gate* (University of New Mexico Press).

BARRY LOPEZ is the author of *Arctic Dreams* (Scribner), for which he won the National Book Award, and *Crossing Open Ground* (Scribner), a collection of essays.

JOHN PFAHL's books include *Picture Windows* (New York Graphic Society) and *Arcadia Revisited: Photographs of the Niagara River and Falls from Lake Erie to Ontario* (University of New Mexico Press). A retrospective of his work, *A Distant Land: The Photographs of John Pfahl,* is forthcoming from the University of New Mexico Press.

NAN RICHARDSON is a writer who lives in New York and is a former editor of *Aperture.*

REBECCA SOLNIT's *Secret Exhibition: Six California Artists of the Cold War Era* is being published by City Lights Books this year. A San Francisco-based writer and environmental activist, she is currently working on a history of landscape ideologies.

ACKNOWLEDGMENTS

"Beyond Wilderness" owes a great deal to the ideas and suggestions of many people. Barry Lopez, in particular, provided invaluable advice, both practical and philosophical; his concern and insight helped clarify the questions underlying this issue, giving them a focus at once general and specific—and thus doubly useful. In addition we would like to thank Jim Baker, of the Anderson Ranch Arts Center, Snowmass, Colorado, which sponsored the "Political Landscape" conference in October 1989, addressing many of these same questions; Doug Hagley and the staff of *Witness* (Ann Arbor), for sharing a pre-publication copy of their Winter 1989 issue, which also deals with similar concerns; Harry Foster, Houghton Mifflin, and Dan Frank, Viking Penguin, for providing helpful suggestions of important writers on the land and landscape; Jay Townsend, Greenpeace; Trish Burns, Wilderness Society; Larry Evans, *Outside* magazine; David Quammen; Kim Stafford; Peter Goin; Ellen Manchester; and the many others who generously shared their thoughts and their concern for the land with us, providing us with welcome guidance in preparing this issue. Above all our thanks to the photographers and writers who allowed us to consider their work for the issue, enabling us in the process to obtain a deep sense of the importance of the questions of land use and wilderness—and the role of humans in it—which this issue considers.

CREDITS

Note: Unless otherwise noted, all photographs are courtesy of, and copyright by, the artists.

Front cover: photograph by John Pfahl; p. 3 photograph by William Clift; pp. 4–5 photographs by Barbara Bosworth; pp. 6–7 photographs by A. J. Meek; pp. 8–9 photographs by William Clift; pp. 10–11 photographs by Robert Dawson; pp. 12–13 photographs by Alan Tibbetts; pp. 14–15 photograph by Mark Klett; pp. 17–19 photographs by Philip Hyde; pp. 21–23 photographs by Robert Glenn Ketchum; pp. 25–29 photographs by John Pfahl; pp. 30–35 photographs by Richard Misrach; p. 37 photograph by Gary Braasch; p. 38 photographs by Ken Graham; p. 39 (top) photograph by Ken Graham; p. 39 (bottom) photograph by Michael Baytoff; pp. 40–43 photographs by Sam Kittner; pp. 44–49 photographs by Len Jenshel; pp. 51–55 photographs by Terry Evans; pp. 57–63 photographs by Robert Dawson; p. 64 photograph by Peter deLory; pp. 65–66 photographs by John Ganis; p. 67 photograph by Masumi Hayashi; pp. 68–71 photographs by Stuart Klipper.

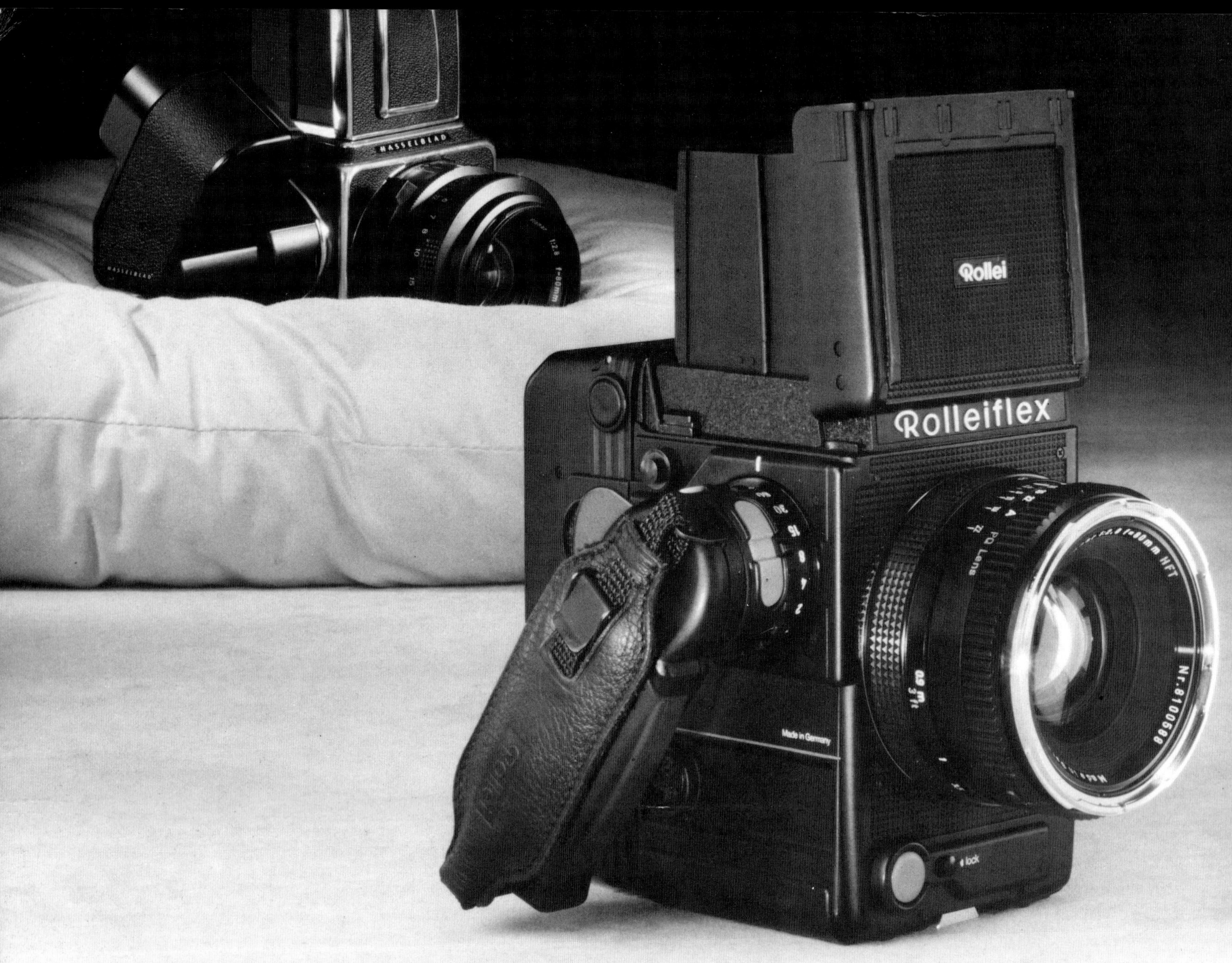

While Hasselblad has slept, Rollei has turned dreams into reality.

Hasselblad® has made essentially the same wonderful cameras for decades. Yet, technological advances have made much higher medium-format performance possible.

Rollei has turned these possibilities into realities and embodied them in the 6000 series cameras, extremely advanced Zeiss and Schneider lenses, and accessories that perform a vaster scope of tasks: with greater speed, accuracy, control and ease-of-use.

While Hasselblad has evolved dedicated flash and such, Rollei – in the new 6008 model – has introduced 13 medium-format "firsts." For superb accuracy, pick your spots: center weighted multi-zone, multi-spot, or tight-spot readings cover-ing under 1%! Save time when you select auto-bracketing: $\pm \frac{2}{3}$ stop automatically. For situation versatility, switch "modes operandi": Shutter Priority AE mode; Aperture Priority AE mode; and Programmed AE mode; plus Manual Metering. For more exacting control, the leaf shutter

adjusts from 30 to 1/500 stops in $\frac{1}{3}$ stop increments; with 2 increments beyond 1/500! Now see all and know all: all vital data is numerically displayed within your view yet not in the "live" screen viewing area.

Discover the benefits of auto ISO speed-settings; exposure compensation from $-4\frac{2}{3}$ to $+2$ stops; open aperture metering; 2 frames/second motor drive; a removable action-grip for single hand operation. And more. New Rollei PQ lenses from Zeiss and Schneider (including 80mm 2.0 and 180mm 2.8 lenses!) make a total of 19 Rollei lenses. And every accessory (some enabling photographic "wizardry") is fully compatible between 6006 and 6008 models (except, alas, the neckstrap).

The stuff of dreams is ready to be put in your hands. Don't sleep on it – explore the possibilities at your Rollei dealer.

Rollei
fototechnic

We're looking at things from your point of view.

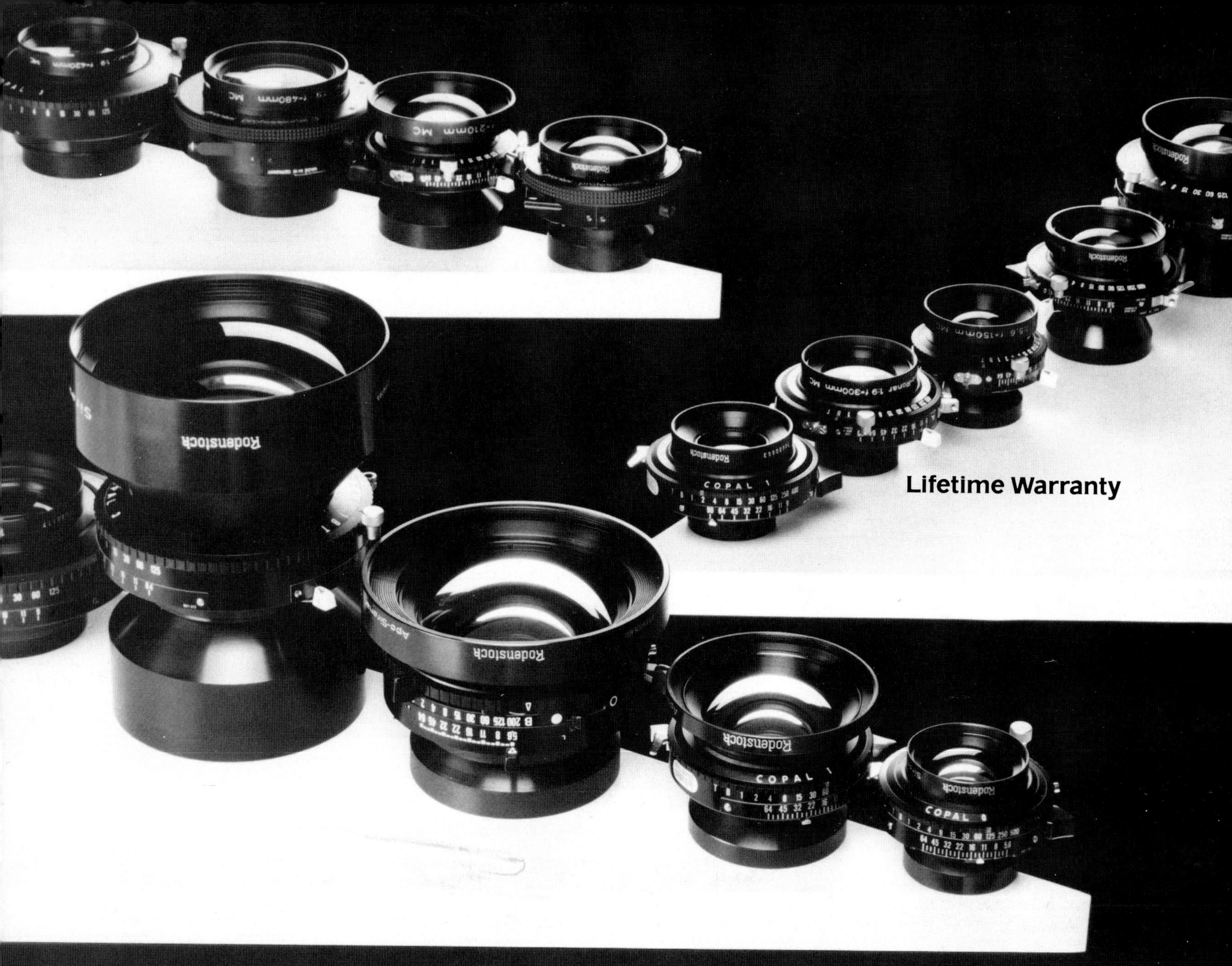

Apo-chromatic lenses.
Some "plane" talk from the people who make the most.

Rodenstock has been making apo-chromatic lenses for almost 5 decades. So, not surprisingly, we offer the world's most extensive selection. Apo-chromatic large-format lenses provide pinnacle performance for the most demanding of photographers. They focus all wavelengths of the visible spectrum at the film plane. Thus yielding sharper, more highly defined images; both in color and black & white. Rodenstock offers 18 Apo lenses. Including Apo-Sironar, Apo-Ronar and the Sironar-N series.

Lateral Chromatic Aberration, Corrected.

The Apo-Sironar series includes our latest and most highly advanced Apo's: the 150mm and 210mm. At f22, they cover 80° delivering image circles of 252mm with the 150mm 5.6 and 352mm with the 210mm 5.6.

They have reduced distortion and eliminated color fringing more than hitherto possible. Rodenstock has corrected the lateral chromatic aberration of the secondary spectrum to 0.03% of the focal length! Yet this major optical breakthrough is achieved in surprisingly small and lightweight sizes. Copal, Compur or Prontor professional shutters are all available— and the prices of these lenses are very competitive. Compare them and their technical advantages. As with all Rodenstock large-format lenses, our Apo's have a Lifetime Warranty.

Rodenstock's superior quality and quantity of "taking" and enlarging lenses give you the greatest chance to solve *any* photographic problem—without sacrificing *any* quality. Come to your Rodenstock dealer and get more "plane" talk.

Marketing Corp.

16 Chapin Rd., Pine Brook, NJ 07058, 201/808-9010

In Canada: Daymen Photo Marketing Ltd., Scarborough, Ontario M1V2J9

Rodenstock
The world's greatest depth of quality.

Lois Conner

William Eggleston

Lee Friedlander

David Graham

Len Jenshel

David Levinthal

Helen Levitt

John Maggiotto

Joe Maloney

Ray K. Metzker

William E. Parker

Judith Joy Ross

Michael Spano

Josef Sudek

Val Telberg

Susan Unterberg

Catherine Wagner

Estate of Larry Burrows

SUSAN UNTERBERG / JOSEF SUDEK

13 September–13 October 1990

LAURENCE MILLER
CONTEMPORARY PHOTOGRAPHS
138 SPRING STREET NYC 10012 212.226.1220 FAX 212.226.2343

BURDEN GALLERY

SYLVIA PLACHY'S UNGUIDED TOUR
September 10 – October 27, 1990

BRUCE CHARLESWORTH/NEW PHOTOGRAPHS
November 13 – December 22, 1990